THE JUDAIC STATE

THE JUDAIC STATE

A Study in Rabbinic Political Theory

MARTIN SICKER

PRAEGER

New York
Westport, Connecticut
London

Library of Congress Cataloging-in-Publication Data

Sicker, Martin.
  The Judaic state.

  Bibliography: p.
  Includes index.
  1. Politics in rabbinical literature. I. Title.
  BM496.9.P64S56   1988   320.5'5   87-25818
  ISBN 0-275-92845-4 (alk. paper)

Copyright © 1988 by Martin Sicker

All rights reserved. No portion of this book may
be reproduced, by any process or technique, without
the express written consent of the publisher.

Library of Congress Catalog Card Number: 87-25818

ISBN: 0-275-92845-4

First published in 1988

Praeger Publishers, One Madison Avenue, New York, NY 10010
A division of Greenwood Press, Inc.

Printed in the United States of America

∞

The paper used in this book complies with the
Permanent Paper Standard issued by the National
Information Standards Organization (Z39.48–1984).

10 9 8 7 6 5 4 3 2 1

This book is dedicated to the memory
of my parents,
Hyman and Lillian Sicker.
May their memories serve as a blessing.

Contents

1	Introduction	1
2	The Nature of Man	7
3	The Origins of Political Society	17
4	The Individual and the Polity	31
5	Political Authority and Obligation	43
6	The Structure of the Polity	53
7	The Priesthood	61
8	The Prophetic Institution	73
9	The National Executive	87
10	The Monarchy	97
11	The King and the Law	107
12	The Judiciary	123
13	The Magistrates	131
14	Priest, Prophet, King, and Judge	141
	Bibliography	151
	Index	159
	About the Author	163

THE JUDAIC STATE

1
Introduction

As indicated by the subtitle of this study, the primary emphasis here is on "rabbinic"—as distinguished from "Jewish"—thought. This differentiation is necessary because, while rabbinic thought represents a highly significant component of Jewish thought, the terms are not synonymous. There are—and have always been—schools of Jewish thought that not only diverge in important ways from the main thrust of the rabbinic intellectual tradition, but in some cases are completely at odds with it.

There is no strict agreement among students of Jewish history and literature on the precise parameters of rabbinic thought—neither from the standpoint of content, nor period. In this study, rabbinic literature is considered to include the vast corpus of writings by philosophers and scholars, exegetes and poets, legalists and pietists, who reflect in their religious and secular work the fundamental concepts, teachings, and traditions held by them to have been transmitted from generation to generation in an unbroken chain since the days of Moses. This is the common thread that holds together the tangled skein of rabbinic thought.

To understand more clearly the conceptual framework within which this study has been undertaken, a brief examination of the notion of "rabbinic tradition" may prove useful.

The term "rabbinic" has a traditional significance that is almost totally obscured by contemporary usage. Currently, "rabbi" is widely used to describe "a communal official whose duties include not only religious activities (in which preaching and public speaking play an important part) but also embrace educational, pastoral, social, and interfaith activities."[1] Except for the educational aspect, such usage bears little resemblance to the traditional view of the rabbi.

For some grasp of that view, it is necessary to turn to the classical rabbinic literature itself.

The point of departure for the formulation of the rabbinic concept of "rabbi" is found in the following discussion, which appears in the Talmud in regard to this biblical text: "And the elders of the congregation shall lay their hands upon the head of the bullock" (Lev. 4:15):

It is taught: The laying on [of hands], and the laying on [of hands] of the elders is performed by three. What is meant by "laying on [of hands]" and "laying on [of hands] of the elders"? R. Johanan said: [The latter] refers to the ordination of elders.... R. Aha the son of Raba asked R. Ashi: Is ordination effected by the literal laying on of hands? [No,] he answered; it is by the conferring of the degree. He is designated by the title of Rabbi and authorized to adjudicate cases of *kenas* [involving penalization through fines].[2]

Thus, in contrast to contemporary usage (particularly in the United States and Europe), the traditional concept of the rabbi carries juridical connotations. Because of this, the most fundamental qualification for acceptance into the rabbinate was considered to be knowledge of Jewish law as embodied in Scripture and in the traditional teachings believed to have been transmitted along with it from biblical days. This body of law—the Torah—deals not only with the questions usually defined as "religious" or "cultic"—governing the relations between man and God. It has an equal—if not greater—concern with matters that affect the relations between man and his fellow—which includes not only personal ethics but also the broader questions of the relationship of man and society in general, and man and the state in particular. Consequently, the political aspects of rabbinic thought—while not treated as discrete subjects for study within specialized treatises—are to be found throughout the vast corpus of rabbinic literature.

The juridical aspect has constituted the dominant characteristic of rabbinic thought throughout its history—even though the judicial role of the rabbi has undergone considerable modification, over time. With the declining political fortunes of the great Jewish communities of the Near East—especially under the rule of the Persian Sassanids in the fourth century—ordination in the classic juridical sense came to an end. By the time of the final redaction of the Talmud (circa 500 c.e.), ordination or *semikhah* was replaced by the *hattarat hora'ah* or *facultas docendi*—an academic device designed to ensure the perpetuity of the rabbinic tradition through the process of certifying those entrusted with responsibility for the education and religious leadership of the community.

An attempt to reestablish juridical ordination—a first step toward resurrection of the Sanhedrin (the rabbinic high court) as the central authority for Jewish life—was undertaken in 1538 by Jacob Berav.[3] However, this effort was soon abandoned because of the strenuous opposition of most of the rabbinic authorities of the period. In contemporary times, a comparable effort has been made in the

State of Israel by the renowned rabbinic scholar J. L. Maimon, who has argued that the time is ripe to reestablish the Sanhedrin as the central judicial institution of the Jewish state.[4] Similarly, the legal scholar Kalman Kahana has argued a brief for the Israeli government's adoption of Jewish Civil Law—that is, the law of the rabbinic codes.[5] Thus far, neither of these efforts has borne any fruit. However, it would be premature to rule out the long-term possibility of the incorporation of rabbinic law as the basis for a reordering of the internal legal framework of the state.

In the traditional rabbinic perspective, the law—as reflected in the Torah, the Scriptures, and the accompanying interpretive traditions—is complete, and already contains essentially everything that can ultimately be said about the domain of its concerns. This would appear to leave little room for accretions from nontraditional sources. While it can hardly be doubted that rabbinic thinkers have indeed come under the influence of the intellectual currents of their day, it is important to note that—even where such influence seems obvious—the rabbinic writers rarely acknowledge such a debt. Instead, the usual aproach is to ground their ideas in traditional sources, rather than ascribe them to alien origins—even where such ascription is fully justified. Thus, just as the rabbis of the Talmud sought to base their views on Scripture—no matter how tenuous the connection—so with the scholars of later generations, who sought to root their opinions in the teachings of earlier ages—especially the Talmud and the other literatures of the classical rabbinic period, which covered the better part of the first millennium of the common era.

The approach taken in this study is to examine some of the key rabbinic concepts relating to the basis and organization of the properly constituted political society that are to be found scattered throughout the literature. The determination of which works represent an adequate sample of rabbinic thought is surely arbitrary at best. However, some rough criteria have been employed as a basis for selection: First, the examined work should generally be considered an authoritative or significant contribution to rabbinic tradition. Second, it should be a work that has generally been available to scholars (although, in some cases, the rabbinic tradition is best exemplified by works only relatively recently discovered). Third, the selected authors should span the historic range of the tradition, to reflect its continuity.

A cursory perusal of the Bibliography will probably elicit the complaint that many major authors and works meeting these selection criteria have been neglected. This may have occurred as a result of either the nonrelevance of the work in question or the insufficient knowledge of the present writer. With regard to the former, it should be noted that a great many of the most important and best-known rabbinic works simply do not deal with the themes examined in this study. For example, the codex literature compiled after the time of Maimonides in the thirteenth century generally does not deal with any aspects of rabbinic law that did not have operative relevance at the time of composition. Consequently, matters relating to the prophetic, monarchic, or sacerdotal institutions—which were essential components of the structure of the Hebrew Commonwealths in the biblical and postbiblical periods—do not appear in this body of literature. Similarly, a great volume of rabbinic literature deals exclusively with questions of ritual, ethics, and matters of a social but not necessarily political nature—for example: marriage, divorce, and inheritance. In addition, there is a very substantial corpus that deals with Jewish civil laws covering contracts, loans, torts, and damages. Finally, there is a large body of literature of a devotional and homiletic nature, including liturgical and poetic works.

Discounting this enormous volume of literature for the purpose at hand, there still remains a prodigious residue that is of direct relevance, from which a representative selection has been culled to provide the primary materials for this study. Aside from the talmudic and midrashic collections, the rabbinic literature that does deal with political ideas may be classified into four general categories. The first (and possibly most fruitful) category contains the commentaries on the Bible—which reflect the essence of rabbinic political philosophy and theory. The second is the codex literature—which helps to generally define the parameters of Jewish life and thought, within the context of rabbinic tradition. The third category contains works of philosophy—which, for the most part, are written in the spirit of apologetics, but have nonetheless proven to be important repositories of rabbinic thinking (often expressed in nonrabbinic style). Finally, the fourth category is one of miscellany—which includes poetry, apologetics, history, and grammatical works.

Ostensibly, many of the writers considered in this study have little in common with each other—by virtue of widely differing backgrounds, interests, temperaments, styles, and philosophic orientations. Yet, despite the sometimes vast gulfs separating these men, there is a common thread that binds them together in such a manner as to permit one to suggest that they are links in a 2,000-year-old chain of rabbinic tradition.

As intimated above, the subject under study here—rabbinic political theory—is increasingly seen as being of more than mere antiquarian interest. The contemporary Israeli scholar B. S. Jacobson has observed that "The present restoration of our statehood has given impetus to a renewed interest in the governmental agencies and institutions of our glorious past, their origin, purpose and development . . . [particularly] the teachings, opinions, and commentaries of the sages of Israel's past about the form of statehood most appropriate for us."[6]

NOTES

Talmudic references are to the Babylonian Talmud unless prefaced by *Jer. T.* to indicate the Jerusalem Talmud. Citations of works by Maimonides that are prefaced by *Hilkhot* (see Chapter 5, note 9) refer to sections of his code—the *Mishneh Torah*.

1. See Werblowsky and Wigoder, eds., *The Encyclopedia of the Jewish Religion*, "Rabbi," p. 320.

2. *Sanhedrin* 13b.
3. Berav, *Sefer Sheilot uTeshuvot*, pp. 199–209.
4. Maimon, *Hiddush haSanhedrin beMedinatenu haMehudeshet*. It should be noted that Rabbi Maimon's efforts in this regard aroused significant opposition within the rabbinic community. It was similar opposition some four centuries earlier that had frustrated the attempt by Jacob Berav.
5. Kahana, *The Case for Jewish Law in the Jewish State*.
6. Jacobson, *Meditations on the Torah*, p. 285.

2
The Nature of Man

The point of departure for rabbinic social and political thought is the biblical paradigm of quintessential man. Depicted in the early narratives of the Book of Genesis in a manner calculated to exemplify the uniqueness of man in the cosmic scheme, paradigmatic man emerges as the centerpiece of Creation.[1] Man is brought into being as the culmination of the creative process, its highest stage; he transcends the mineral, vegetable, and animal—the inorganic and organic orders that preceded him. As though to emphasize the distinctiveness of man from the rest of the natural world, Genesis presents us with a purposive inversion of the processes that govern the natural orders of creation. Thus, while the universal experience of the reproductive process is the biological birth of the male from the female, in the biblical narrative of the origins of man it is the reverse that occurs. Man "gives birth" to woman.

Similarly—and in bold contrast to those ancients who conceived their gods in the image of man, gods that faithfully mirrored the weaknesses of man—the biblical author conceives of man as having been created in the "image of God," reflecting the strengths of his Creator. Constrained by the inherently limited capacity of the language of the Bible for dealing with abstractions, this radical idea is given expression in figurative anthropomorphisms, which many fundamentalists and literary critics alike insist on taking literally.[2] However—as has been repeatedly argued and demonstrated throughout the history of biblical interpretation—it is not a corporeal image that is intended, but rather a partial reflection of certain aspects of divine personality. Just as God who created the natural order must of necessity transcend it; so, too, does man, with respect to those attributes of his being that—however faintly—reflect the divine. Thus, while man is a product of divine creativity and thereby an inherent part of the universal natural order, he is nonetheless qualitatively different from—and, in important respects, transcends—the rest of Creation.

This fundamental idea is vividly expressed in the biblical description of the creative process. Animal life is depicted as evolving directly from the earth in response to the divine imperative, "Let the earth bring forth the living creature" (Gen. 1:24). Animate existence is brought into being as an immediate and natural extension of inanimate nature. Man, however, is different. He cannot be brought into being simply as a direct natural extension of the inanimate. Man, who is to reflect the image of the Creator, must follow a different evolutionary course than the rest of animate nature. The complex creature who is to embody special faculties such that—at least in some respects—it, too, will display an inherent power of creativity cannot be merely a natural product of the earth. Nature itself cannot produce what by definition transcends its domain. Consequently, "the Lord God formed man of the dust of the ground, and breathed into his nostrils the breath of life; and man became a living soul" (Gen. 2:7). In contradistinction to the rest of animate nature, man is compounded of what is explicitly inorganic and hence lifeless on earth—its dust— and is formed into the shape of what is yet to become a human being. As a mere product of the earth, man remains a form without life. What gives life to man comes from beyond created nature. It is the Creator who, through direct intervention in the established natural order, supplies man with the vital life-force—transforming the molded frame of inert matter into a living personality. This uniquely "human" personality is formed in the image of God, endowed with the faculties of will and intellect—faculties foreign to the direct products of nature.[3] It is the possession of these distinctive and divinely granted faculties that determines and defines the essential humanity of this creature compounded out of the dust of the earth and the "breath" of the Creator.

Man is thus endowed with a dual nature. His physical existence is governed by the immutable laws of the natural order, as we understand them. His human personality, as reflected in the activity of his will and intellect, is subject to a uniquely human nature—a realm with laws that are indeed mutable.[4] The realm of human nature is conceived in traditional rabbinic thought as coming under man's conscious control. Man alone of all creation has the capacity to commit an act of will. He is not a passive participant in a cosmic production over which he can exert no influence. He is no mere puppet on the stage of brute nature— just responding to instinctual drives that determine the course of his very existence. He is free to structure the human realm in accordance with his own intellectually informed and deliberate choices. He is free to be creative and to augment nature through the positive development of his essential humanity. He is also capable of being destructive—thereby diminishing what is distinctively human, and reducing the human realm to an approximation of that of animal nature. Without this essential freedom, the recitation in the Bible of the divine command to Adam to refrain from the fruit of the "tree of the knowledge of good and evil" would be pointless; and the description of Adam's transgression of that divine imperative, meaningless. The ultimate significance of the episode—as introduction to the biblical recounting of the moral history of mankind—arises precisely out of the recognition that not only can man elect to disobey so as to assert his volitional independence, he can also translate his choice into deliberate actions. On the other hand—having such an innate freedom—man can also choose to obey. He can elect to withstand what would deter him from an appropriate course consonant with an enhancement of his intrinsic humanity, even in the absence of an explicit divine imperative. Man is thus conceived of as being ethically autonomous.

How is man to discern the proper course of action for him to pursue? How is he to know what enhances man's humanity, as well as what detracts from it? The quintessential norm by which man is to be guided in his ethical behavior is *imitatio Dei*—emulation of the Creator's beneficence, as depicted explicitly and implicitly in Scripture. Thus, just as God is characterized in the Bible as merciful, gracious, righteous, just, and tolerant, so should man aspire to merit similar attributions.[5] The realization of these qualities reinforces man's moral posture, and advances his essential humanity. However, in pursuing this ethical course, man is confronted by the conflicting demands of the fundamentally different aspects of his nature. The perennial challenge to man is to maintain the optimum balance between his human nature—reflecting the divine gift of personality and responding to the ethical imperative of *imitatio Dei*—and his fundamentally animal nature—governed by the inherent need to meet and satisfy the biological and physical demands imposed by it.

This dual nature of man—each aspect of which appears to be constantly struggling for self-expression and dominance—is characterized in classical rabbinic literature by the somewhat misleading notions of the "good and evil impulses" that condition man's moral state. This terminology is unfortunate, in that its use of the word "evil" suggests that the associated impulse is inherently bad. However logical, such an influence would be fallacious within the context of rabbinic thought. It would be inconceivable from the rabbinic perspective to conclude that God would create something essentially evil. Indeed, we are informed by Scripture that "God saw everything that He had made, and behold, it was very good" (Gen. 1:31). What then is intended by the "evil impulse"?[6]

"Evil impulse" is a rabbinic term used to convey the idea of potential. It refers to a natural disposition toward behavior that will likely result in evil. The evil impulse is a natural appetite that—if indulged without restraint—would eventuate in evil, but that is nonetheless inherently good because it is essential to man's overall well-being. Thus, without a natural sexual drive, man would neither mate nor replenish his species.[7] However, the evil impulse to overindulge that drive may lead to promiscuity and lust, with a consequent diminution of man's ability to fulfill the norm of *imitatio Dei*. Similarly, an acquisitive drive may be essential to achieving a necessary and desirable degree of economic autarky and viability, while an excess of such drive may result in greed and avarice. The evil impulse is therefore as much an inherent and necessary aspect of man's total complex nature as is the good impulse. It becomes man's task to bring about and maintain the appropriate balance of the forces raging within him—to impose the divine gift of reason on his natural appetites.[8] He must learn to constrain his response to the aesthetic, which seduces him through his senses, with the moral imperatives transmitted by his intellect—"that ye go not about after your own heart and your own eyes, after which ye use to go astray" (Num. 15:39). He must avoid both gluttony at one extreme, and exaggerated asceticism at the other. The test of man's humanity is the manner and extent to which he exhibits conscious and enlightened control of his appetites, while seeking fulfillment of his transcendent potential as one created in the image of God.

The biblical paradigm clearly depicts man as a responsible personality—thereby distinguishing him from the rest of created nature. Indeed, man is locked in continual struggle with nature. His very survival is contingent on his ability to successfully overcome the vicissitudes of climate, disease, predatory beasts, hunger, health, and premature death. It is within such a challenge-laden environment that man must strive to maintain his essential distinction from the rest of the natural order. God's first commandment to man is to take the necessary steps to conquer nature "and subdue it" (Gen. 1:28). This is a precondition to man's life as a human; he is a reflection of the Creator, and—while intimately involved with nature—he is not at one with it. In a sense, man's affinity with God may be considered to vary inversely with his subjugation to the imperatives of nature. In this struggle, man must conquer or else be vanquished and reduced to the level of the nonhuman animal—subject to the regime of brute nature.

To the extent that man is part of nature, he is subject to its physical and biological laws. Natural appetites are stimulated in response to the demands of physiological and biochemical processes. In this respect, man is not very different from other animals. However, to the extent that man can exercise his will—and thereby assert his moral autonomy from the yoke of nature—he affirms the reflection of divinity within him. Nature itself is morally neutral. In the biblical view, nature is essentially good, in that it serves the divine purpose. Man, too—insofar as he is an element of nature—is essentially good. It is man's God-given capacity to transcend the natural—to place limits on it and curb its powerful influences on his behavior—that creates the possibility of evil (that is, that which does not serve the divine intent and purpose).

The postulation of man's essential freedom of moral choice (and the concomitant will to act on that choice) is the critical underlying premise of all Judaic ethical and political thought. But this assertion of man's moral autonomy also presents a fundamental dilemma. As creator of the universe and the natural order that governs it, God must—of necessity—be omnipotent. But, if God is omnipotent, how can man be free to oppose His will? God is also presumed to be omniscient, and must therefore know what man will choose. How then can man's moral decision be characterized as free and autonomous? Yet, if man's freedom of will is denied, the punishment of man for his transgression against the will of the Creator—as described in Scripture—becomes absurd.

The attempt to resolve these patent contradictions—the reconciliation of the two irreconcilables: free will and determinism—has constituted a major theme of philosophic concern throughout the past two millennia. The earliest such endeavor in Judaic thought—that reflected in the Talmud—takes the position that the apparent contradiction exists solely in the mind of man, as a consequence of his inherently limited capacity to understand the mystery of God's ways. However—it is argued—reality is in no way contingent on man's ability (or lack thereof) to describe it in categories and terms acceptable within a framework of rational discourse. The rabbinic sages would simply have us recognize that being created in the image of God is still quite different and far from constituting an absolute analogue of the Creator. Thus, Rabbi Hanina could unequivocally declare that "Everything is in the hands of heaven, except the fear of Heaven," with regard to the matter of God's omnipotence;[9] and Rabbi Akiva could assert that "All is foreseen, yet freedom of choice is given," with regard to His omniscience.[10]

There is no denying that these teachings are truly paradoxical—frontally challenging the *doxa* of a logic that cannot abide or cope with such contradictory assertions. Yet, the truths in these teachings—unacceptable to the proponent of orthodox logic as being obvious violations of the law of contradiction—may well be harmonized by the metarational logic of faith. Consequently, from the perspective of the sages, there is little profit in wasting one's time and energy on fruitless speculations, in the attempt to give intellectual legitimacy to a reality that is beyond man's understanding. Man is counseled not to concern himself with what is beyond his reach. He is urged to occupy himself instead with those matters over which he can exercise dominion—that is, his own humanity and that of the society in which he plays out his divinely apportioned role.[11]

With the revival of classical learning in the Middle Ages, the talmudic response was reverently set aside. Renewed confidence—or, perhaps more to the point, renewed faith in the absolute rational ordering of the universe—once again demanded "rational" resolution of the problem of reconciling divine omniscience and man's freedom. Maimonides propounded a semantic solution to the dilemma—which, in essence, constituted a reformulation of the classic argument of the sages. In his view, the universe is indeed rationally ordered. However, the very language with which we describe and analyze that order is a human construct, subject to the limitations of its inventors. Consequently—while, for purposes of general communication, we speak of God in human terms, reason itself cannot demand that God's freedom be constrained by the limitations of human speech. Therefore, the apparent contradiction between everything being foreseen and man's simultaneous freedom of action is merely a formal one. When we speak of the inherent conflict of omniscience and freedom, we do so from the standpoint of man's understanding, which precludes the simultaneous validity of such contradictory propositions. However, in speaking of divine omniscience, we also implicitly make the logically unwarranted assumption that, when applied to God, this term persists in describing an explicit divine attribute that corresponds to an accepted universal definition.[12] This—Maimonides would argue—we may not do without committing violence to reason itself. We do not know God's nature, and consequently cannot meaningfully ascribe any humanly defined attributes to Him.[13] At most, we can suggest that certain attributes predicated of man cannot reasonably be applied to God. We cannot say with any confidence what God is, but only what reason dictates that God is not.

In the following century, Gersonides[14]—followed in part by Don Isaac Abravanel[15] in the fifteenth century and M. L. Malbim[16] in the nineteenth century—rejected Maimonides' approach to the problem, in favor of one considered more acceptable. Faced with the choice of restricting either man's freedom or God's omniscience in order to resolve the paradox, Gersonides elected to place limitations on the idea of omniscience. It is imperative that man be conceived as unbound in his moral life, if he is to be held accountable for his ethical conduct. Consequently, God's all-knowingness cannot extend to the individual choices made by man.

How can this radical limitation on God's foreknowledge be reconciled with the basic propositions propounded by the sages in regard to God's omnipotence and omniscience—propositions so fundamental to Judaism? God—it is asserted—is indeed all-knowing, in that the outcomes of the totality of events are foreseen. However, the particulars of the component elements of a cause-and-effect sequence in human affairs are under the discretionary control (as if by delegation of authority) of man's free will. The general and ultimate outcomes in history correspond faithfully to the divine plan, and cannot deviate therefrom. The course of events reflects providential manipulation of the general circumstances and conditions; in response to which, particular choices are made by men. However, the final outcomes are not necessarily contingent on any unique set of events that may take place as a consequence of deliberate human choices. A predetermined effect may be engendered by more than any particular set of causes.

Under this concept of man's moral freedom, God's omniscience is quite evidently constrained and delimited in that He does not know what choice a man will make in any given circumstance, even if the probable decision seems certain. To Hasdai Crescas—perhaps the outstanding Jewish philosopher of the fourteenth century—such an approach to the problem of the paradox was completely unacceptable.[17] Given the choice between restricting God's knowledge or man's free will, Crescas saw no alternative other than to limit the latter to ensure the integrity of the former. He attempted to salvage man's free will through the rather complicated argument that—while God's omniscience is absolute and perfect, and He foresees causes leading to specific effects—the individual choices made by man remain inherently free. In other words, while each choice is free insofar as man is concerned, the factors that will cause him to make a given choice are already known to God. In a sense, this argument brings us full circle to the idea that we simply cannot reconcile the paradox of divine omniscience and human free will within the framework of classical logic; it is only through the higher logic of faith that the dilemma can be dealt with— an idea that reaches back to the sages of the Talmud.[18]

One consequence of the postulation of man's free will in the face of divine omnipotence and omniscience is the corollary concept that man can ultimately exercise a significant degree of influence—and perhaps even control—over human nature itself, and the manner in which it is manifested in history. Because of his moral autonomy, man is conceived as a covenanted partner with God in the creative process. His role is that of perfecting what has been created, including mankind itself.[19] This idea, which is one of the central concepts of rabbinic political and social thought, postulates the imperative for activism in the affairs of man.[20]

In structuring the paradigm of quintessential man, the Bible provides the data of creation, but not the underlying purpose or plan.[21] We do not know the why of creation; nor have the extensive exegetical and speculative endeavors of commentators and theologians succeeded in devising explanations that satisfy the questioning mind. Nevertheless, although the question of why cannot be answered, rabbinic tradition insists that we proceed on the basis that man has a special role to perform in the cosmic scheme—a role predicated on man's intrinsic responsibility for his conduct. The sage Rabbi Akiva maintained that man's unique status in the universe is exemplified by his having been explicitly made aware that he was created in the image of God.[22] It is man's consciousness of this divine beneficence that provides the inspiration to carry on with the struggle to fully realize his humanity in the course of human history.

The uniqueness of paradigmatic man in the order of Creation is further emphasized by his singularity as portrayed in a dramatic and explicit manner in the biblical narrative. In stark contrast to the rest of animate nature—which is created in pairs, male and female, to ensure natural reproduction and continuity of the species—man is depicted in the Creation narrative as having been created alone. Fashioned in the image of God—who is conceived as singular and unique—man is held to intrinsically reflect that uniqueness. Constituting the capstone of creation, man is also conceived in the classical literature as bearing the responsibility of being the Creator's viceroy with respect to the earth and all that is on it. Therefore, each individual may justifiably view the world as having been created to enable him personally and individually to fulfill an assigned role in the divine scheme.[23]

Paradigmatic man enters the world alone. He is a limited reflection of the divine personality. Being endowed with the attributes of free will and reason, he is fully liable for his conduct as long as he remains in control of his faculties.

Confronted by the competing demands of good and evil impulses struggling within him, each man is held ultimately and individually accountable for his moral state. Man is responsible because he is free!

NOTES

1. See Saadia ben Joseph al-Fayyumi, (Saadia Gaon), *The Book of Beliefs and Opinions*, p. 181; and Kimhi, *Perush RADAK al haTorah*, commentary on Gen. 1:26.

2. The generally accepted rabbinic view of the use of anthropomorphisms in the Bible is that, as the Talmud puts it, "The Torah speaks in the common language of man" (*Kiddushin* 17b; *Baba Metzia* 31b).

3. While the "image of God" is interpreted by some to encompass a number of other human attributes (such as love), the majority of commentators define it in terms of intellect and will. For example, Maimonides: "On account of the Divine intellect with which man has been endowed, he is said to have been made in the form and likeness of the Almighty" (Maimonides, *The Guide for the Perplexed* I:1); Judah Loew ben Bezalel (MAHARAL): "But man, who was created in the image of God has this distinguishing characteristic, that by virtue of his own volition he is as the Blessed Name who does as He pleases; and thus man has the power to do as he desires. He is one who wills" (Judah Loew ben Bezalel, *Derekh Hayyim*, p. 112); Meir Simhah HaKohen: "Divine image means 'free will,' without natural compulsion but rather derived from a free expression of will and intellect" (Meir Simhah HaKohen, *Meshekh Hokhmah*, p. 3).

4. Rabbi Abbahu taught: "The God of Israel said, '... I rule man; who rules Me? [It is] the righteous: for I make a decree and he [may] annul it'" (*Moed Katan* 16b). Elaborating on the matter of the mutability of nature, Samuel Judah Katzenellenbogen (MAHARSHIK) writes: "It is well known in the sayings of our sages that the righteous that are in Israel have in them the capability of changing nature... and this power and authority are given to them because of the elevation and brilliance of their spirit" (Katzenellenbogen, *Shnaim Assar Derushim*, # 2, p. 12). MAHARSHIK is well aware of the logical as well as philosophical problems inherent in this position. His argument in defense of the rabbinic view amounts to saying that, since man's rational faculties are constrained by the natural order, it should not be surprising if man cannot rationally understand something transcending this same natural order. He states: "I am fully aware that when man considers this matter in a natural, rationalistic, examination, it will be difficult for his understanding to accept that man, whose origin is in the dust, should ascend to such a marvellously lofty stage as to be, in his own being, a dwelling place for the Divine Presence, and to alter nature and nullify decrees as previously mentioned. Of course, the intelligent man will have the capacity to know and understand that matters touching on the divine transcend nature and are not to be brought under an examination based on man's understanding of the natural" (# 10, p. 55). See also note 9 below.

5. "As God is called the Merciful, the Gracious, so also shall you be merciful and gracious, and beneficent to all. Just as God is called righteous in all His ways, so also shall you be righteous. Just as God is called kind in all His doings, so shall you be kind" (*Sifre Deuteronomy*, "Ekev" 11:22).

6. Maimonides notes that "we call 'good' that which is in accordance with the object we seek" (Maimonides, *The Guide for the Perplexed* III:13). Eli Munk writes: "*Tov* [good]

is something which complies fully with an intended state, whether physical, spiritual, moral, or in any other way. It could not be 'better,' namely by that standard. Whatever we call 'good,' is good by a certain standard, but may not be good by a different standard. It would then be called *ra* [bad], a term describing something which is not perfect, irrespective of the degree of deficiency. *Ra* is, therefore, not necessarily 'evil.' When Isaiah says (45:7): [I make peace, and create evil] *uvorey ra*, he means: the Creator of what was not created in its final state" (Munk, *The Seven Days of the Beginning*, pp. 47–48). Munk goes on to say that "the Law was revealed at Mount Sinai by the Creator. Thus, a standard of correct behaviour is set for man and known to him. Compliance with this standard achieves the 'intended state' of man, *tov*... Deviation from the standard would then be *ra*, sub-standard. Man's ability to form a decision complying with the standard is known as *yetzer hatov* [the good impulse]: forming an action to standard. His ability to deviate from the standard is known as *yetzer hara* [the evil impulse]: forming a sub-standard action. Such deviation stems either from his natural tendency to satisfy his desires impulsively, or from a conscious intention to act, whether through negligence or of choice, against his better knowledge" (p. 90).

7. "If not for the evil impulse men would not build homes, marry, have children and carry on the necessary activities of life" (*Genesis Rabbah*, "Bereshit" 9:7).

8. "The Holy One, blessed be He, created two impulses, one good and the other evil.... The good impulse controls the righteous.... The evil impulse controls the wicked.... Both impulses control average people" (*Berakhot* 61a–61b). Man is seen as being able to control the influences of his natural appetites. This is exemplified in the teaching of Rabbi Simon: "If your impulse seeks to incite you to frivolous conduct, banish it with words of Torah.... Should you say that it is not under your control... [God says,] I have declared unto you in the Scriptures, 'Unto thee is its desire, but thou mayest rule over it' (Gen. 4:7)" (*Genesis Rabbah*, "Bereshit" 22:15).

9. *Berakhot* 33b. Rabbi Hanina's dictum is based on Deut. 10:12, "And now, Israel, what doth the Lord thy God require of thee but to fear." Samuel Eliezer Eidels (MAHARSHAH) suggests that the interpretation by R. Abbahu of the biblical text to imply man's capacity to alter God's decrees (see note 4 above) is an extension of R. Hanina's dictum (Eidels, *Hiddushei Aggadot* to Moed Katan 16b.).

10. *Avot* 3:15.

11. This idea receives early formulation in the *Wisdom of Ben Sira* in the Apocrypha literature, and is cited with approval in *Haggigah* 13a. "Do not seek for what is too hard for you, and do not investigate what is beyond your strength; Think of the commands that have been given you, For you have no need of the things that are hidden. Do not waste your labor on what is superfluous to your work, For things beyond man's understanding have been shown you" (Ecclus. 3:21–23). Similarly, and in recognition of the intense frustration that awaits those who devote their efforts to speculation on what is beyond man's capacity to understand, the sages taught: "Whoever reflects on four things, it were a mercy if he had never come into the world, viz., what is above, what is beneath, what is before and what is after" (*Haggigah* 2:1).

12. Maimonides, *The Guide for the Perplexed* III:20.

13. "All this is according to the language of man; he ascribes to God what he considers a perfection, and does not ascribe to Him what he considers a defect. In truth, however, no real attribute, implying an addition to His essence, can be applied to Him, as will be proved" (Maimonides, *The Guide for the Perplexed* I:47).

14. Gersonides, *Milhamot haShem*, pt. 3, ch. 2.

15. Abravenel, *Perush haTorah*, "Bereshit", end of ch. 37.
16. Malbim, *HaTorah vehaMitzvah* on Gen. 37:14.
17. Crescas, *Or haShem*, pt. 2, sec. 5.
18. It should be noted, however, that—while it remains a subject of philosophic concern—the resolution of the free will vs. determinism question has never been considered a matter of practical importance in traditional Judaism. In any case—from the standpoint of Jewish law and ethics—man is obligated to act *as if* he could exercise his will autonomously and in freedom.
19. In commenting on the covenant between God and Abraham (Gen. 17:2), Malbim notes that the wording of the text implies "that the binding obligation rests on both parties to the covenant, because Abraham also obligated himself to be a partner with God in the act of creation by perfecting what was created and participating in its improvement. And the beginning of improvement will take place in the microcosm that is the individual person" (Malbim, *HaTorah vehaMitzvah* on Gen. 17:2).
20. The idea of the mutability of human nature and its perfectibility through each person's own efforts precludes an interpretation of the Genesis narrative that would permit a doctrine of "original sin," as conceived in Christianity. To the extent that a notion of original sin is found in Judaic sources, it is always in connection with the idea that the punishment of Adam's "original" transgression introduced biological death as an ultimate constraint on human behavior; and even this rudimentary idea is not permitted to pass unchallenged. See I. Epstein, *Judaism: A Historical Presentation*, p. 142.
21. This point is reflected in the following midrashic parable: "For nine months the infant dwelled in the mother's womb. When the time arrived for it to emerge into the light of day, the angel came and said: The hour for you to emerge has come! The infant answered: Why do you wish to bring me out into the light of day? The angel answered: My child, know that perforce were you created, and now know further that perforce you are born, and perforce you die, and perforce you will have to render account before the King of Kings, the Holy One, blessed be He" (*Midrash Tanhumah*, "Pekudei" 3). Also cited in part at the end of *Avot* 4.
22. Rabbi Akiva is cited as teaching: "Beloved is man that he was created in the image of God. It is a mark of even greater love that it was made known to him that he had been created in the image of God" (*Avot* 3:14).
23. "For this reason was a man created alone, to teach thee that whosoever destroys a single soul, Scripture imputes [guilt] to him as though he had destroyed a complete world.... The Holy One, blessed be He, fashioned every man in the stamp of the first man, and yet not one of them resembles his fellow. Therefore every single person is obliged to say: The world was created for my sake" (*Mishnah Sanhedrin* 4:5).

3
The Origins of Political Society

In the biblical paradigm, man is caused to enter the world alone to exemplify his uniqueness within the universe of Creation—his singular ultimate worth as a reflection of the image of God. However, once having made this point dramatically clear, Scripture proceeds to indicate that "it is not good that the man should be alone" (Gen. 2:8). As a "higher" being, man has more complex needs than the rest of animate nature. His requirements for food, clothing, and shelter present a challenge to him far greater than that confronting other creatures, yet man is surprisingly ill equipped to adequately satisfy those needs by himself. If all his time and energy are not to be expended in the continuing struggle for existence in a world under the regime of brute nature—if he is to have the leisure necessary for the development of his higher faculties—he must have assistance. It is only through sharing the burdens of subsistence that he can muster the resources necessary to master and subdue nature. And, it is only through division of the requisite labor among others that man can achieve sufficient efficiency in his primitive economy to provide the leisure so essential to the fulfillment of his role in the divine scheme.[1]

Accordingly, the Creator provides man with a counterpart—a "help meet," another complete individual personality comparable in every essential respect to his own—to complement his endeavors.[2] Together, they constitute original society—the primeval social structure designed to more effectively satisfy man's intrinsic social and economic needs.

Finding himself in the most elemental of societal structures—association with another integral human being—man must develop a pattern of relationships that will enhance and promote the viability and practical utility of that association. The fundamental principle serving as the foundation for this uniquely human social structure is that of the inherent equality of all human beings. Just as the first man is created in the image of God and is therefore special—reflecting ultimate value—so, too, is his counterpart and companion as well as all subsequent human beings.

Alone, and acting on the divine imperative to master nature and subdue it—that is, to forge a civilization out of the brute environment—man can exercise his free will as he chooses. He is in a state of absolute liberty. However, it readily becomes self-evident that, once man enters into association with another, his freedom of action can no longer be absolute. Absolute liberty fundamentally contradicts the maintenance of essential equality among members of society. If all are equally at liberty to conduct themselves as they please, there will inevitably be some encroachment of one upon another. Such encroachment would entail a basic denial of the ultimate worth of another human—and, consequently, of human equality.[3] Paradigmatic man is thus confronted by a fundamental conflict of values: liberty versus equality.

Since, from the standpoint of its originally intended purpose, the existence of society cannot have ultimate meaning and value if absolute liberty is held to be an inviolable principle, it becomes necessary to impose certain constraints on the liberty of the individual in order to permit the quintessential equality of men in society to be sustained. In so doing, liberty becomes defined in negative terms. Within some stipulated limits, man is free to act as he wishes, without regard to the effects of his actions on others. Beyond these bounds, he must desist from such behavior as will have detrimental effects on others. However, since the essential principle undergirding society is that of equality, this principle must also be applied to man's negatively defined liberty. In other words, the properly constituted society is characterized by an equality of negative liberty among its members. That is, the limits of one's freedom of action should be the same for all—irrespective of the natural inequalities that may exist among men.

This principle of equality of negative liberty was held by the sage Hillel to be the central doctrine of biblical and Judaic teaching. As formulated by Hillel, the principle is: "What is hateful to yourself, do not do unto your fellow man." However, it is obvious—given the natural diversity of character among men—that the threshold of acceptability of a particular action might vary widely according to individual idiosyncrasies. This would place the practicability of application of the principle in jeopardy. Consequently, Hillel went on to indicate that, while the principle of equality of negative liberty as reflected in his formulation was indeed the central teaching of the Torah, the Torah itself also provided the required interpretation of the principle. He thus concluded his dictum with the exhortation: "That is the whole of the Torah, and the remainder is only commentary. Go and learn it!"[4] That is, the teachings of the Torah reflect the standards or norms of conduct to be used in application of the principle in order to optimize the effective equality of negative liberty for the society as a whole.

However, there is a divergence in rabbinic thought regarding the interrelationship of man and his society when the needs of each are in conflict—a divergence that can affect how one understands the norms of the Torah. One position—exemplified in the writings of Judah Loew ben Bezalel (MA-HARAL)—maintains that a society is something rather more than a simple aggregation of discrete individuals. It is seen instead as an entity that, once formed, takes on an organic characteristic of its own. As the primary social organism, society provides the context for the emergence of the individual personality.[5] Consequently, the needs of society should be accorded higher priority than those of any of its component elements. The individual is thus conceived as naturally subordinate to the body from which it derives its identity.[6]

For Malbim, on the other hand, the individual—and not society—is the basic social unit. It is through his own self-development that the individual attains to the good. When carried to its logical conclusion, this view insists that political society in itself is inherently incapable of realizing the good, and therefore can make no valid claim to be an "organic" necessity. The moral perfectibility of society derives from the perfection of its component elements. From individual man "alone will perfection extend to all creation."[7] Consequently, the needs of the individual must—in principle—be given priority over those of the broader society.

The essence of his position—rooted in the Talmud—is that man possesses a divinely allocated attribute that enables him to bring about fundamental changes in the order of things, by force of his positively directed will.[8] However, if it is within man's capacity as an individual to achieve moral perfection, then the purpose of society and its institutions can only be to assist the individual in becoming sufficiently free from external hindrance to allow him the maximum unrestricted scope for his pursuit of the good. Men everywhere do live in society, and therefore require some order that will permit them to pursue their lives in tranquility—at least until such time as man achieves the distant goal of transforming the prevailing moral order. In Malbim's view, the role of political society is to impose restraints on man's absolute liberty to do as he pleases without regard to the effects on others—a negative but necessary function.

Under the concept of an organic political society, the institutions of government will assume an aggressively positive role in determining and ordering the behavior of the people. However, the predominant rabbinic view comports with the position that ascribes central importance to the individual, and is not prepared to readily subordinate the interests of the person to those of society. Nonetheless, society is implicitly recognized by most as an integral entity that is something more than the mere sum of its parts—a corporate body having its own intrinsic value and importance for the well-being of all its members. However, in theory and in principle—although not necessarily always in practice—society is ultimately subordinated to the critical needs of its individual members. In the words of a contemporary scholar, "Judaism is based upon the fundamental concept that in our national and individual lives we can continue to function properly only so long as we believe in the dignity of every individual, in the inviolability, infinite worth and sacredness of each human being."[9]

For some, there is implicit in the rabbinic view of man the idea that it is the individual alone—not generic man, but particular man—that is the concrete reality and a complete microcosm, whereas the society of which he may be a member is nothing more than an abstraction that man reifies whenever it serves his purpose. As such, society has relevance for the individual only insofar as he is a living being and can have recourse to it for whatever benefit it may provide. However, once the individual is confronted by the threat of death, society becomes a meaningless metaphor for him. His obligations to society pale in significance, when confronted with the principle of self-preservation.[10] In this view, the ultimate purpose of society must of necessity be the preservation and sanctification of the individual lives of its members—even at the risk of its own destruction.

This position is given normative sanction in the talmudic dictum: "If they say to you: Give us one of you that we may kill him, and if not we will kill all of you, they shall risk slaughter rather than hand over a single person."[11] Just as the moral permissibility of the actions of an individual must be assessed in view of their consequent effects on others, so too with men in the aggregate—in society. Society's actions must also be evaluated for their moral acceptability in consequence of their effects on the individual. Furthermore, there can be no question of the ends justifying the means. Ends and means are intrinsically linked in a moral continuum. The end cannot justify the means, because the very character of the end itself is affected and modified by the means employed in its realization. If the end is to withstand the test of morality, the means must ethical.[12]

With regard to human life, all are considered intrinsically equal. Therefore, society may not arrogate to itself priority of survival, simply because it represents a multitude of members. Where the life of the individual is at stake, society loses its significance as a corporate entity, and becomes simply an aggregation of individuals. The natural primary drive for self-preservation becomes transformed into an ethical principle taking moral priority over competing tenets. This unchallenged principle is set forth by Rabbi Akiva in the dictum that, all things being equal, "Your life takes precedence over that of your fellow man."[13] One may choose—out of love for his fellow human being or concern for the well-being of his society—to sacrifice himself so that others may live. Such self-sacrifice would indeed be a supreme act of loving-kindness—an act to be held in the highest esteem. However, there can be no positive moral obligation to perform such an act of self-abnegation—regardless of whether it is a single life or a multitude of lives that are at stake.

Since, of necessity, man lives within the framework of a society of men, he must be concerned not only with the effects that his actions may have on others. He must also be concerned with the manner in which he is affected by such association. Consequently, the idea of each individual's responsibility for his personal conduct is extended by the sages into the concept of the collective moral responsibility of each man for his fellow.[14] It is recognized that, in his ongoing struggle for self-mastery, man is readily susceptible to corrupting influences from the social environment. If he is not to succumb, he must commit himself to an overt and serious effort to mitigate the prospective effects of such evil, at its very inception. "Thou shalt surely rebuke thy neighbor, and not bear sin because of him" (Lev. 19:17). Indeed, for the sages of the Talmud, the test of a morally viable society is the extent to which responsible involvement in the affairs of one's fellow is deemed socially acceptable and proves efficacious in improving the quality of the social environment.[15]

The corruption of society is considered to reflect the failure of its members to fulfill their basic responsibilities to themselves and each other. Such failure cannot but result in social upheaval and dislocation.[16] Conversely, the proper fulfillment of the individual's self-responsibility requires that he actively pursue his true well-being by taking the actions—both personal and social—necessary to ameliorate the moral condition of his society. It is a burden that is incumbent on each individual to bear as a personal responsibility. Scripture repeatedly demands of man that "thou shalt put away the evil from the midst of thee" (Deut. 17:17, 19:20, 22:21, 22:24, 24:7). The individual is therefore obligated to play an active role within his society, and may not defer to others the responsibility for its moral quality. He may not be successful in his endeavor, but he must not desist from the attempt.[17]

There is also a strain of optimism in rabbinic thought, which implicitly suggests that man and his fellow—living and working in association—are fully capable of ordering their lives and interrelationships on an exclusively voluntary basis. Man is conceived as having it within his power to achieve a stance of moral rectitude, and even perfection—solely by dint of his own efforts, if he be but determined to do so. In this view, before undertaking any action, a person should reflect on the consideration that he is a being created in the image of God and placed in the world to serve God's purpose, and that he most assuredly will be held accountable before his Creator for any deviance in the morality of his conduct. He should then carefully assess the nature and consequences—both desired and unintended—of his proposed actions, and be guided accordingly.[18] In this manner, by evaluating his every act in the context of whether it truly serves the divine purpose as reflected in the Torah, he and his fellow man can organize their lives in cooperative social arrangements and achieve a fundamental societal harmony without need of or reference to any external human authority. In effect, he could achieve a reconstitution of the idyllic society of paradigmatic man—the prototypical utopia of the Garden of Eden.

Since the original basis for the constitution of society is the benefits for the individual to be garnered from productive association with other men, any anticooperative behavior manifested by a member of society would be seen as an aberration and as ultimately inimical to the individual's rational self-interest. However, to the extent that such conduct has negative effects on the prevailing social harmony, it would have to be contained. Thus, Joseph Albo argues that, because the complexities of the human economy require that men live in association with one another, it is necessary that they establish a political order—the expressed purpose of which is to "keep men from quarrelling in their transactions and business relations with one another," and generally to "enable the people to live in welfare."[19] Implicit in Albo's view is the assumption that, even though society is founded on the need for interpersonal cooperation, there will always be sufficient deviance from such beneficial relationships to require the establishment of an authoritative political regime to ensure social peace, if not harmony.

In his reflections on government, Malbim takes Albo's position a step further, and argues that the character of man's social relations and the government institutions established to deal with them correspond closely to the level and form of society's economic organization. Social conflict is seen as increasing in some positive relationship to the increase in personal wealth, as well as to the increase in the holdings of private property. The structure of the legal system—and, therefore, the state—follows suit. Under a system of relatively equal distribution of wealth—unencumbered by the institution of private real property—conflict is at a minimum. This residual level of conflict—present even in an essentially propertyless society—results from man's conscious deviation from the path of optimum conduct, and can be eliminated through the process of man's progressive moral improvement. However, the conflicts and the resulting institutions brought into being in a society where economic well-being is based on the ownership of property are in themselves by no means necessary or natural, except insofar as they are reflective of the state of man's progress along the course of his moral history.[20]

Similarly, Samson Raphael Hirsch takes the position that there is no natural need for government at all. Man's consciousness of his place in the divine scheme and his accountability before God for his moral conduct "should be sufficient deterrents from all sin and excesses, even without the intervention of a human authority." However, since "human society is still in that state of moral imperfection where it fears even the lowliest visible human authority more than the unseen omnipotence of the King of Kings," government is now required to perform the functions specified by Albo—namely, to regulate social behavior. But—Hirsch adds—society is nonetheless perfectible under the aegis of governmental authority.[21] The implication here is that, under the proper conditions of moral progress, the need for government intervention in the ordering of human relationships could be rendered moot, and the political society—the state—could devote all its attention to securing the external interests of its members. It would no longer be necessary to impose social order. Instead, man would once again be capable of reconstituting his social relations with others on the basis of true justice, without recourse to human authority. The Torah itself would become the authoritative basis for the ideal society.

Another less optimistic view of man reflects the implicit proposition that not only is man a rational being, he is also naturally prone to rationalization. Indeed, it is his innate ability to rationalize his behavior and actions that permits him consciously and deliberately to violate established social norms and to trespass the bounds of acceptable conduct, while maintaining an attitude of moral vindication. Man's acquisitive instincts may thus become transformed into a rationalized drive for power and possession that—when permitted to operate without restraint—can unleash a predatory competitiveness that—in its turn—may result in the disruption of the prevailing social order. The ensuing social chaos would be contrary to the divine purpose, and therefore would constitute a debasement of man and a perverse distortion of the image of God. The sages viewed the biblical saga of Cain and Abel as exemplifying the ultimate destructiveness of such unrestricted competitiveness.[22]

The slaying of Abel is considered by some to represent an ethical watershed in the moral history of mankind. Prior to this primeval incident, man is seen as living in social harmony with his fellow—engaged in a voluntary cooperative enterprise for the benefit of all, and without the need for an external human regulatory authority. The emergent competitive struggle between Cain and Abel for social preferment or dominance shattered the prevailing natural social order. The killing of Abel constitutes a second "original sin"—that of man against man. The intolerability of Cain's ultimate trespass of the essential inviolability of the life of another human necessitates a fundamental reordering of the bases of social life. An authoritative political order must replace the now disrupted natural voluntary order, if man is to reestablish the personal security required by him in order to freely pursue his part in the divine plan. Thus, Genesis informs us that, subsequent to this original social outrage, an organized political society comes into being. Cain builds the first city, and—by implication—establishes the first government to rule over it. His purpose in so doing is presumably to devise a scheme of social regulation that will—at a minimum—protect him against a repetition by others of the very transgression against the principle of man's inviolability that he himself had just committed. From this perspective, political society comes into existence as a universal moral necessity—a need to provide societally enforceable constraints on individual liberty, which will continue to characterize all subsequent human history.[23]

The concept of political society as a universal necessity is predicated on a view of man—at least in the post-Cain phase of man's moral history—as a willing servant of an egocentricity that places him in a virtual state of belligerence with all other men. He finds himself in an inherently aggressive—and often destructive—competitive environment, which has superseded the cooperative character of society as originally constituted. He can no longer rely on the application of enlightened and rational self-interest to ensure the observance by others of the bounds of the negatively defined personal liberty so essential to social tranquility. Consequently, a regulative regime must be imposed on man, to prevent a cataclysm of competitive attrition through which only the fittest can survive.[24] Left to its own devices, man's unfettered egoism cannot but result in the eventual dissolution of society, to its own detriment.

In this view, anarchy—the absence of an ordering regime—becomes synonymous with social chaos and moral depravity. An early proponent of this perspective is the prophet Habbakuk. Commenting on the chaotic conditions in international affairs attending the rise of Chaldean power, the prophet equates men under conditions of anarchy with the "fishes of the sea... that have no ruler over them" (Hab. 1:14). Applying this same metaphor, the Talmud states: "As it is with the fishes of the sea, the one that is bigger swallows the other up, so with man: were it not for the fear of the government, everyone that is greater than his fellow would swallow him up."[25] Perhaps the most extreme expression of this viewpoint is that reflected in the dictum of Rabbi Hanina, who taught at the time of the social and political convulsions that rocked Judea during the final years of the Second Hebrew Commonwealth before its ultimate destruction by the Romans. Rather than accept the consequences of anarchy, he urged the people to "pray for the welfare of the government"—even though this meant the Romans, for all practical purposes.[26] Presumably, even the social and political order established by an alien enemy was preferable to anarchy and its resultant chaos at the hands of one's compatriots. This view of man and the supposition of his critical need for an authoritative regime to lend order and stability to his social environment dominate subsequent rabbinic political thought.

Maimonides argues that the Torah—as the foundation of human society—has a twofold purpose consistent with the dual character of man. It is concerned with "the well-being of the soul, and the well-being of the body." While he considers the well-being of the soul to be of greater ultimate importance, "the well-being of the body, the government of the state, and the establishment of the best possible relations among men, is anterior in nature and time."[27] Maimonides' view reflects the implicit argument of the seemingly paradoxical dual talmudic adage, "Where there is no Torah, there is no flour. Where there is no flour, there is no Torah."[28] That is, without the Torah, man is incapable of satisfying those basic physical requirements necessary for his very subsistence. On the other hand, man must have his basic physical wants satisfied before he can direct his energies toward the ennoblement of life. In other words, unless the perfection of political society is pursued as a matter of priority, man's higher purpose will not be realized.

Menahem Meiri elaborated further on Maimonides' argument by taking the position that not only is government necessary to restrain man's propensity for aggression and violence, it is also required to facilitate the very conduct of the religious life. In his analysis, human conduct falls under two distinct categories, which he classifies as the religious and the political. Presumably, the religious conduct of man refers to those matters that concern the relationship between man and God, while man's political conduct refers to his relations with other men—singly, or in the context of society at large. The former is considered by Meiri to come under the jurisdiction of the sages (that is, the religious teachers and leaders); the latter falls within the province of the political authorities. Meiri goes on to argue that, while the two categories of leadership represent distinct spheres of concern and authority, they are interrelated in a nonreciprocal manner. He sees the loss or absence of competent religious leadership—while surely detrimental to the quality of religious life—as not necessarily affecting negatively the stability of society, so long as the political leadership remains viable. The normal social relations among men may continue in relative harmony and tranquility. However, the converse is not equally true. In Meiri's view, the loss or absence of competent political leadership will—of necessity—adversely affect the very nature and quality of religious life. An adequate spiritual life requires the social stability that can only be assured under a sound political order. Anarchy and the attendant collapse of the social structure will necessarily divert the attention of men from religious matters to the more mundane concerns of personal security and survival under the threatening circumstances characteristic of social chaos.[29] A stable political order is thus seen as a critical prerequisite—if not the very basis—for a mature religious and spiritual life. In a typical exposition of this perspective, Nissim Girondi (RAN) said it was common knowledge that humans required an institutional authority to regulate their affairs. Indeed, so critical is a political society to the effective conduct of human relations that even a band of thieves must establish an authority structure, if the group is to maintain its essential viability.[30]

However, Malbim would caution against making the leap from this conclusion to the idea that a universal society might be an effective means of dealing with society's problems. In examining the character of political society in the period following the Deluge, Malbim finds the inherent nature of a universal polity itself serving as a source of discontent and corruption—further exacerbating the internecine strife plaguing mankind. Commenting on the breakup of primitive political society as described in the Genesis narrative (11:1–9), he interprets the sequence of events as follows: Initially, in the second—post-Cain—phase of human history, there is but a single human society. This universal society is characterized by a common culture and language, and exists under the regime of a set of social arrangements established in accordance with divine guidance. The primitive social equilibrium is upset when the descendants of Noah elect to establish a new political order, symbolized by the Tower of Babel—a political system not based on the elemental divine guidance. The Creator reviewed the situation and "saw the consequences that would spring from this matter of the city and political society, namely, that violence, ruin, theft and murder would increase among men with an increase in insolence and the rule of tyrants.... And He saw that the conclusion would be that man would become totally corrupted."[31]

The essence of Malbim's argument is simply that, despite the widely held view that a universal political society (if attainable) would equate to some sort of utopia, the truth—as suggested by the biblical saga—is quite to the contrary. Thus, he concludes his interpretation of the biblical text (Gen. 11:7) that describes how the Lord decides to confound men by causing men to speak different languages—which will precipitate the unraveling of the intended universal political order—as follows: Malbim imagines the Creator saying, "We shall not wait until humanity is totally corrupted. Instead, We shall now separate mankind through a diversity of language so that language itself shall diffferentiate among men, and this will be to the benefit of man generally, because an aggregation of villains is both bad for them and bad for the world."[32]

In Malbim's view, a world state would only accelerate the self-destruction of mankind. Consequently, a multinational state structure is necessary to preclude a universal tyranny. Man therefore needs a national political society—even if only as a necessary evil—since the achievement of universal harmony is fully dependent on the reform of man himself, rather than on the elimination of the distinctive national orientations of existing political societies.

Rabbinic political theory is thus clearly not monolithic in character. There is a basic divergence in approach to the question of the origin and basis of political society. On the one hand, some argue that man enters into political society out of a natural need for cooperative association within a framework that can cope with the problems caused by deviance from basic social norms. Others contend that man enters into such a regulated social environment as a consequence of his egocentricity and proclivity for competitive behavior, and therefore in order to secure his own well-being. In essence, the first perspective holds that man has need of political society to preserve himself, while the latter maintains that man needs political society to restrain him from destroying himself. Thus, there is universal agreement that, at least in the post-Cain phase of man's moral history, man clearly requires some sort of authoritative political order to regulate his common affairs.

Given the consensus that political society and government are practical—if not natural—necessities, the critical issue for rabbinic theory is how to ensure that the state does not become a self-serving end in itself. Furthermore, if the polity is to serve an ethical end—namely, the good of man—it must be motivated and directed in accordance with some guidance that will assure the desired behavior of the political regime as well as the members of the polity. In the rabbinic view, this guidance is contained in the Torah.[33] As stated by Gersonides, "The Torah was ordained in order to remove mutual injury from man in order to bring about the perfection of political society."[34]

NOTES

1. The Talmud portrays a person musing to himself: "How much labor Adam must have expended before he obtained bread to eat! He ploughed, sowed, reaped, piled up the leaves, threshed, winnowed, selected the ears, sifted the flour, kneaded and baked and after that he ate; whereas I get up in the morning and find all this prepared for me. And how much labor must Adam have expended before he obtained a garment to wear!... All artisans attend and come to the door of my house, and I get up and find all these things before me" (*Berakhot* 58a). See also Maimonides, *The Guide for the Perplexed* I:72.

2. See Hirsch, *The Pentateuch* I:65 on Gen. 2:18. Hirsch argues that text clearly implies the complete equality of the sexes.

3. The Midrash expresses this concern in the following homily: "It is comparable to a group of men who found themselves seated in a boat. One of them took hold of an augur and began to bore a hole beneath him. His companions challenged him: What are you doing? He retorted: What concern is it of yours? Am I not doing it under my own seat?" (*Leviticus Rabbah* 4:6).

4. *Shabbat* 31a. In my opinion, this formulation by Hillel has been long misunderstood and misinterpreted. Starting perhaps with *Targum Yonatan* on Lev. 19:18, Hillel's statement has been treated as the negative formulation of the Golden Rule: "Thou shalt love thy neighbor as thyself." Since then, scholars have offered a wide variety of explanations as to why Hillel may have seen fit to recast the positive form of the rule in Lev. 19:18 into the negative formula that he taught. However, little attention has been paid to the consideration that, if Hillel's teaching is really simply a restatement of the Golden Rule, there emerges a basic disagreement between Hillel and Rabbi Akiva over what constitutes the central teaching of the Torah. For, while Hillel here states the concept of equality of negative liberty to be the central teaching, Rabbi Akiva is cited in *Sifra* 19:45 as holding that the Golden Rule is simply "a great principle of the Torah." If Hillel's formulation is considered a restatement of the Golden Rule, he would then have to maintain that the Golden Rule is the central teaching of the Torah—while Rabbi Akiva would maintain that it is merely *a* great teaching, rather than *the* teaching of the Torah. Given the stature of these two sages in the talmudic literature—whose teachings are considered authoritative—it is interesting to note the complete absence of any reference to the obvious discrepancy between their views on this matter. My contention, however, is that there is no disagreement between the two sages because they are talking about two different matters. Hillel is not reformulating the Golden Rule—it being, as indicated by Rabbi Akiva, one of the great teachings of the Torah. Hillel is concerned with defining the core teaching of the Torah, which lays the foundation for the truly moral society.

5. MAHARAL writes: "There is no individual man in the universe, but man receives his reality from the totality, in that he is among the whole and belongs to the whole" (Judah Loew ben Bezalel, *Derekh Hayyim*, p. 101). As noted by one student of MAHARAL's thought, "In maintaining this position, MAHARAL predates the majority of social researchers. The public is an actual social unit—not a collection of individuals—and it is prior in its formation as a unit to the individual. . . . The public is not a synthetic entity. It is not an aggregate of independent individuals" (Gordin, *HaMAHARAL miPrague*, p. 56).

6. "The whole is the most important, not the private person, because the individual is subject to change . . . [whereas] the public has a firmer foundation" (Judah Loew ben Bezalel, *Derekh Hayyim*, p. 56). MAHARAL describes the organic nature of society by drawing an analogy between it and the human organism: "Know that man is composed of many limbs, such as hands, feet, and the remaining organs . . . and none of them has any independent life except for a single one: the one that is at the seat of the regime [of the body], which receives existence first . . . and as this primary organ is the heart, nullify its existence and all the other organs are void and without further life. And thus all mankind is conceived as a single person. There are people that relate to one another in the same manner as the primary organ relates to man, and so with the remaining organs . . . each one in a proper relationship to every other one. . . . The prince or king

that rules over man is called 'head,' in that he is as the head of a man; and the sages ... leading the people in their wisdom and by their law, just as the courts and the judges are called 'eyes of the people'... in that they are like the eyes... and man follows after his eyes.... It is necessary that all the organs be joined to the heart. Similarly, man should be associated to that which is at the same level as the heart, and receive thereby the life force" (Judah Loew ben Bezalel, Be'er haGolah, p. 143).

7. Malbim, HaTorah vehaMitzvah on Gen. 17:2.
8. See Chapter 2, note 4.
9. Belkin, Essays in Traditional Jewish Thought, p. 40.
10. This argument is pursued extensively and vigorously by Abraham Hen: "Every government in the world, since the foundation of the earth, and especially since the flowering of civilization, is based on society, on the state, on the majority; that is to say, on the sacrifice that the individual must bring to the altar of the many. In actuality, the individual is always sacrificed on the altar of some tyranny, of some dictator or some accepted slogan which we are too lax to examine and recognize as a mere fabrication. ... The individual by himself, in his independent and private life, is nothing but an expendable quantity—such is the secular state. The Jewish Kingdom is designated to be the very antithesis to this sanctified viewpoint; it must be based only on the individual man, on the three 'qualitative aspects of existence': the truth of being, the right to exist and the sanctity of existence. Simply, the existence of each individual. Our Torah, which is the central essence and ultimate foundation of that promise—absolute justice, is nothing but a complete antithesis to the order of the world that is based on the law of the majority. Under every expanse of heaven there is nothing but individual man. No man has authority over another other than man over himself.... In all of this there is no denial of the state, of society, of the people. On the contrary, there is nothing more sacred to the Jew and his Torah, nor more exalted, than the life of society, the totality and the people.... A lonely life, a life of segregation and separation from the totality is for the Jew a life of boredom, desolation, waste, and above all else, a life of iniquity and impurity. Consequently, there is nothing in the world that it would not be worth sacrificing for the benefit of the totality, society and the nation. Everything in the world... except... for a petty thing... except for life itself" (Hen, BeMalkhut haYahadut I:101–104).
11. J. Terumot 8:6.
12. See M. H. Luzzatto, Mesillat Yesharim, p. 34.
13. Baba Metzia 62a.
14. See Sanhedrin 27b: "All of Israel are responsible for one another." This same idea is expressed in the Midrash, as follows: "Why is Israel compared to a nut? Just as with a nut, if you remove one from the heap the rest tumble down and roll one after another, so it is with Israel. When one is affected, all feel it" (Canticles Rabbah 6:17). In another variation on this theme, the Midrash asks: "Why is Israel compared to a sheep? Just as with a sheep, if it receives a blow on the head or on one of its limbs all of its limbs feel it, so it is with Israel. When one sins, all feel it" (Leviticus Rabbah 4:6).
15. "As long as censure and admonition are effective in social life, there will be peace and comfort in life, and evil will vanish" (Tamid 28a). On the other hand, should they be absent, the direst of consequences may follow. "Jerusalem was destroyed only because they did not rebuke each other; for it is said, 'Her princes are become like harts that find no pasture' (Lam. 1:6); just as with the hart, the head of one is at the side of the

other's tail, so Israel of that generation hid their faces in the earth, and did not rebuke each other" (*Shabbat* 119b).

16. In the rabbinic view, the prevalence of evil in society—particularly in Judaic society—is its own indictment. The consequent upheavals and dislocations are seen as predicted by the text, "Ye shall therefore keep all my statutes, and all my judgements, and do them: that the land, whither I bring you to dwell therein spew you not out" (Lev. 20:22). The Midrash states: "The land... cannot tolerate men of transgression. It is to be compared to the son of a king, whom they made to eat food that was indigestible, which he is compelled to vomit out" (*Sifra* 20:14).

17. This is reflected in the teaching of Rabbi Tarfon: "It is not thy duty to complete the work, but neither art thou free to desist from it" (*Avot* 2:21).

18. Akaviah ben Mahalalel—a contemporary of Hillel—taught: "Reflect upon three things and you will not come into the grip of sin: Know whence you came, where you are going, and before whom you will in the future have to render account and reckoning" (*Avot* 3:1). This same theme is struck by Rabbi Judah the Prince, who taught: "Reflect upon three things, and you will not come into the grip of sin: Know what is above you— a seeing Eye, and a hearing Ear, and that all your deeds are recorded in a book" (*Avot* 2:1).

19. Albo, *Sefer Ha'Ikkarim* I:72.

20. Malbim, *HaTorah vehaMitzvah* on Deut. 1:9.

21. Commenting on *Avot* 3:2, Hirsch argues that "the orderly, undisturbed development towards that happiness to which all men are entitled is dependent upon the preservation of the authority of earthly powers and officials" (Hirsch, *Chapters of the Fathers*, p. 40).

22. The Midrash offers the following interpretation of the fraternal conflict leading to the death of Abel: "About what did they argue? They said: Come let us divide the universe between us. One took possession of the earth, and one possession of all movable estate. The one then argued: You are standing on my property. The other argued: That which you are wearing is mine. One said: Begone!—the other shouted: Undress! In the midst of this argument Cain rose up and slew Abel" (*Genesis Rabbah* 22:16).

23. See Malbim, who writes: "After he had become the first murderer that destroyed the natural order of things, which resulted in man becoming as the fishes of the sea, each man swallowing his neighbor alive, Cain wanted to rectify this situation by building a city wherein men would join in a political society and establish laws and statutes among themselves in such a manner as to assist them in withstanding those who would rise against them... the erection of this city was the beginning of political society" (Malbim, *HaTorah vehaMitzvah* on Gen. 4:17).

24. See Saadia ben Joseph al-Fayyumi (Saadia Gaon), *The Book of Beliefs and Opinions*, p. 141.

25. *Avodah Zarah* 4a.

26. Ibid. Also *Avot* 3:2.

27. Maimonides, *The Guide for the Perplexed* III:27.

28. *Avot* 3:17. See Judah Loew ben Bezadel (MAHARAL), *Derekh Hayyim*, p. 118.

29. Meiri, *Sefer Bet haBehirah: Perush Massekhet Avot*, pp. 115–116.

30. Nissim Girondi, *Shnaim Assar Derushim* # 10, p. 74.

31. Malbim, *HaTorah vehaMitzvah* on Gen. 11:5.

32. Ibid. on Gen. 11:7.

33. See the discussion of kingship in its relation to Torah in Shalom, *Nevei Shalom* I:107.

34. Gersonides, *Perush al haTorah al Derekh Biur* I:84. See also Hirsch, *Chapters of the Fathers*, p. 57.

4
The Individual and the Polity

Much of rabbinic political theorizing is predicated on the fundamental premise that political society and its institutions are justified only to the extent that they serve the true interests of their constituents. They are never to be viewed as ends in themselves. It follows from this that the principles and legal precepts on which the institutions of political society are based must be such as to both establish a harmonious and beneficent relationship between man and the polity of which he is a member, and provide means of restricting the potential for abuse of authority and power by officials of the institutions. The formulation of the appropriate legal foundation for this purpose becomes critical to the success of the enterprise.

It was soon recognized by the early expositors of the rabbinic teachings that, although the ultimate perfection of man and his society is contingent on willing conformity with the precepts of the divine law embodied in the Torah, the particular application of those precepts in the context of concrete historical conditions must remain relatively flexible, if the needs of man and society are to be met. Were this not the case, the social structures and arrangements appropriate to the environmental circumstances of the period of the revelation of the Torah to Moses and Israel would have become fixed and intractable for all time. In later periods and in radically different environmental contexts, men would be arbitrarily compelled to fashion their lives in accordance with the demands and requirements of archaic and anachronistic social, political, and economic institutions. The proper relationship of man and society would become distorted. Instead of serving to facilitate the perfection of man under a given set of temporal and spatial conditions and under the prevailing social reality, the institutions of the polity would in themselves become the objects of man's attentions—the towering center of his universe. Man would become subverted into serving the arbitrary ends of institutions, which—more properly—should be serving him. In this way, the very purpose and justification for the establishment of a politically organized society would be undermined. Thus, Rabbi Yannai—one of the sages of the Talmud—taught: "If the Laws of the Torah had been fixed in advance, the world would have no basis for existence."[1]

The obvious problem of reconciling the eternality of the precepts of the divine law—the Torah, as embodied in the written word of the Five Books of Moses—with the temporality of interpretation and application is resolved in Rabbinic Judaism by the concept of Oral Law.[2] It is the function of the Oral Torah to ensure the viability of the written Torah as the basis for the ideal organization of the life of virtue for the individual and his society. Immanuel Jakobovits has compared the relation between the oral and the written laws "to that between the hard soil of mother earth and the lush vegetation growing from it. The one is rigid and static, in itself lifeless and yet unchanging; the other flexible and dynamic, ever fresh and rejuvenated."[3] The Oral Law—the Torah in its extended sense—is considered by rabbinic tradition to be coeval with the written law—Torah in its narrower connotation, the Five Books of Moses.

Since the Oral Law is presumed to have originated at the same time as the written Torah and is handed down as a tradition from one generation to another, one might assume that it would not entail any greater flexibility than the written law in terms of its adaptability to the needs of a particular time and place. However, the Oral Law is conceived as being broader in content than the written law. It includes not only the correct exegesis of the latter, but also the hermeneutical methods for interpreting the Torah in a manner that will assure its continuing relevance as the supreme guide to the life of justice and virtue. It contains matters of a revelatory nature that augment the written texts of the Five Books of Moses. Finally, it incorporates principles and precepts that are derived from and dependent on human reason.[4] Accordingly, the range of subject matter that comes within the purview of human discretion is very broad indeed. At the same time, however, rabbinic teaching maintains that the Torah as revealed at Sinai—both written and oral—is all-encompassing and already contains within it the essence of everything that can be attributed to it through exegesis and interpretation. As stated in the Talmud, "Whatever an expert was destined to find anew in the Torah was given already to Moses on Sinai."[5] Consequently, intellectual endeavors regarding the formulation of laws and rules of conduct appropriate to man's existential situation consist fundamentally in uncovering what already exists conceptually, rather than in creating something new.[6] This suggests that there exists a carefully circumscribed framework of divine law, within which man is essentially free to adapt eternally valid precepts and principles of interpretation for practical application to specific contemporary issues and concerns. Thus—as asserted by Joseph Albo—"the law of God can not be perfect so as to be adequate for all times, because the ever new details of human relations, their customs and their acts, are too numerous to be embraced in a book. Therefore Moses was given orally certain general principles, only briefly alluded to in the Torah, by means of which the wise men in every generation may work out the details as they appear."[7]

Given the great variation among men and the extreme unlikelihood that they would easily and unanimously agree to a particular interpretation and application of a precept of the Torah in any specific instance, how are such decisions to be reached? What formula will enable a common understanding of the guidance provided by the Torah to become accepted and operative? The answer given in the Talmud by Rabbi Huna is that "throughout the Torah there is an established rule that a majority is like the whole."[8] Or—as stated in another place— when Moses pleaded with God, "Lord of the Universe, inform me as to the Law; [the Lord] said to him: Follow the rule of the majority."[9]

The notion of decision by a majority in this context is highly problematic. Does it imply that the authoritative interpretation and adaptation of the precepts of the Torah are to be subject to the vagaries of popular opinion? Such a position would surely contradict the very essence of rabbinic teaching and tradition. Should mere numbers alone be relied on to determine what is morally right or wrong, or what policies will best serve to realize the goals of the Torah? The rabbis were certainly well aware that the public is subject to manipulation by the unscrupulous who can shape majorities to serve their own purposes, for ends that may be fundamentally inimical to the real interests of the majority. What of the exceptional individual? Should not the views of an outstanding legal scholar be accorded greater weight than the opposing views of a majority of more ordinary men? The rabbinic response to these questions entails a reformulation of the principle. The law should be interpreted in accordance with the opinion of the majority, but the majority that is intended by the talmudic dictum is a majority of those learned in the Torah.[10] As for the outstanding individual—regardless of his stature and recognized scholarship—the opinion of the individual cannot stand against that of the majority.[11] The emphasis on a majority of the learned would seem to imply that the control of society's affairs should be placed in the hands of an intellectual elite. Government of the society would then be carried out by an aristocracy—not of the blood, but of the mind.

This view of the political role of an intellectual aristocracy reflects the dominant tendency in rabbinic political theory as it attempts to grapple with the many problems of structuring the ideal Torah-based polity. At the same time, it should also be recognized that the ranks of the intellectual elite in Judaic society are open to all, and not just a privileged few. All have the opportunity (indeed, the obligation, within the limits of their natural capacities) to become learned in the Torah—to become part of the learned community that is entitled to prescribe for society.

Since the overall purpose of the Torah is to guide men toward the achievement of moral self-perfection, both the Torah and the bases on which particular laws or judgments are derived from its precepts must be widely known and understood by the general public, if they are to gain popular acceptance and command faithful observance. Seen from this perspective, the Torah must not become the special province of the magistrate and scholar. Its teachings are the legacy, and should be the concern of the entire people of Israel. Knowledge of the Torah—the Law—is thus of preeminent importance in the rabbinic scheme of things. It is only through an intimate familiarity with its various aspects that the individual can establish and pursue his relations with other men on the basis of true justice. It is only by having a highly educated general public that the political society and its governing bodies can be held fully and effectively responsible for the commonweal.[12]

Accordingly, Rabbinic Judaism places great emphasis on public education. The efficacy of the Torah as the basis for establishing and maintaining an ordered society is considered directly related to the extent that its laws are known, understood, accepted, and honored by the members of the polity. It is only through the individual's personal familiarity and conformity with the tenets of the Torah that society and its institutions can be perfected, and thereby provide the social tranquility required by man in pursuing his higher purposes undisturbedly. Indeed, the view is expressed in the Talmud that the study of the Torah surpasses in merit all other precepts of the Torah,[13] because it brings in its wake an understanding of the other precepts that will lead to their greater and more comprehensive observance and fulfillment.[14]

To help achieve such universal familiarity with the laws, a special burden is placed on those officials of the polity who bear responsibility for the administration of justice and for the education of the public. To clarify the nature of the legal order governing the relationships between man and society at any particular place and time, the jurist is enjoined to commit to writing the basis for his decisions—to issue a judicial opinion that is documented for all to see and learn from. At the same time, such a practice exposes the judge's decisions to the scrutiny of the entire community of the learned, which serves to reduce any elements of arbitrariness. Thus—according to one medieval scholar—"It is proper for every man who fears Heaven to write down the reasoning behind his judgment."[15] This pedagogic responsibility of the jurist is an important facet of accomplishing the aim of a well-educated public.[16]

A corollary to the concern for immersing the citizen in deep understanding of the law is the proposition that the laws imposed on society must be reasonable with respect to the capacity of the general public to observe them faithfully. Adherence to this principle ensures that the laws governing society reflect a viable jurisprudence capable of serving the essential needs of man and society under the varying circumstances of time and place. This idea is explicitly embodied in the talmudic dictum, "A restriction is not to be imposed upon the community unless the majority of the community can maintain it."[17]

Popular acceptability is thus seen in rabbinic political theory as a determining factor in the determination of burdens that may be placed on the public by its constituted authorities. But—as observed by Samson Raphael Hirsch—"it is quite clear, of course, that maximum dissemination of the knowledge of the

Law could act as a powerful agent to predispose the people for the acceptance and observance of such enactments."[18] In a polity structured in accordance with—and informed by—the precepts of the Torah, there will thus be found a creative tension between the citizenry and the government—which will keep each party from overstepping the bounds of reason and propriety.

The earliest sages of the talmudic period urged their disciples to "make a fence for the Torah."[19] Such a "fence" was to be a protective wall around the precepts of the Torah—designed to permit them to flourish under all historical conditions. The fence would serve to preclude violation or abandonment of a precept, by interposing a safeguarding rule. Thus, by placing additional constraints on the behavior and actions of men in confronting the challenges of life at any particular point in time and circumstance, such a fence would help preserve intact the sanctity, dignity, and eternal validity of the precepts of the Torah, which would thereby remain an island of constancy in a world of flux— a buoy to hang onto in a sea of turmoil.[20] However, "they did not make fences other than such as are capable of being sustained."[21] Restrictions imposed by the authorities were legitimate only when the majority of the community acknowledged them as such, and were prepared to modify their behavior and practices accordingly. Noncompliance by the public at large constituted an effective veto over such legislation—making passive resistance an integral component of the process of government. Under such a concept of public law, a highly educated and motivated citizenry was clearly necessary, if the rule of reason were to prevail in the governance of society. A poorly informed public might be prone to accept views and practices that could obstruct the imposition of additional regulations essential to its own longer term interests.

As a counterpart to the positive law enacted by the authorities and subject to the popular constraints just discussed, there is also to be found in rabbinic jurisprudence a strong element of customary law. In the latter case, the law is legislated—in effect—by popular practice, and subsequently incorporated into the legal corpus by the juridical authorities. Thus, the Talmud relates an instance when a sage was requested to pronounce a ruling in law and responded by saying, "Go see how the people conduct themselves."[22] In another place, we find the dictum, "For every law that is under question in the court, and those with whose nature you are unfamiliar, go and observe. The way the public practice is, is the way it should be."[23]

The broad involvement of the public in the governmental process is a clear reflection of the fundamental tenet of rabbinic political theory concerning the nature and purpose of political society and its institutions. In this construct, the public has a moral obligation to help assure that both law and government ultimately serve the interests of a Torah-oriented society.

To ensure that the legal order be rendered capable of fulfilling its role in establishing and promoting social justice and the general welfare, it is necessary that the provisions of that order be not only lawful, but inherently just. The essential principle of social justice within the functional context of the legal order is therefore the idea of the fundamental equality of all men before the law.

The rabbinic concept of the intrinsic equality of men is a corollary to the biblical description of the creation of man. He is created alone and in the image of his Creator. Thus, all men have a common origin in respect of ancestry.[24] Furthermore, Scripture explicitly declares: "Ye shall have one manner of law, as well for the stranger, as for the homeborn" (Lev. 24:22).[25]

This concept of equality before the law may perhaps be best understood as a synthesis of the professed natural equality of men in respect of their Creator, and the acknowledged natural inequality of men in respect of one another. The former is expressed in the Midrash as follows: "R. Judah b. Shalom said: If a poor man comes and pleads before another, that other does not listen to him; if a rich man comes, he receives and listens to him at once. God does not act in this manner; all are equal before Him—women, slaves, rich and poor."[26] The natural inequality of men in respect of one another is addressed in the Midrash as well—perhaps with a poignant touch of irony—in its retelling of a purported dialogue between King David and the Lord: "David said, 'Lord of the Universe, make equality in Thy world.' God replied, 'If I made all equal, who would practice faithfulness and lovingkindness?' "[27] This reference is concerned with man's moral posture, rather than the more obvious distinctions of intellectual and physical capacities. However—as Emmanuel Rackman has argued—"since God created all men equal, their natural inequality can only be justified with reference to His service, which means the fulfillment of the very equality God had willed."[28]

While the rabbinic concept of social justice is predicated on the ideal of intrinsic equality, it also takes account of the fact that the tangible differences between men may be very great—both in terms of innate capacities, as well as with regard to social and economic circumstances. Consequently, if persons characterized by such intrinsic and extrinsic inequalities were treated as equals before the law—without special consideration being given to those differences—the fundamental principle of justice might be severely compromised in the process of arriving at an authoritative judicial decision. True justice therefore requires that differences between persons be taken fully into account, so that unequals may become equalized before the law.[29] Recognizing the differences among men—both innate and contingent or acquired—it becomes a basic responsibility of government to so order society as to bring about the equivalent of equality, while preserving those essential qualities manifested in the differences that derive from the gift of the Creator or from the practical consequences of the operation of His law in the social and economic spheres. The scales of justice must be balanced in such a manner as to produce the greatest possible social cohesion and harmony. The precepts of the Torah are considered to have been provided as the necessary guidelines for the successful accomplishment of this momentous task.

The rabbinic concern over the application of the law in justice goes beyond being a mere aspiration for the realization of social justice in the polity. It reflects an earnest intention to structure the Judaic legal order in accordance with the biblical charge, "Judges and officers shalt thou make thee in all thy gates . . . and they shall judge the people with righteous judgement" (Deut. 16:18). The process of government must be such as to ensure the equalization of the inequalities of men in the interest of social harmony. However, the principle of "righteous judgement" is not self-executing. It becomes operative only through the intervention of the right men. As Maimonides observed, "The well-being of society demands that there should be a leader able to regulate the actions of man; he must complete every shortcoming, remove every excess, and prescribe for the conduct of all, so that the natural variety should be counterbalanced by the uniformity of legislation, and the order of society be well established."[30] This places an awesome responsibility on the shoulders of those whose task it is to make sure that justice prevails in the polity. The business of political leadership and the exercise of political power and influence must therefore be approached with great seriousness and deliberation.

The exercise of righteous judgment on behalf of the polity is to be governed both by procedural and substantive norms and safeguards. From a procedural perspective, at a minimum there must be due process, whereby all are treated equitably—that is, nonpreferentially. As Obadiah Sforno argued, "The process of litigation should be such that the law is administered righteously; that it should not be soft for one party and harsh for the other."[31] From the substantive standpoint, there is a heavy moral burden on the judges not only to ensure the legality of the proceedings, but also to ensure that substantive justice is rendered in the judgment. In Malbim's opinion, "It is insufficient that one should adjudicate only according to the rules of law. He should see to it that his judgement be truly just, and if it appears to him that the law is deceptive [from the standpoint of justice] he should not pronounce sentence based on it."[32]

While the many complex issues regarding the relationship between the letter of the law and justice are beyond the scope of this discussion, it is evident that rabbinic political theory is motivated by the central proposition set forth at the outset—namely, that political society and its institutions are justified only to the extent that they truly serve the interests of their constituents. Those interests must, however, be carefully weighed on the scales of justice.

NOTES

1. Jer. T. Sanhedrin 4:2. Moses Margoliot explains Rabbi Yannai's teaching as meaning that "there would be no continued existence for the world because the Torah requires that its various aspects be interpreted for each particular situation" (Margoliot, Pnei Moshe, ad loc.).

2. Joseph Albo explains the inherent purpose and nature of the "oral law" as follows: "A thing is perfect if we can not conceive it to receive addition or diminution. Now

since David characterizes the Torah as perfect, it follows that it can not in any respect be deficient in the realization of its purpose. Now every written document of whatever nature it be, can be understood in two different ways, one of which corresponds to the intention of the writer and the other is very far from it. . . . For this reason it was necessary, in order that the divine Torah should be perfect and should be understood in the correct way, that when God gave the Torah to Moses in writing, He should explain it to him in the proper manner. Similarly Moses explained it to Joshua, Joshua to the elders, the elders to the prophets, and so from generation to generation, so that there should be no doubt in the correct meaning of the written document. This interpretation of the written law . . . is called the oral law, because this interpretation can not be in writing, else the same uncertainty of which we spoke would attach to this writing as to the first, and we should require an interpretation of the interpretation, and so on without end. . . . It is clear, therefore, that the written Torah can not be perfect unless it is accompanied by this oral interpretation, which is called the oral law" (Albo, *Sefer Ha'Ikkarim* III:201–203).

See also Hoffmann, *HaMishnah haRishonah*: "The Bible word read from the written book and the teachings heard from the mouth of the Sages are for the Israelite the two sources from which he draws the Torah received by Moses from God on Sinai. The Torah is one, although the source from which it comes is twofold, the teaching which comes to us from the Mishnah of the Sages is of the identical date and identical origin as that which is derived by interpretation of the scriptural word, all is given by one God and communicated by one and the same prophet. Hence, when we speak of written law, *Torah Shebikhtab*, and the oral law, *Torah Sheb'al Peh*, we have in mind one and the same law of God derived in part from the divine word committed to writing and in part from the authoritative statements of the teachers of tradition" (translation from first German edition of 1882 by Harry C. Schimmel in his *The Oral Law*, pp. 19–20).

3. "Foreword" to Schimmel, *The Oral Law*.

4. As defined by Malbim, the substance of the oral law is divided into three categories (Malbim, *HaTorah vehaMitzvah* on Deut. 17:18):

A) Matters that depend upon human reason and understanding, such as the length of the year and the determination of the calendar, which are dependent on a knowledge of the progress of the stars and the science of mechanics. . . .

B) Matters that are traditionally conceived to be laws given to Moses at Sinai, and which are not alluded to in any manner within scripture. . . .

C) The laws of the Torah that are derived from scripture by means of the rules of exegesis that are applicable to the Bible, and by means of linguistic rules that we have also received as a tradition in the first instance.

5. Jer. T. Peah 2:6.

6. This view is set forth most forcefully by Zvi Hirsch Chajes: "After the sealing of the Torah [the Pentateuch], the Lord did not command either prophet or sage, through prophecy or inspiration . . . with regard to anything concerning law and justice; nor does the Lord instruct man with regard to the conduct and study of the laws and rules. For the divine law is perfect, encompassing all possible issues, and the Lord transmitted to us at Sinai general and particular rules and details of the law, and the methods by which exegesis may be accomplished, and they will be adequate for every matter essential to the proper conduct of mankind" (Chajes, *Torat Neviyyim*, p. 17).

7. Albo, *Sefer Ha'Ikkarim* III:203. Similarly, another writer of the fourteenth cen-

tury—Vidal Yom Tov of Tolosa—argues: "Our perfect Torah provided general principles for the improvement of the morals of man and for his conduct in the world.... And the intent was that he should conduct himself in a straight and good manner with his fellow men. And it would have been inappropriate to dictate details in this regard, because the precepts of the Torah apply necessarily to every time and period and every issue, but the morals of man and his behavior vary according to the period and the personalities" (Vidal Yom Tov of Tolosa, *Maggid Mishneh* on *Shulhan Arukh*, "Hilkhot Shekheinim" 14:5).

8. *Horayot* 3b.

9. *Jer. T. Sanhedrin* 4:2. See also Margoliot, *Pnei Moshe*, ad loc. Similarly, an anonymous sixteenth-century commentator notes: "Within each law there are aspects of permissiveness and prohibition, and who would be able to discern the truth [in advance]? Therefore it is said that the law should be in accordance with the majority view" (*Perush* on Jerusalem Talmud in the Cracow edition of 1609, reprinted in *Talmud Bavli ve-Yerushalmi*).

Naftali Zvi Berlin suggests that "one should follow the view of the majority because the straight and the good probably are in accord with its opinion" (Berlin, *HaAmek Davar* to Ex. 23:2).

10. Albo writes: "The power of deciding must always be given to the majority of the learned. And though it is possible that a single individual may be wiser than every one of them, and his view more in agreement with the truth than that of all the rest, nevertheless the rule is as the majority decide, and an individual has no authority to oppose them in a practical decision.... If we abandon the majority and follow an individual in one matter, there will be a serious division in Israel in every generation. For every individual will claim that he is right and that the law shall be as he decides. This would destroy the Torah entirely. We must not therefore abandon the general rule, which is to follow the majority and ignore the individual or the minority, provided, however, that the majority consists of learned men and not ignoramuses, for the masses and the ignorant people are easily persuaded of a thing that is not so, and strenuously insist that it is" (Albo, *Sefer Ha'Ikkarim* III:205–206).

11. The question of the exceptional individual opposing the majority is dealt with in legendary form in the Talmud in regard to a controversy between Rabbi Eliezer and Rabbi Joshua—the latter representing the majority: "Again he [R. Eliezer] said to them: If the *halakhah* agrees with me, let it be proved from Heaven! Whereupon a Heavenly Voice cried out: Why do ye dispute with R. Eliezer, seeing that in all matters the *halakhah* agrees with him! But R. Joshua arose and exclaimed: 'It is not in heaven' (Deut. 30:12). What did he mean by this?—Said R. Jeremiah: That the Torah had already been given at Mount Sinai; we pay no attention to a Heavenly Voice, because Thou hast long since written in the Torah at Mount Sinai, 'After the majority must one incline' [Ex. 23:2]" (*Baba Metziah* 59b).

12. Samson Raphael Hirsch writes: "The Torah is ... meant to be the common possession of the entire community, and the maximum dissemination of the knowledge of the Law is viewed as our supreme task and our most sacred concern.... In this way every Jew was to be rendered capable of consulting the original sources of the Law by himself to find guidance for his daily life. At the same time, this means that the decisions handed down by the judges and the expounders of the Law would be subject to control by the largest possible number among the general Jewish public. In all likelihood the sages of Jewish religious doctrine are now and have always been the only teachers in any religion

on earth to regard it as the supreme goal of their endeavors to render their own services superfluous" (Hirsch, *Chapters of the Fathers*, p. 6).

13. "We have learned that these are the things that a man does and reaps their benefits in this world while the principal remains for him in the world to come, and they are honoring one's father and mother, the practice of active lovingkindness, and the bringing of peace between man and his fellow; but the merit of the study of the Torah surpasses all the others" (*Shabbat* 127a; and *Peah* 1:1).

14. "The following question was asked: Which is greater, study or performance? R. Tarfon answered and said: performance is greater. R. Akiva answered and said: study is greater. [Afterwards] all answered and said: study is greater because study leads to performance" (*Kiddushin* 40b). See also Maimonides, *Hilkhot Talmud Torah* 3:3; and Moses of Coucy, *Sefer Mitzvot Gadol*, "Mitzvot Aseh," # 12.

15. See Hayyim ben Isaac "Or Zaruah", *Sefer Sheilot uTeshuvot*, p. 6, # 13. Jacob ben Wolf Kranz, the Maggid of Dubno, regrets that there is such a paucity of judges in Israel because, "if there were to be a judge for every ten people, there would be sufficient time for them to instruct every inquirer and provide him with insight into the reasons of the law" (Kranz, *Mishlei Yaacov*, p. 51b).

16. However, it should be noted that, under certain circumstances specified in the Talmud, the principle under discussion here is somewhat modified. Thus, for example, in cases of ritual purity (*Avodah Zarah* 37b) or the acquisition of property rights in the public domain (*Baba Kamma* 30b)—where the law is clearly established—the judges are nonetheless prohibited from giving advisory opinions that would tend to permit the inquirer to take undue advantage of the permissiveness of the law. This does not preclude the inquirer himself from learning the law, through examination of the relevant source texts.

17. *Baba Batra* 60b; *Avodah Zarah* 36a; *Baba Kamma* 79b. See also *Jer. T. Shabbat* 1:5: "R. Yohanan . . . said: It is an accepted principle with me that every restriction that a court imposes on the public that the majority of the public does not accept, has no force." Using this principle as the point of departure, an anonymous scholar of the post-talmudic period argues: "Certainly [laws] may be abolished for several reasons; one, because it is said that the laws are open to retraction in order to meet the needs of the many, and also because it does not make sense to levy restrictions on the public that the public cannot uphold" (*Shaare Teshubah: Responsa of the Geonim*, p. 4a, # 33).

Maimonides restates this principle in a more elaborate formulation: "A court that sees fit to impose a restriction, enact a regulation, or establish a custom must give careful prior thought to whether the majority of the public can maintain them. Where a court did so legislate, and thought that a majority of the community could maintain it, and after it was enacted people disputed it and it did not become accepted by the majority of the community, the enactment is nullified and they may not compel the people to conform to it. If it was enacted and it was thought to have been accepted by all of Israel, and the matter rested as such for many years, and long after another court arose and investigated throughout Israel and saw that the restriction was not being observed generally, the court has the authority to nullify it, even though the court is of a lesser stature, both in number and in wisdom, than the original court that issued the restriction" (Maimonides, *Hilkhot Mamrim* 2:5).

18. Hirsch, *Chapters of the Fathers*, p. 7.
19. *Avot* 1:1.
20. In discussing the process of fence-making in the development of rabbinic law,

Zacharias Frankel notes: "Sometimes they built fences and enacted decrees according to the needs of the hour and period. They also made legal provisions in accordance with the prevailing political and social conditions; because it was known that in the course of time issues would come into being that the earlier teachers had not addressed, both with regard to the needs of men as well as the conduct of the state and the relationship of its residents to one another. Because of this they had need of new norms and laws" (Frankel, *Darkei haMishnah*, p. 2).

21. *Tosefta Sheviyit* 3:7. Also *Jer. T. Sheviyit* 4:2.

22. *Berakhot* 45a.

23. *Jer. T. Peah* 7:6. In an attempt to place customary law in an appropriate context within rabbinic tradition, Eliezer Levi provides the following formulation: "All the customary practices that spring from the people—even if they come about as the result of foreign influences—are based on the views of Abraham with regard to true justice, integrity, and the love of man, and therefore... on the foundations of the Torah, and have thus received the concurrence of the sages" (Levi, *Yesodot haHalakhah*, p. 159).

24. The Talmud suggests that one reason why man was created alone was "for the sake of peace among men, that one might not say to his fellow, 'My father was greater than yours'" (*Sanhedrin* 37a).

25. This passage is interpreted by Samson R. Hirsch as meaning, "just as all the rights and all the high value of human beings are rooted in the Personality of God, so does this form the basis for complete equality in law and justice" (Hirsch, *The Pentateuch* on Lev. 24:22). The Midrash declares: "All are equal before the law. The duty of observance is for all" (*Sifra Deuteronomy*, "Ekev" 11:22).

26. *Exodus Rabbah* 21:4.

27. Ibid. 31:5.

28. Rackman, *One Man's Judaism*, p. 145.

29. Samson R. Hirsch epitomizes the rabbinic concept of social justice in the following formulation: "Respect every being around thee and all that is in thee as the creation of thy God; everything belonging to them as given them by God or in accordance with law which he has sanctioned. Leave willingly to each being that which it is justly entitled to call its own. Be not as regards aught a curse. Especially honor every human being as thy equal, regard him in his essence, that is to say, in his invisible personality, in his bodily envelope and in his life. Extend the same regard to his artificially enlarged body, his property; to the demands which he may be entitled to make upon you for assistance by grants of property or acts of physical strength; in measure and number; in recompense of injury to his person or possessions. Have regard, also, to his rightful claim of truth; of liberty, happiness, and peace of mind, of honor and undisturbed tranquility. Do not abuse his weakness of heart, mind, or body; do not unjustly employ thy legal power over him" (Hirsch, *The Nineteen Letters of Ben Uziel*, pp. 109–110).

30. Maimonides, *The Guide for the Perplexed* II:40. This same idea is treated in a somewhat different though related fashion by Menahem Meiri, who bases his remarks on the biblical passage where Moses requests a successor so "that the congregation of the Lord be not as sheep which have no shepherd" (Num. 27:17). Meiri writes: "Because just as the shepherd suffers and undertakes great pains in his need to lead his sheep in varying ways, the healthy and strong sheep in one way, and the weak in a different manner, one that follows a straight path in one direction, and one that tends to wander from the path in another, in the matter of leadership, sheep and men are equivalent; the proud shall be led in one way and the humble in a different way, the wise in one

way and the simple in another, the good in one way and the wicked in another. And they shall each be given their laws in accordance with their natures until all can be brought into a single path" (Meiri, *Teshuvot Rabbenu HaMeiri*, p. 20).

31. Sforno, *Perush R. Obadiah Sforno* on Deut. 16:18.
32. Malbim, *HaTorah vehaMitzvah* on Deut. 16:18.

5
Political Authority and Obligation

In order that the polity be rendered capable of fulfilling its responsibilities toward its constituents, once established it must command the general obedience of the public. That is, it must be able to act authoritatively. The source of such authority is a matter of grave importance in rabbinic political theory. Authority must be legitimate if the public is to incur the obligation to pay heed to it. Accordingly, the Torah—constituting the ultimate source of political authority—declares: "According to the law which they shall teach thee, and according to the judgment which they shall tell thee, thou shalt do" (Deut. 17:11). The "law" referred to in the biblical text is considered within rabbinic tradition as including "those regulations, restrictions and practices that they may impose on the public for the purpose of fortifying their religious beliefs and improving their well-being."[1] The public is thus under an explicit biblical obligation to obey the wide range of laws and regulations that may be promulgated by the legitimate authorities. Furthermore, while the core of the Torah—the written law—is available to all, it is nonetheless deemed essential that the polity be regulated according to authoritative interpretations of the principles and precepts of the Torah, rather than permit each member of the society to be guided by a personal understanding of what the Torah requires. Given the variety of men's opinions and their differing levels of comprehension, the latter approach would prove too divisive, and would likely produce social chaos.[2] Consequently, for purposes of providing practical guidance for the promotion of justice and virtue—both for the individual and the society of which he is a member—the meaning of the teachings of the Torah becomes not what the texts seem to be saying, but rather how those texts are authoritatively interpreted.

However—while willing and wholehearted obedience to the dictates of the established authorities was and remains the desideratum—it is also recognized that, in a less than perfect world, even legitimate authority needs to be bolstered by a capacity to invoke sanctions against those who might challenge the validity of its commands. Thus, Scripture continues: "And the man that doeth presumptuously, in not hearkening unto the priest . . . or unto the judge, even that man shall die; and thou shalt exterminate the evil from Israel" (Deut. 17:12). It seems reasonable to infer that the "evil" spoken of in this text refers to the evil inherent in the social chaos that might result from the perpetuation of an ineffectual and poorly defined political and legal regime.[3]

The biblical injunction is echoed in the expression of fealty offered to Joshua by the tribal leaders, upon his assumption of the national leadership of Israel: "Whosoever he be that shall rebel against thy commandment, and shall not hearken unto thy words in all that thou commandest him, he shall be put to death" (Josh. 1:18).[4] In another place, men are cautioned against seditious conduct that might threaten to undermine legitimate authority: "Thou shalt not revile God,[5] nor curse a ruler of thy people" (Ex. 22:27).[6] Noting these and other related biblical passages, the Talmud records Rabbi Eleazar's teaching that "these passages are a warning to the congregation [of the people] to revere their judges, and to the judges to bear patiently with the congregation. To what extent [is such patience required]?—R. Hanan says: 'As the nursing father carrieth the suckling child' (Num. 11:12)."[7]

Notwithstanding the extensive legitimate authority conferred on the political and judicial leadership by Scripture, the exercise of that authority is to be neither arbitrary nor excessive. Political authorities must never lose sight of who and what they are and why they have been chosen to wield power on behalf of the polity. They must remain continually cognizant that the authority with which they are entrusted derives its legitimacy from a higher source—mediated through the acknowledgment of such legitimacy by the very public they serve. Consequently, the decisions they render and the actions they take should comport with the principles and precepts of the Torah, rather than their own subjective and arbitrary inclinations. Indeed, those officials of the polity who would propose to dispense justice according to their private insights—on the basis of their presumed wisdom—are considered to have exceeded their proper authority, and to have placed the very legitimacy of their actions in jeopardy.

Furthermore, the sages were deeply concerned about the corrupting effects that the possession of political authority and power might have on an individual—particularly the tendency toward tyrannical behavior. Displaying a caution perhaps necessitated by the exigencies of the period of its composition, the Talmud alludes to this concern in its understated teaching that "any leader who levies excessive dread on the public, that is not for the sake of Heaven, is not seen as a wise person."[8] With Maimonides, however, this tepid maxim is transformed into a strong indictment of authoritarian conduct: "It is forbidden for a person to lord it over the public and to behave crudely, but he is to act only with humility and awe. And every leader who levies excessive dread on the public, that is not for the sake of Heaven, will be punished."[9] The punishment of which Maimonides speaks will be at "the hands of Heaven," rather than at "the hands of man"—since there are no provisions for bringing the tyrant to the bar of justice without a successful revolution. Nevertheless, the principle of Torah reflected in these statements is clear. Authority granted to public officials must not be exercised for its own sake or for purposes that do not directly serve the true public interest. The proper use of political power must always be governed and delimited by legitimate purpose.[10]

The exercise of public authority is thus considered to be legitimate (irrespective of the particular institutional structure) only if that authority is exercised "for the sake of Heaven"—that is, if it is administered in accordance with the precepts of divine law and justice set forth in the Torah. The corollary to this proposition is that, where the exercise of authority is legitimate, it is incumbent on the public to accept and scrupulously obey such authority. However, where the exercise of power by the authorities clearly violates the precepts of the Torah—which is the ultimate arbiter of political legitimacy—or where positions of power and authority are arrogated by means inimical to the rule of law and are therefore inherently illegitimate, the moral obligation of the public to obey the regime is severed.

The rabbinic theory of political obligation is summarized in the midrashic commentary on the teaching of Ecclesiastes (8:2–4): "I counsel thee to keep the king's commandment... for he doeth whatsoever pleaseth him. Because the word of a king is power; and who may say unto him, What dost thou?" The sages interpreted this passage to mean: "The Holy One says, I adjure you that if the kingdom decree persecutions against you, you shall not rebel against anything that it imposes on you, but you shall 'keep the king's commandment.' But if it decrees that you should abrogate the Torah and its precepts, then pay no heed to it."[11]

This midrashic passage contains two fundamental propositions that merit careful consideration. On the one hand, it announces the general principle that there is no intrinsic right of rebellion against lawful authority. On the other hand, it also informs us that, if an issued decree is essentially flawed and therefore illegitimate, the chain of obligation is broken, and obedience to such authority is unwarranted. Clearly, the notion being conveyed here is that all human authority is subject to a higher law, which alone legitimates the actions of government—even one that is popularly chosen. A command to violate the precepts of the Torah—the higher law itself—cannot bear any legitimacy.[12] Confronted by such an improper demand, the public's obligation of obedience to authority reverts entirely to the higher law, which—as indicated by the Midrash—calls for civil disobedience. Resistance to illegitimate authority is thus not only sanctioned, but ordained.

Furthermore, should the ruling authorities demand that the public itself take steps to lend legitimacy to the regime's improper or unjust impositions, such as enacting authorizing legislation—even where there is no demand for any direct violation of the precepts of the Torah—the public is urged to withstand the regime's pressures, if it can. However, where the public is coerced into formally extending a fig leaf of legitimacy to the illicit actions of the government, such legislative acts are not considered binding. *Force majeure* does not create a binding obligation.[13]

While there is broad agreement in rabbinic thought on the principle of civil disobedience, there remains some ambiguity with regard to what is considered the acceptable mode of such behavior. There appears to be a general and explicit consensus with regard to the appropriateness of passive resistance. However, it is less clear that a comparable consensus exists with regard to active resistance to a legitimately established regime.[14] Maimonides seems to lend strong implicit support to the permissibility of active resistance to government, in his restatement of the *halakhah*: "He who nullifies an enactment of the king in order to occupy himself with the precepts [of the Torah], even though it be only a minor precept, is guiltless."[15] This dictum surely lends itself to the argument—noted by Meiri—that, since it permits a person to ignore a command of the king in order to pursue even a minor precept of the Torah, it would certainly allow one to ignore a command to violate a precept—which is unquestionably illegitimate from a rabbinic perspective.[16] This argument, which would make the acceptability of passive disobedience derivative from the active disobedience clearly indicated in Maimonides' statement, surely affirms the legitimacy of the latter under the appropriate circumstances.

Perhaps one of the strongest affirmations of the duty of active resistance to the illegitimate use of authority to be found in classical rabbinic literature is the responsum of the great Babylonian authority, Hai Gaon. He takes the position that, in a case where the behavior of the judicial authorities is such that the poor are maltreated because of their vulnerability—in direct violation of the precepts of the Torah—it is the responsibility of those well versed in the law not only to ignore the existing authorities, but to select new leaders from among themselves.[17] In this responsum, Hai Gaon goes far beyond active civil disobedience. In effect, he calls for revolution and the establishment of a new regime responsible to the higher law of the Torah. However, it must be recognized that such overt rebellion against established authority may not be undertaken merely as the outgrowth of a sense of social outrage at purported injustices. Where such active resistance to legitimately constituted authority is being considered, it is imperative that such a determination be solidly grounded in the precepts of the Torah. Such an extreme step may only be taken when determined to be absolutely necessary by those recognized as competent in the teachings and requirements of the Torah. This is not to suggest a cabal by a few self-appointed spokesmen for the public. In the rabbinic view, the tenets of justice are proclaimed in the principles and precepts of the Torah, and—as such—are fully accessible to all who are willing to make the required effort to attain competency in them. Therefore, knowledge and understanding of the law by the greatest possible number of people is a critical factor in ensuring competent participation in the political affairs of the polity.[18]

Civil disobedience—when appropriate—must be based on sound and competent judgment, in every instance. Hai Gaon's teaching is predicated on the explicit assumption that "you yourselves have knowledge of the law," and that the representatives of the people will be "wise men who are circumspect with regard to the honor due to the Torah." However—notwithstanding the right of the public to challenge the legitimacy of the acts of government—it is not clear what the precise methods or mechanisms are, by which the determination to resist the authorities is to be made and promulgated. Presumably, the traditional rabbinic authorities did not consider the conditions under which overt resistance to the government would be justified as likely to occur, and therefore made no explicit provisions for dealing with the question. In the absence of such provisions, a popular decision to resist would appear to have to rely on a spontaneous decision by an indeterminate number of persons considered competent by the public (within the context of a given place and time) to assess the actions of government, and to conclude that the legally constituted authorities have acted outside the law—thereby nullifying the obligation of obedience owed to them.

Although civil disobedience to the political authorities is clearly established as an appropriate last-resort course of action, it must—as noted earlier—be approached with great care and deliberation. Apparent arbitrariness on the part of the legitimately constituted authorities cannot automatically be equated with violation of legitimate authority. It is with this caveat in mind that the passage from the Midrash stating, "if the kingdom decree persecutions against you, you shall not rebel against anything that it imposes on you"—cited earlier in this discussion—should be recalled. Oppressive actions by the government are not always intrinsically unjustified, and therefore illegitimate.

Meiri attempts to rationalize the apparent paradox of legitimate arbitrariness by arguing that what may seem arbitrary to the governed may prove to be a legitimate necessity for the government and truly in the longer range interest of the governed as well.[19] However, unthinking and slavish acquiescence to this idea can result in justification of even the most unwarranted tyranny. It is thus only through a highly educated and articulate public that the goal of a properly ordered society can be realized. The leaders of the polity must never be permitted to lose sight of the instrumental purposes for which they have been entrusted with authority and power, and of their obligation to fulfill their responsibilities to the public with prudence and obedience to the higher law of the Torah. An alert, deeply concerned, and well-informed public becomes the major obstacle to abuse of power by the government.

The view expressed by Meiri fully comports with the fundamental idea that political authority must be firmly established and accorded significant discretion, to prevent the social chaos inherent in a situation where each person feels independently free to determine the appropriateness and limitations of the law. As observed by Malbim, "The ruler of a land that is appointed in accordance with the laws of the state has the authority to interpret the law in accordance with his view of what is right."[20] Furthermore, effective political authority implies the capacity to apply sanctions for noncompliance with its demands. For those individuals who may disagree with a particular rule or regulation, the application of such sanctions as a demonstration of the coercive power of the regime may be seen as arbitrary and capricious, but this in itself does not invalidate the legitimacy of the government's actions. Until such ostensibly arbitrary abuse of governmental power evokes a broad public outcry resulting in acts of civil disobedience that undermine the proper functioning of government, the presumed legitimacy of the authorities remains unimpeached.

Where political authority is legitimately constituted and exercised, there is no unequivocal right to revolt, and the bearers of that authority are allowed wide discretion and powers of coercion to enforce their will. The legitimacy of such power is categorically stipulated by Maimonides: "For all who rebel against the king, the king has the right to put them to death. Even if he decreed that one, from among all the people, should go to a certain place and he did not go, or that he should not go out of his house and he did go out, he merits the death penalty. And if the king desires to put him to death, he shall be put to death... and so too all who mock the king or shame him, the king has the right to put them to death."[21] Implicit in this dictum is the idea that the effectiveness of political authority is related to the dignity with which it is maintained and the honor and respect accorded to it by the members of the polity. This principle is expressed in the Talmud in the rule that a king (ruler) cannot waive the honor due him.[22] However, the fundamental and necessary condition for such a sweeping grant of coercive power cannot be overemphasized. The ruler must have attained his position through legitimate means.[23] The obligation of the members of the polity to respect political authority is—in the first instance—entirely contingent on the fundamental legitimacy of the regime.[24]

In the rabbinic perspective, the well-ordered political society is considered to be primarily dependent on the quality of its members and leaders, rather than on the quantity and elaborateness of its institutions. In a polity imbued with the principles and precepts of the Torah, a highly informed and educated public will serve in most cases as an effective constraint on excesses by the government. Rabbinic political theory thus posits a system of creative tension between the governors and the governed, within a framework of a higher law that ultimately guides the proper conduct of both. As the common point of reference for all elements of the polity, the Torah constitutes the only unimpeachable source of authority and obligation.

NOTES

1. Berlin, *HaAmek Davar* on Deut. 17:11.
2. Moses ben Nahman (Nahmanides) argues that "as it is well known that general agreement on anything is rare, disagreements will multiply and the Torah will be trans-

formed into a multiplicity of Torahs. Therefore Scripture determined that we should pay heed to the high court... with regard to all that it may dictate to us concerning the interpretation of the Torah, whether such interpretation was handed down by witness to witness since it was received by Moses from the Almighty, or whether they inferred it from the sense of the text or its intent" (Nahmanides, *Perushei haRAMBAN al haTorah* on Deut. 17:11).

3. See comment of Levi ben Gerson (Gersonides, *Perush al haTorah al Derekh Biur* II:223b.

4. Simon Federbusch argues that "it is evident from this that the basis for the law of rebellion rests in popular consent. From the days of Joshua onwards the king and the court have the right to punish the rebel, because they thought, it would seem, that this authority was granted by the people not only to Joshua alone, but also to every head of state, whether a king or a popularly chosen ruler" (Federbusch, *Mishpat haMelukhah beYisrael*, p. 83).

5. The name of the deity is taken here to refer to the judges who render judgment in accordance with the divine law. See the discussion in *Sanhedrin* 66a.

6. Obadiah Sforno considers this injunction necessary because the proscribed behavior "is generally bad and damaging to the public" (Sforno, *Perush R. Obadiah Sforno* on Ex. 22:27).

Aaron HaLevi of Barcelona writes: "The intent of the text is to caution us with regard to whomsoever may assume a position of leadership over Israel, under both the regime of the state and the regime of the Torah. The roots of this precept reflect the impossibility of human society where one of its members is not made the head over others who will carry out his commands and observe his restrictive enactments. Because men's views differ one from the other, and all will never agree unanimously to a single viewpoint and to a common action... it is therefore necessary for them to participate and succeed in the activities of the world. On one occasion they will find great benefit in his counsel, on other occasions the opposite. But this is still better than conflict which results in total waste" (Aaron HaLevi of Barcelona, *Sefer haHinukh*, # 71).

7. *Sanhedrin* 8a. Samson R. Hirsch elaborates on this view and the text of Deut. 1:16. He sees it as "warning the judges of the tiresomeness of their office and of the necessity for their having patience even with outrageous conduct of the public, to know that a judge is appointed to train the public and patience is expected from him" (Hirsch, *The Pentateuch* on Deut. 1:16).

8. *Rosh haShannah* 17a. See also Hananel ben Hushiel, *Perush Rabbenu Hananel*, ad loc. The talmudic dictum is based on Job 37:24. See commentary of David Altschuler, *Metzudat David* on Job 37:24. The essential point made by Altschuler and other commentators is that a person with authority is not intrinsically different from anyone else, and must answer to God equally with those over whom he exercises his authority.

9. Maimonides, *Hilkhot Sanhedrin* 25:1.

10. Moses of Coucy states: "It is within the power of the judge to take issue, and to strike, and to curse in accordance with the needs of the hour... and he also has the authority to bind hands and feet and to imprison in a place of detention, to push away and to drag on the earth.... But even though the judge has the authority to do all this, it is forbidden to him to levy excessive dread on the public" (Moses of Coucy, *Sefer Mitzvot Gadol*, "Mitzvot Lo Taaseh" # 208).

11. *Midrash Tanhumah*, "Noah," 12, p. 31. For other versions, see *Midrash Tanhumah*, ed. by Buber, "Noah," 15; and *Midrash Agadat Bereshit* 7:1.

12. See Gersonides, *Perush haRALBAG* on Josh. 1:18; Solomon ben Isaac (RASHI), *Perush RASHI* on *Sanhedrin* 49a; and Ibn Zimra (RADBAZ), *Perush haRADBAZ* on Maimonides, *Hilkhot Melakhim* 3:8.

13. The responsum of an anonymous rabbi of the gaonic period reflects this position, when he states: "A king or government or tax official who causes the community to dedicate property for his personal needs and desires . . . and it is not possible for the community to do otherwise, because of its oppressive character every such dedication is without force" (*Shaare Teshubah: Response of the Geonim*, p. 20a, # 195).

14. Referring to the grant of authority made to Joshua—"Whosoever he be that shall rebel against thy commandment, and shall not hearken unto all thy words in all that thou commandest him, he shall be put to death" (Josh. 1:18)—Don Isaac Abravanel sees in this passage an injunction to deal both with passive and active disobedience to authoritative commands. He considers the phrase "that shall rebel against thy commandment" to refer to positive actions that are opposite to what is commanded, and the phrase "shall not hearken unto thy words" as referring to not doing what is commanded—or, in other words, passive resistance (Abravanel, *Perush al Neviyyim Rishonim*, p. 19). Abravanel's analysis is adopted almost verbatim by Malbim in his *Mikra'ei Kodesh* on Josh. 1:18. From this standpoint, not only passive resistance (a refusal to carry out an act commanded by the authorities), but also active resistance (the pursuit of actions proscribed by the authorities), would seem to come within the range not only of the permissible—but the requisite—behavior of a responsible citizenry.

15. Maimonides, *Hilkhot Melakhim* 3:9.

16. Meiri, *Bet haBehirah al Massekhet Sanhedrin*, p. 204, on *Sanhedrin* 49a.

17. Hai Gaon writes: "Where there are judges that mortgage the beds of the poor and their possessions illegitimately, and creditors come and steal their homes and remove their beds and utensils, which are not to be legitimately mortgaged [according to the Torah], and you cannot restrain them. May their souls depart from such judges, they are the judges of Sodom, thieves. . . . Therefore it is necessary to raise up a cry against them among all your neighbors, and in those places in close proximity to you, to shame them and prevent them from judging you, for they do not pay attention to the Torah and the words of the Sages. And since you yourselves have knowledge of the law and the rabbinical provisions, give attention to this matter, take counsel among yourselves and draw out men from among you who fear Heaven, wise men who are circumspect with regard to the honor due to the Torah, and place them at your head" (*Shaare Teshubah: Responsa of the Geonim*, p. 9a, # 86).

18. See Chapter 4, note 12.

19. Meiri writes: "The king has the right to put to death according to his own laws anyone who raises his voice in rebellion with regard to some matter, or who rebels against any aspect [of his rule] . . . for the intent is not [for the king] to transgress the commandments of the Law, but rather to build a fence around the Law according to the requirements of the generation and the hour" (Meiri, *Bet haBehirah al Massekhet Sanhedrin*, p. 197, on *Sanhedrin* 46a–46b). The question of the relationship between the laws of the regime and those of the Torah are discussed later on in this study.

20. Malbim, *HaTorah vehaMitzvah* on Gen. 23:8.

21. Maimonides, *Hilkhot Melakhim* 3:8.

22. *Kiddushin* 32b. Isaac Abravanel considers this as required "for the honor of the kingdom and the needs of the people" (Abravanel, *Perush al Neviyyim Rishonim* on Joshua 1:18).

23. In a different but related context, Maimonides writes: "In what regard are these things said? With regard to a king whose seal has currency in those lands, in that the people of that land have agreed upon him and determined that he is their lord and they his servants. However, if his seal bears no currency, he is considered as an armed and mighty robber—and just as in the case of a group of armed bandits whose rules have no legitimate force—such a king and all his servants are considered robbers in regard to all matters" (Maimonides, *Hilkhot Gezeilah* 5:18). See also Nissim Girondi, *Perush haRAN al Nedarim* 28a.

24. Commenting on the statement of Maimonides (see note 23 above), David ibn Zimra notes: "This king is one who reigns by virtue of prophetic appointment or by the consent of the people. However, if an individual arises and rules . . . by force, the people are under no obligation to pay heed to him, and he who voices his opposition is not categorized as a rebel" (Ibn Zimra, *Perush haRADBAZ* on Maimonides, *Hilkhot Melakhim* 3:8).

6
The Structure of the Polity

As the revelation of God's will to man, the Torah constitutes the ultimate authority in regard to human affairs. In the rabbinic view, it reflects God's sovereignty in the universe, to which mankind—rulers and ruled alike—owe fealty. This idea has served as a foundation of biblical and rabbinic political theory since the earliest days of Jewish history. It can be seen most clearly in the biblical episode where Gideon is solicited by the elders of the tribes to become their ruler. "And Gideon said unto them: 'I will not rule over you, neither shall my son rule over you; the Lord shall rule over you'" (Judges 8:22–23).

A thousand years later, the Jewish historian Joseph ben Mattathias (Josephus Flavius) discussed the question of political structures: "Now there are innumerable differences in the particular customs and laws that are among all mankind, which a man may briefly reduce under the following heads: some legislators have permitted their governments to be under monarchies, others put them under oligarchies, and others under a republican form; but our legislator had no regard to any of these forms, but he ordained our government to be what, by a strained expression, may be termed a Theocracy; by ascribing the authority and the power to God."[1] And, a millennium still later, Maimonides discussed the same issue: "The government of a city is a science imparting to its masters a knowledge of true happiness.... It also lays down laws of righteousness for the best ordering of the groups. The sages of the peoples of antiquity made rules and regulations, according to their various degrees of perfection, for the government of their subjects. These are called *nomoi*; and by them the people were governed.... But in these times we do not need all these laws and *nomoi*; for divine laws govern human conduct."[2]

Given that the Torah is considered in rabbinic political theory as the constitutional embodiment of the divine law—and, as such, the reflection of God's sovereignty in the world of man—the matter of appropriate political institutions becomes an issue of grave importance. Laws, rules, and regulations are not self-executing. In a less than perfect world, conflicts that arise between members of the polity cannot be resolved just because there is an availability of proclaimed precepts of justice. Misinterpretations of both principle and fact must be corrected by impartial arbiters. A myriad of practical decisions must be made on behalf of the members of society as a whole, if it is to prove equally beneficial to all. The Torah may embody divine sovereignty, but it cannot govern. Only men can govern, in accordance with its principles and precepts. In short, the Torah itself cannot prevent anarchy, without a government of men dedicated to carrying out its imperatives. The critical question is how the appropriate form of government shall be structured, so as to translate the precepts of the Torah into effective operational guidelines for a functioning polity. The problem of the proper organization of the institutions of Judaic political society must be resolved, if this end is to be realized.

Since the Torah is conceived as constituting the foundation of all Judaic thought, it would seem reasonable to assume that the question of how society is to be politically organized and governed would be dealt with in the Torah itself. In the rabbinic perspective—as will be discussed throughout the remainder of this study—such is clearly the case. Viewed in part as a political constitution for Judaic society, the Torah specifies the major organs of the political structure and delineates their functions—although not in a manner that precludes significant differences in interpretation by students of the written texts and oral traditions.

The primary biblical sources for this aspect of rabbinic political theory are to be found in a section of Deuteronomy (16:18–21:9) that may be considered a basic constitutional framework for the Judaic polity. This section opens with the commandment: "Judges and officers shalt thou make thee in all thy gates." In his commentary on this passage, Obadiah Sforno introduces the subject matter under discussion, as follows: "After the commandments were given to the people as a whole [in earlier sections of Deuteronomy], He commanded with regard to the matter of their leaders. And they are the kings, the judges, the priests and the prophets through whose efforts the public interest would be well-served and through whose corruption it too would become corrupted."[3]

Notice that the enumeration given by Sforno does not provide for the distinct category of "officers," as specified in the biblical text. This omission would seem to suggest that Sforno does not consider officers to represent an element of political importance comparable to those he does mention—notwithstanding the explicitness of the text. Sforno's implied position here may be seen as reflecting one of two basic and conflicting rabbinic conceptions regarding the scope of judicial authority and power.

The preponderant view, which Sforno implicitly reflects, is one that imputes inherent executive power to the judiciary. It argues further that the officers mentioned in the Bible are clearly intended to serve as instruments of the coercive powers of the judiciary, and therefore do not constitute a distinct coequal element of government with the judges. The officers are thus considered to be included as a component of the judiciary, where they are clearly subordinate to the authority of the judges. This position finds its source in the Talmud, where it is noted somewhat cryptically that "an officer has a superior appointed over him."[4] Rabbinic commentary on this statement tends to the view that the function of the officers is to carry out the judgments rendered by the judicial authorities.[5] In other words, the "officers" are officers of the court.

On reflection, it seems that this perspective implicitly construes the executive powers of the judicial institution as limited to the enforcement of decisions rendered by the judges in specific cases brought before them for adjudication. The judiciary—acting through its coercive instruments, the officers—is thus seen to exercise the police powers of the state only after a matter has been brought to its attention, and a ruling issued. The question as to who has the police power to initiate actions before the courts remains a matter of contention.

Maimonides resolves this matter by a significant extension of the concept of the executive powers of the judiciary. He defines "officers" as the "wielders of the rod and lash, and they stand before the judges. They circulate in the market places and in the streets and in the shops to rectify prices and measures and to strike the dishonest. And all their actions are at the direction of the judges, and all in whom they detect something dishonest they bring to court."[6] It is evident that, in Maimonides' view, the police power of the state is exercised by officers acting under authority of the judiciary, both prior to and after specific judicial action. A similar view of judicial executive power is held by Gersonides, who defines "officers" as "those who subdue the people, who have the coercive means to bring them to court and to lead them in accordance with the law as stated by the judges."[7]

Another group of writers and commentators adopts a somewhat more ambitious stance on this issue. Meyuhas ben Elijah essentially repeats the view of his contemporary, Maimonides, with regard to the relationship between the officers and the courts, and then goes on to associate the officers with the functionaries identified in the Talmud as the *agardamim* appointed over the marketplaces.[8] This latter designation is a corruption of the Greek term *agoranomos*,[9] meaning a market commissioner—the official referred to in the Talmud as being appointed for the purpose of superintending honest weights and measures.[10] Thus—while Maimonides sees the functions of the officers as including the policing of trade practices in the marketplace—he does not tie that function directly to the position of the *agoranomos*, as does Meyuhas. Primary control over such positions would indeed represent a significant extension of the judiciary's executive power into the economic sector.

Some among this latter group of authors tend to assign even greater implied powers to the officers—without clearly addressing the question of their relation to the judiciary. Thus, Abraham Rapa of Porto defines the "officers" as "those who have in their hand the power and the dominion to bring to realization the law of the judges."[11] Although still linked to the authority of the judiciary, there is implicit in this definition a somewhat greater autonomy with regard to the source of their power, if not their exercise of it. An even further departure from the restrictive view of the school represented by Sforno—discussed earlier— is that of Jacob ben Abba Mari Anatoli. He maintains that the officers are not exclusively the instruments of the judiciary, but seem rather to be the general enforcers of public order—subject to the direction of a number of political authorities.[12] Samuel ben Hofni Gaon goes so far as to consider the officers as those who are also commanders of the army.[13] However, they still do not seem to possess any independent statutory authority of their own.

As observed earlier, this range of interpretation generally reflects the dominant perspective in rabbinic thought regarding the executive powers of the judiciary— notwithstanding the diversity of opinion regarding the precise delimitation of the scope of such powers. However, there is also a minority view, which essentially denies any executive powers—whatsoever—to the judiciary. This perspective is predicated on a clear differentiation of functions between the adjudicators and executors of the law. In one midrashic exposition of the text of Deuteronomy, the argument is made that, since the judiciary has no executive powers to enforce its decisions, it must rely entirely on the executive branch of government for this purpose. Indeed—in this view—where there is no effective executive arm, the judiciary itself is seen as superfluous.[14] Clearly supportive of this position is Hayyim ben Moses ibn Attar who concludes his examination of the midrashic text with the comment: "The text demonstrates that if there are no officers there is no obligation to appoint judges; that is, in so far as it is known that the people will not listen to the judges and that the judges cannot compel them, there is no obligation to appoint judges. However, where the people generally pay heed to the judges even without officers, they are obligated to appoint judges."[15] Evidently—in Ibn Attar's view—the only intrinsic executive authority possessed by the judiciary is strictly moral in character. From the standpoint of this school of thought, the judiciary is not considered as having the authority to establish its own enforcement agencies.[16]

Other major advocates of this position among the classical rabbinic commentators include Abraham ibn Ezra[17] and David Kimhi.[18] However, perhaps the strongest and most outspoken proponent is Samuel David Luzzatto. He emphatically states: "There is no doubt that the officers are not agents of the court that subdue with a rod." He notes that the use of the term elsewhere in Deuteronomy[19]—as well as in 2 Chronicles[20]—is in clear reference to the political leadership, rather than the judiciary. Thus, "the judges dealt with the matters between man and man, or with witnesses that testified to a transgression, and the officers would oversee the well-being of the state and would enact regulations and customs for the people."[21]

Taking the dominant rabbinic view on this issue as the point of departure, we have an implied theory of the differentiation and distribution of political power. Sforno's omission of "officers" from the category of significant political leadership positions may be understood on the basis of the dominant position: that they have no independent authority. It may thus be inferred that each of the organizational entities enumerated by Sforno—that is: the kings, judges, priests, and prophets—has an independent basis for its authority within the overall scheme of a Torah-oriented and directed political society. In other words, the Torah provides the constitutional source from which the specified institutions of government derive their legitimate authority, and which establishes the interrelationships between these authorities in such manner as to assure the harmonious ordering of the polity.

However—as indicated in the preceding discussion and in contrast to other types of constitutional documents—the biblical text is so worded as to obscure the specific delineation of powers to the identified institutions of government, as well as the separation of enumerated powers among them. Superficially considered, the authorities explicitly established in Deuteronomy seem to flatly contradict the concept of separation of powers. Instead, the text seems to promulgate clearly overlapping jurisdictions—which would appear incapable of creating anything resembling a well-ordered political structure. For example, after having established the basis for an independent judiciary in Deut. 16:18, the text of Deut. 17:9 declares: "And thou shalt come unto the priests the Levites, and unto the judge that shall be in those days; and thou shalt inquire; and they shall declare unto thee the sentence of judgment." This passage would appear to establish the judiciary and the priesthood as coequal entities—each exercising independent but identical juridical authority.

Similarly, while the text of Deut. 17:5 explicitly states that "Thou shalt in any wise set him king over thee, whom the Lord thy God shall choose," it does not give any clear description of the functions of the king, nor does it set forth any specific authorities that may be exercised by him. By contrast, Deut. 18:15 establishes the prophetic institution, and immediately endows it with an authority that the people become obligated to acknowledge: "A prophet will the Lord thy God raise up unto thee, from the midst of thee, of thy brethren, like unto me: unto him ye shall hearken." Surely, one may not reasonably assume that the prophet—and not the king—is intended to be the focal point of executive power within the political society. Yet, such a conclusion could be reached by an uncritical reading of the biblical texts.

Consequently, from the rabbinic perspective, one must turn to the traditional literature for competent exposition and elucidation of the biblical texts. At the same time, it should be noted that these same texts are considered by that tradition to have been the bases of the historical Hebrew commonwealths. While this study will not undertake an examination of the historical validity of this contention, it should be borne in mind that—since it is rabbinic political theory that is under consideration here—for disciples of that tradition, the Bible is *the* fundamental historical document as well as the repository of the law. The approach taken in this study is to consider the rabbinic exposition of the biblical constitution as establishing a set of norms for the model polity, rather than to engage in an effort to prove or disprove their actual application in ancient Jewish history. The historical Hebrew commonwealths are not considered by rabbinic tradition to have been ideally organized and administered societies that were truly based on the precepts of the Torah, and therefore worthy of replication. To reiterate, our concern in the following chapters will be with the constitution of the Judaic state constructed in accordance with the specifications of the Torah—as understood in the rabbinic tradition—and not with a historical analysis of man's capacity for twisting and abusing those ideals in practice.

NOTES

1. *Against Apion* 2:17 in Josephus Flavius, *Complete Works of Josephus*. Clearly, Josephus's use of the term "theocracy" has no relation to its subsequent connotation of rule by religious authorities. See Jacobson, *Meditations on the Torah*, p. 291.

2. Maimonides, *Treatise on Logic*, p. 64. In his commentary on Maimonides' work, Moses Mendelssohn suggests that the meaning of "in these times we do not need..." is simply that "the Torah commanded to us by Moses is that which corrects our ways in divine matters and in the ways of honesty in matters between man and man. We have but to reflect on it and learn from it those things that a man should do and thereby enhance his life" (Mendelssohn, *Biur Millot haHigayon*, p. 67b).

3. Sforno, *Perush R. Obadiah Sforno* on Deut. 16:18.

4. *Sotah* 42a.

5. Commenting on the talmudic statement, RASHI notes, "The judge is appointed over the officer, since the officer is appointed in order to apply pressure on whomever the judge shall order to be compelled" (Solomon ben Isaac, *Perush RASHI* [T], ad loc. note 4 above). In another place, RASHI describes the officers as *galearii* (Latin: "common soldiers") "who, on the word of the judges, strike with rods all who will not pay heed" (ibid. on *Sanhedrin* 16b). Still elsewhere, in commenting on the use of the term in biblical texts, RASHI defines "officers" as "those who subjugate the people in accordance with their commands [that is, of the judges]; those who strike and compel with rod and lash until they accept the legal decision of the judge" (Solomon ben Isaac, *Perushei RASHI al haTorah* on Deut. 16:18). See also RASHI's commentary on Deut. 1:15.

Similarly, Samuel ben Meir (RASHBAM) observes: "The judges direct the officers to those who are recalcitrant with regard to matters of law" (Samuel ben Meir, *Perush haTorah asher Katav haRASHBAM* on Deut. 16:18). Here again, the implication is that the officers are merely sheriffs of the courts. This same view is also held by Jacob ben Asher who defines "officers" as "wielders of the rod and lash that stand before the judges in order to subdue at their word" (Jacob ben Asher, *Arba Turim: Tur Hoshen Mishpat* I:2a). Isaac Abravanel reflects the same notion in his characterization of the officers as those who subdue the people "in order to compel them to uphold the decision of the judges" (Abravanel, *Perush haTorah*, "Devarim" on Deut. 16:18). A comparably unequivocal position is taken by Obadiah of Bertinoro who declares that "the officers are those appointed according to the instructions of the judges" (Obadiah of Bertinoro, *Sefer Amar Neke* on Deut. 16:18).

6. Maimonides, *Hilkhot Sanhedrin* 1:1. See also Mecklenburg, *HaKtav vehaKabbalah*, "Devarim," p. 39.

7. Gersonides, *Perush al haTorah al Derekh Biur* II:223a.

8. Meyuhas ben Elijah, *Perush al Sefer Devarim*, p. 84.

9. See Jastrow, *A Dictionary of the Targumim, the Talmud Babli and Yerushalmi, and the Midrashic Literature*, p. 14.

10. Discussion of the appointment of an *agoranomos* is found in *Baba Batra* 89a.

11. Rapa, *Minhah Belulah*, p. 181b.

12. Anatoli, *Malmad HaTalmidim*, p. 167a.

13. Samuel ben Hofni Gaon, *Perush haTorah leR. Shemuel ben Hofni Gaon*, p. 520.

14. "Judges—these are the adjudicators; and officers—these are the managers that lead the community. R. Eleazar said: If there is no officer, there is no judge. How is that? When a person has been declared in court obligated to compensate his neighbor, unless there is an executor to collect from him . . . the judge has no power over him" (*Midrash Tanhumah*, ed. by Buber, "Shofetim" 3). The same discussion is found in less explicit form in standard editions of the *Midrash Tanhumah* (such as ed. by Rosen), where it is located in "Shofetim" 2.

15. Ibn Attar, *Or haHayyim* on Deut. 16:18.

16. The dichotomy in rabbinic thought on this issue is brought into sharp relief by Elijah Mizrahi. In discussing RASHI's commentary on the text of Deuteronomy, he writes: "There are those who maintain that the officers are the rulers . . . and that it is they who have in their hands the power and the authority to bring to the light of the law of the judges, and except through them the judges have no power or authority over the litigants at all other than to point out the law alone. After pointing out the law, it is only the officers that have the power and authority to coerce the guilty to accept the legal decision . . . for the judges have no power to command, but only to indicate the law. However, Maimonides . . . and Jacob ben Asher wrote . . . it is evident that the officers are the servants that wait upon the judges to command them to strike and coerce the crooked, since all authority and power is the judge's alone and the officers have neither power nor authority except such as is derived from the judges" (Mizrahi, *Perush R. Eliyahu Mizrahi* on Deut. 16:18).

In similar fashion, Judah Loew ben Bezalel (MAHARAL), while attacking the minority view, points out the crux of the opposing positions: "There are those who interpret [the biblical text] to mean that the judge has no power or authority over litigants. Thus we find, according to their view, that the officer is more important than the judge . . . but *a fortiori* the officer is the agent of the judges" (Judah Loew ben Bezalel, *Gur Aryeh* on Deut 16:18).

17. Ibn Ezra, *Perushei haTorah leR. Abraham ibn Ezra* on Deut. 16:18.

18. Kimhi, *Sefer haSharashim*, p. 383.

19. "So I took the heads of your tribes, wise men, and full of knowledge, and made them heads over you, captains of thousands, and captains of hundreds, and captains of fifties, and captains of tens, and officers, tribe by tribe" (Deut. 1:15).

20. "And behold, Amariah the chief priest is over you in all matters of the Lord; and Zebediah the son of Ishmael, the ruler of the house of Judah, in all the king's matters; also the officers of the Levites before you" (2 Chron. 19:11). Note that the phrase "the officers of the Levites" may also be read "the Levites shall be officers" (Israel W. Slotki's commentary in the Soncino edition of the Bible, p. 247).

21. S. D. Luzzatto, *Perush SHADAL al Hamishah Humshei Torah*, p. 532.

7
The Priesthood

Simon Federbusch once wrote: "The vision of the Torah in the foundation of the Hebrew state was the education of the people to moral perfection, to become 'a kingdom of priests and a holy nation' " (Ex. 19:6).[1] This conception of a "kingdom of priests"—rather than a "kingdom ruled by priests"—is useful in attempting to properly understand the role of the priesthood in the biblical political scheme, as conceived in rabbinic theory. The ultimate transformation of the Hebrew state into a "kingdom of priests" is seen as the logical outcome of a society educated and impelled to live in accordance with the precepts of the Torah. This becomes Israel's mission in the world: to be a light to the nations, so that "out of Zion shall go forth the law, and the word of the Lord from Jerusalem" (Isa. 2:3). Similarly, the function of the priesthood within Israel is to help bring it to the stage of internal harmony and moral development that will allow the nation to achieve its higher purpose. The priesthood is thus seen as bearing a societal responsibility that far transcends its role in the performance of sacerdotal acts in the context of a highly complicated sacrificial rite.

Within the constitutional configuration provided for in the biblical system, the priesthood plays a unique and perhaps somewhat anomalous role. For, while the priesthood is explicitly designated as a formal element of government, the overall political structure is not theocratic—except in the sense discussed in the preceding chapter. Indeed, Elijah Benamozegh has argued: "In the Hebrew priesthood we discern a characteristic approach which places the political constitution beyond any danger of theocracy; the priest is the agent and representative of the people in respect of God, and not the representative of God to the people."[2]

Without articulating it as such, rabbinic political theory appears to include a concept of separation of church and state—sufficient enough to deny the priesthood formal legitimate access to the reins of executive power, which it sees as institutionalized within the framework of the biblical constitution. However, it should be recognized that, when we speak here of the separation of church and state, the emphasis is exclusively on the institutional aspects of the structure of the polity. In the rabbinic perspective, there can be no fundamental separation of religion from the state. The laws governing the relationship between man and Heaven and those establishing the proper relations between man and his fellow or society are seen as but two sides of a single coin: the Mosaic Law—the Torah. Yet, the biblical constitution does draw a distinction between the other institutions of political society and the sacerdotal—the political role of the latter being structurally circumscribed in the exercise of political authority and power. The question of the separation of church and state must therefore be considered within the context of an ethical state inspired and governed by the all-encompassing principles and precepts of the Torah.

First of all, the uniqueness of the priesthood derives from the fact that its membership is exclusively familial. That is, all members of the priesthood must stem patrilineally from the male descendants of the four identified sons of Aaron, beginning with those who were born after their fathers' elevation to the priesthood by Moses. Moses is commanded on Mt. Sinai: "And bring thou near unto thee Aaron, thy brother, and his sons with him, from among the children of Israel, that they may minister unto Me in the priest's office, even Aaron, Nadab and Abihu, Eleazar and Ithamar, Aaron's sons" (Ex. 28:1).[3]

It is evident that the priesthood is not conceived in Judaism as a vocation involving voluntarism as a criterion for recruitment. The priesthood *in* Israel is clearly a closed society—in contrast to the priesthood *of* Israel, which is open to all who would bear its burdens. Because the priesthood is hereditary and is not based on individual merit or capacity, it is not viewed in Judaism as a "higher calling"—but, rather, simply as a functional distinction that was necessary for the general welfare of the nation. This factor contributes to the uniqueness of the priesthood as a political institution, as well.

Finally, the priesthood may also be seen as unique because of its place within the original basic tribal structure of the biblical polity. The family of Aaron derives from the tribe of Levi, the third son of Jacob—one of the constituent components of the Hebrew nation and society, which was also assigned a unique national role.

It appears from the Bible that, in the period immediately following the Revelation on Mt. Sinai, certain semi-sacerdotal (as well as lay) functions in support of the religious rite were performed by the firstborn sons of the families of all the tribes. However, they were soon disqualified from performing sacred service, on account of their involvement in the incident of the idolatrous worship of the Golden Calf. As a consequence, these secondary religious functions were transferred entirely to the Levites.[4] The dedication of the entire tribe of Levi to the support of the sacerdotal functions of the priests entailed structural factors that were to have far-reaching effects on the organization of the society. Most significantly, it resulted in the total exclusion of the Levites from the major active sectors of the national economy. They were constitutionally precluded from owning real property, in a primarily agricultural society.[5] In such a society—characterized by heavy labor and relatively little leisure—the Levites found themselves in a unique position to become the intellectual elite of the nation. Unencumbered by economic entanglements that might divert them from their basic mission, they could find compensating status as mentors of the people. Indeed, their very economic disenfranchisement would become a major factor contributing to the expansion of their sacerdotal mission to include the assumption of the intellectual leadership of the nation. Propertyless, they became an educator class.[6]

The deliberate establishment of the Levites in general and the priests in particular as an educator class—segregated from active participation in the productive economy—was bound to have a significant impact on the political structure of the society. This is particularly true with regard to the judicial aspects of the structure, because of the intimate relationship of law and religion in Judaism. Thus—as Nissim Girondi observed—"The majority of the judges were from the tribe of Levi because of their greater availability, since they were not fully occupied in other activities because they had no portion or inheritance in Israel . . . so that they should be free for the study of the law, that they might judge the people in righteous judgement."[7] The involvement of the priests and the Levites in the judicial arena is exemplified by the biblical injunction that "thou shalt come unto the priests the Levites, and unto the judge that shall be in those days; and thou shalt inquire; and they shall declare unto thee the sentence of judgement" (Deut. 17:9).[8]

As suggested, the deep involvement of the Levites and the priesthood in the judicial process may be the direct consequence of their purposive segregation from the mainstream of Israelite society. Given the rabbinic perspective on the vital role of an educated public as the countervailing force to the arbitrary use of authority by the political leadership, the total dedication of a significant component of society to this task of improving the popular understanding of the Torah and its precepts would seem to be an ideal method of achieving that high purpose. Who would be better qualified to transform the nation into a "kingdom of priests" than a tribe of priests and Levites wholly dedicated to the task? The enforced leisure of the priests and Levites also made them ideally suitable and available for other public service, as well. For example, the Talmud states that "at first, officers were appointed only from among the Levites."[9]

It should not be concluded, however, that their judicial role was a mere appendage to the primarily sacerdotal functions of the priests and Levites. As indicated earlier, the judiciary has an independent base of authority in the biblical constitution; it is coequal with that of the priesthood. Thus, while great emphasis is placed on Levitical participation in the court system, such participation is not considered as impinging on the role of the judiciary as an autonomous organ of government.[10] The primary criterion for service in the judiciary is juridical competence. It is simply assumed that persons with the necessary qualifications are most likely to be found among the priests and Levites, for the reasons discussed above. However, such membership is not an automatic perquisite of the priesthood. Maimonides expresses this position categorically in his dictum, "No one is appointed to the Sanhedrin except priests, Levites and non-Levites who are properly qualified for the highest office."[11]

The problem of the apparent overlapping of jurisdictions between the priesthood and the regular judiciary does not appear to be definitively resolved in the rabbinic literature. One basis for such a resolution relies on the interpretation of a midrashic text indicating that, within the Temple precincts in Jerusalem, there were three distinct courts. These courts—one of which was the court of the priests—may have constituted elements of an appellate system that culminated in the Great Sanhedrin.[12] The priestly court—the "one at the entrance to the Temple courtyard"—does not appear to have been considered a court in the usual legal sense of the term. It seems to have been an authoritative law institute or service to which people might turn for legal advice—much as they would, in later times, turn to individual lawyers for such information.[13]

The primary political role of the priests and Levites is thus considered to revolve around their pedagogic functions. They are the teachers of the law—not necessarily its adjudicators or legislators. They are the upholders of the legal tradition, but not its innovators. They are the caretakers of the Mosaic Law, but not its executors beyond the realm of the sacerdotal. The pedagogic function outlined here appears to be the wholly assigned province of the priests and Levites, considered as an educator class or as the intellectual aristocracy of the biblically constituted society.[14] Responsibility for learning the law remained with every member of the society—as did the responsibility for teaching it to one's children—"and thou shalt teach them diligently unto thy children" (Deut. 6:7). However, in terms of a clearly defined public responsibility for education, the role of the priests and Levites seems clear: "They shall teach Jacob Thine ordinances, and Israel Thy law" (Deut. 33:10).[15]

In addition to their institutional responsibilities as public educators, the priests—individually—were also expected to actively participate in the judicial process by applying their knowledge and understanding of the law to practical problems and situations. It is in this double sense of institutional as well as individual involvement of the priests in the judicial sphere that rabbinic commentators tend to interpret the prophetic teaching: "And they shall teach my people the difference between the holy and the profane . . . and in controversy they shall stand in judgement; and they shall judge it according to my judgements" (Ezek. 44:23–24).[16]

There is, however, a divergence of rabbinic opinion over the question of the extent of priestly involvement in the judicial process. As suggested earlier, some maintain that there was a priestly court, which dealt with civil law matters as well as sacerdotal.[17] Others hold that the priests' involvement in civil as well as criminal law matters was restricted to their participation in the general court system on an individual basis.[18] While the resolution of this question cannot be undertaken here, there is nonetheless broad agreement among rabbinic writers on the general relationship of the priesthood to the judiciary: That is, the priesthood as an institution—along with the Levites generally—were entrusted with the responsibility for the education of the people not only in matters of religion and ritual, but also with regard to the precepts of both the civil and criminal laws.[19]

Some rabbinic scholars contend that the role set aside for the priesthood by the biblical constitution was actually carried out during Israel's early history. It is pointed out that—according to the Bible—after the death of Moses, the executive leadership function was taken over by Joshua, while the law was delivered "unto the priests the sons of Levi" (Deut. 31:9)—who became the repository of Torah law and lore.[20] However, while the role cast for the priesthood was predicated on an ideal ordering of society, the priesthood as a class proved itself incapable—in practice—of fulfilling the awesome responsibilities assigned to it. Indeed, it was the priests' failure to meet this historic challenge that is assumed to have led to the organization of bands of prophets by the judge and prophet Samuel (1 Sam. 19:20)—to undertake the mission of public education neglected by the priesthood.[21]

In practice, the constitutionally established authority of the priesthood as primary guardians and disseminators of the Torah, its teachings, laws, and precepts began to erode early in its history. It was still to take a long time, however, before that authority would be so sufficiently undermined as to force any fundamental emendation of the biblical constitutional structure.

The decisive decline in the de facto constitutional status of the priesthood began with the reestablishment of the Hebrew state as the Second Commonwealth at the turn of the fifth century b.c.e. In discussing the historical development of the Sanhedrin, Judah L. Maimon points to the profound challenge that confronted Ezra the Scribe as leader of the reconstituted nation: "Great and fraught with responsibility was the task undertaken by Ezra and his court, the men of the Great Assembly. Ezra knew and understood that a return to Judaism was necessary as a fundamental condition for the reestablishment of the people in their territory and on their land.... However, in order to know and to become familiar with the fundamental religion, it was necessary to return to the living source of the people, to the Scroll, to the Torah.... It would be necessary to extricate the Scroll of the Law from the Sanctuary into the street; from the hands of the priests-Levites.... And this great feat, to bring the Law out to the street to make it the possession of the entire people—Ezra accomplished."[22]

Ezra, the priest-Levite, thus became the instrument through which the constitutional authority and perquisites of the priesthood entered into a steep decline—never again to regain its original stature. However, it is worth noting that the failure of the priesthood to carry out its biblical charter does not in itself invalidate the original constitutional design.

The passage in the Talmud that purports to trace the chain of tradition curiously omits all reference to the explicitly established role of the priesthood, in this regard. It reads: "Moses received the Torah from Sinai and handed it down to Joshua; Joshua to the Elders; the Elders to the Prophets; the Prophets handed it down to the Men of the Great Assembly."[23] It is beyond question that the author of this talmudic teaching was thoroughly familiar with the biblical text that states: "And Moses wrote this law, and delivered it unto the priests the sons of Levi, that bore the ark of the covenant of the Lord, and unto all the elders of Israel" (Deut. 31:9). As related in the Talmud, the deliberate omission of any reference to the priests in connection with the transmission of the tradition reflects the loss of significance—over time—of the pedagogic role of the priesthood. Interestingly, paralleling the silence of the Talmud in this regard is the surprisingly little comment on the matter by rabbinic scholars throughout the ages. Some of the few commentaries that do deal with it tend to base the omission of the priests on the far greater stature and importance of Joshua, as compared to Eleazar the High Priest.[24]

In any case, it seems quite evident that, by the time of the emergence of the rabbinic literature, the priesthood was no longer considered the intellectual elite and guardian of the Torah. From the standpoint of the constitutional separation of powers, the decline in the status and influence of the priesthood may be seen as a necessary occurrence in order to assure that the division of powers set forth in the biblical constitution could be maintained in practice. Zacharias Frankel draws our attention to the fundamental change in the political environment following the establishment of the Hasmonean state in the second century b.c.e.—which made it imperative to revise the role of the priesthood within the judicial system. "In the early days the high priest stood at the head of the Sanhedrin. In the days of the Persians, the high priest was above his brethren in every matter of concern to the king, and similarly in the days of the early Greek kings. However, the high priest did not have the ability to do as he wished, but sought the advice of the members of the community that stood at his side, and with their agreement carried out acts in accordance with the needs of the time and the general good.... After the end of the time of troubles and the victory of the Hasmoneans, there was no longer any high priest appointed as chief of the Sanhedrin. For the high priests of the House of the Hasmoneans were also rulers of the land and the heads of the army before they were chosen to be kings. Nothing remained for the Sanhedrin except to guard the beautiful instrument that is the Torah. And, out of concern that there arise a powerful high priest that would have both the throne and the government of the land, at the head of the Sanhedrin, lest he place his hand on the Torah as well and change its statutes and replace its laws with his own, they established an independent Sanhedrin.... The conduct of the state ... was in the hands of the king, and the guardianship of the Torah, teaching the people its precepts and to uphold its statutes and its ordinances, was the responsibility of the Sanhedrin."[25]

The historical situation described by Frankel would seem to have twisted the biblical constitutional structure into a shape hardly resembling the original. Indeed, it would appear to have established the basis for a theocracy wherein there is an identity between king and high priest—an arrangement quite unacceptable to rabbinic political theory. Thus—as will be shown later—the de jure status of the Hasmoneans as kings in the biblical sense is subject to serious question in the early rabbinic literature—their dynastic rule being seen as a deviation from constitutional norms, rather than an affirmation of a new standard.

The biblical intent to separate the functions of priest and ruler is reflected in the instructions given to Moses in anticipation of his demise: "And the Lord said unto Moses: Take thee Joshua the son of Nun, a man in whom is spirit, and lay thy hand upon him; and set him before Eleazar the priest, and before all the congregation; and give him a charge in their sight. And thou shalt put of thy honor upon him, that all the congregation of the children of Israel may hearken. And he shall stand before Eleazar the priest, who shall inquire for him by the judgement of the Urim before the lord" (Num. 27:18–21).

This text would seem to indicate that Moses left a dual leadership, in contrast to the monolithic one he wielded himself. A stronger indication of the character of this dual leadership—one that reflects a functional division of labor—is found later in Scripture, where it states: "Behold, Amariah the chief priest is over you in all matters of the Lord; and Zebadiah the son of Ishmael, the ruler of the house of Judah, for all the king's matters" (2 Chron. 19:11). Thus, while the executive and sacerdotal functions are distinct, the Bible makes them interrelated—perhaps even interdependent.[26] Malbim suggests that the king and high priest serve complementary purposes, which—in combination—are essential to the biblical scheme: "That is to say, the king was set up to bring about justice in the land between man and his fellow, and the high priest was responsible for the house of the Lord, the worship of the Lord, and for the teaching of the Torah and its precepts to establish righteousness, which are the precepts governing the relationship between man and Heaven."[27] Malbim again emphasizes the functional distinctions drawn in the biblical constitution. The king—the executive power—is to rule in accordance with the precepts of justice. The priest is to concern himself with both the sacerdotal and pedagogy.

While the preceding discussion has attempted to delineate the distinctions between the executive and the priesthood within a common political framework, it remains to examine the intriguing question as to why their functions could not simultaneously be vested in a single individual—as was the actual case with the Hasmoneans.

Although the references to this question in the rabbinic literature are scant, such as may be found tend to view such an arrangement as inimical to the constitutional intent of the Bible. An early statement of the rabbinic position on the legitimacy of the priest-king is to be found in the Talmud, which categorically disallows it. "Priest-kings are not anointed. R. Judan based this dictum on the text, 'The scepter shall not depart from Judah' " (Gen. 49:10).[28] In effect, Rabbi Judan is arguing that—since, by definition, priests are from the tribe of Levi—they are automatically excluded from kingship, which is reserved for the descendants of Judah—most particularly, the Davidic line. Other participants in the talmudic discussion base the dictum on the biblical declaration that neither the priests nor anyone else from the tribe of Levi can have any portion or inheritance in Israel. However, it seems far more likely that this concern for basing the talmudic dictum on the Bible reflects a desire to provide an unimpeachable authority for the rabbis' determination to delegitimize theocracy as an acceptable model for government in the Judaic state.

In any case, it is significant that the dictum opposing the legitimacy of priest-kings is unchallenged. It may well be that this opposition to priest-kings reflects an intrinsic concern over the complete domination of all aspects of society by any single authority—a situation that may lead to autocracy. The biblical constitutional framework precludes such total dominance of the polity by a single authority—notwithstanding the historical aberration of the Hasmoneans.[29]

NOTES

1. Federbusch, *Mishpat haMelukhah beYisrael*, p. 15. It should be noted that not all commentators accept the interpretation of "kingdom of priests" suggested here, although they would agree with the underlying notion. Thus, both RASHI and RASHBAM in their respective commentaries on the Bible consider the term for priest (*kohen*) as used in Ex. 19:6 to carry the same meaning as it does in 2 Samuel 8:18—that is, "ministers."

2. Benamozegh, *Yisrael vehaEnoshut*, p. 241.

3. In explaining why the names of Aaron's sons are specified in the biblical text, Nahmanides states: "So as not to conclude that, because of the accession of the father to the high office, the sons are thereby also so elevated. Rather, each of them was individually elevated, thereby excluding Phineas and the remaining offspring, so that only those four were elevated that were anointed with Aaron, as well as their sons that were born afterward" (Nahmanides, *Perushei haRAMBAN al haTorah* on Ex. 28:1). Phineas, a son of Eleazar born prior to his father's elevation to the priesthood was therefore precluded from succession to the office. Later, he is raised to the priesthood as a specific reward for his actions on behalf of the integrity of his people. See Num. 25:10–13.

4. This event is recorded in the Bible as follows: "And the Lord spoke unto Moses, saying: Bring the tribe of Levi near, and set them before Aaron the priest, that they may minister unto him.... And thou shalt give the Levites unto Aaron and his sons; they are wholly given unto him from the children of Israel.... And I, behold, I have taken the Levites from among the children of Israel instead of every first-born that openeth the womb among the children of Israel" (Num. 3:5,6,9,12).

5. This restriction is spelled out explicitly in the Bible: "The priests the Levites, even all the tribe of Levi, shall have no portion nor inheritance with Israel; they shall eat the offerings of the Lord made by fire, and His inheritance. And they shall have no

inheritance among their brethren" (Deut. 18:1–2). Also, "And the Lord said unto Aaron: Thou shalt have no inheritance in their land, neither shalt thou have any portion among them. . . . And unto the children of Levi, behold, I have given all the tithe in Israel for an inheritance, in return for their service which they serve . . . it shall be a statute for ever throughout your generations, and among the children of Israel they shall have no inheritance" (Num. 18:20–23).

In discussing the underlying rationale for the economic disenfranchisement of the Levites, Maimonides writes: "Why did not Levi benefit from inheritance in the Land of Israel, and the spoils of war along with his brothers? Because they were segregated for the worship of the Lord, to His service, and to instruct the multitude in His honest ways and righteous laws" (Maimonides, *Hilkhot Shemitah veYovel* 13:12). Gersonides somewhat expands on this theme, when he states: "With regard to the admonishment to us not to give the tribe of Levi any share in the spoils of war or any inheritance in the land, the benefit inherent in these caveats is that the Levites should be free for worship of the Exalted Name. Therefore, they were not compelled to go to war nor to have anything to do with the work of the land in a way that could, as a result, spoil their profundity in matters of the Torah" (Gersonides, *Perush al haTorah al Derekh Biur* II:233a).

6. Judah HaLevi observes that "Music was the pride of a nation which distributed their songs in such a way that they fell to the lot of the aristocracy of the people, viz., the Levites, who made practical use of them in the Holy House and in the holy season" (HaLevi, *Book of Kuzari*, p. 108). This emphasis on music, poetry, or song must be understood in its historical context, as the primary vehicle of oral tradition and education.

Eliezer Levi places the significance of song in the appropriate perspective, when he writes: "The Levites took no share in the land. The levitical offerings were insufficient. True, they officiated at various altars but because of the absence of a central Holy Temple they could not find adequate work. Consequently, the Levites lived a life of poverty. From among them, Samuel—who was himself from the tribe of Levi—took persons enthused by the word of the Lord, and formed them into a band of scholars. He taught them poetry and song, and they wandered among the dwellers of the land and taught them the songs of praise to the Lord. And in this way they instructed them in the knowledge of their Father that is in heaven, and the observance of the precepts and the study of the Torah. They became the educators of the generation, the teachers of the people in the worship of the Lord" (Levi, *Yesodot haHalakhah*, p. 61).

7. Nissim Girondi, *Shnaim Assar Derushim*, # 11, p. 79. Similarly, Isaac Abravanel comments: "They are the ones properly fit to serve on the high court since they have no portion or inheritance to trouble them; because they would be free from all burdens they are ready for the study of the law and the precepts and to be members of the Sanhedrin" (Abravanel, *Perush haTorah*, "Devarim," p. 37a).

8. This theme is reiterated in the passage: "Moreover in Jerusalem did Jehoshaphat set of the Levites, and of the fathers of Israel, for the judgement of the Lord, and controversies" (2 Chron. 19:8). In his commentary on this text, Gersonides notes: "The judges that were set up in Jerusalem constituted the high court, and because of this Jehoshaphat placed among them the Levites and the priests and from among the chief of the fathers of Israel" (Gersonides, *Perush haRALBAG* on 2 Chron. 19:10).

9. *Yevamot* 86a. See also Meyuhas ben Elijah, *Perush al Sefer Devarim*, p. 84.

10. Discussing the text of Deut. 17:9, the Midrash explains: "The section dealing with the judges which states 'unto the priests the Levites,' would imply that it is obligatory as a matter of principle that a court must have priests and Levites in its composition,

and that without them it is not properly constituted. Therefore it is written: 'And to the judge,' to advise that even if the court does not contain any priests and Levites it is nonetheless validly constituted" (*Sifre Devarim* 17:20). See also Maimonides, *Hilkhot Sanhedrin* 2:2; and Gersonides, *Perush al haTorah al Derekh Biur* II:223b.

11. Maimonides, *Hilkhot Sanhedrin* 2:1.

12. Deut. 17:8 states: "If there arise a matter too hard for thee in judgement . . . then shalt thou arise, and get thee up unto the place which the Lord thy God shall choose." Commenting on this passage, the Midrash concludes: "From this it is said that there were three courts there [at the chosen place—that is, Jerusalem], one at the entrance to the Temple mount, one at the entrance to the Temple courtyard, and one at the Chamber of Hewn Stone" (*Sifre Devarim* 17:19). See also Malbim, *HaTorah vehaMitzvah* on *Sifre Devarim* 17:19.

The discussion here is not concerned with elucidating the historical structure of the Jewish court system during the Hebrew commonwealths. For an in-depth review of this highly controversial subject, see Hugo Mantel, *Studies in the History of the Sanhedrin* (1961) or the augmented Hebrew translation, *Mehkarim beToldot haSanhedrin* (1969).

13. Bahya ben Asher explains: "Israel makes pilgrimages [to Jerusalem] three times a year, and will find there the priests the Levites and teachers of the Torah, and they can inquire of them as to the Law and the precepts and how to conduct themselves in accordance with them, and they will resolve all their doubts" (Bahya ben Asher, *Biur al haTorah* III:348 on Deut. 16:18). See also Ibn Ezra, *Perushei haTorah leR. Abraham ibn Ezra* on Deut. 16:18.

14. RASHI writes: "They alone have this privilege" (Solomon ben Isaac, *Perushei RASHI al haTorah* on Deut. 33:10).

15. Note also: "For the priest's lips should keep knowledge and they should seek the law at his mouth" (Mal. 2:7). David Kimhi remarks: "Thus it is proper for every priest that his lips should keep knowledge of the precepts and the statutes, and through his lips to instruct Israel in them" (Kimhi, *Perush RADAK al haTorah* on Mal. 2:7). Similarly, David Altschuler interprets this passage as meaning "all this is befitting every priest, for the priest's lips are the ones privileged to keep knowledge for dissemination, and it is therefore proper that Israel should seek the law from his mouth and that he should teach them" (Altschuler, *Metzudat David* on Mal. 2:7).

Elijah Benamozegh takes strong issue with the position being put forth here. He attempts to limit the pedagogic role of the priests and Levites exclusively to ritual matters. However, his argument is primarily concerned with refuting any assertions in favor of the idea that Judaism supports the concept of theocracy in the usual sense—which it clearly does not. See Benamozegh, *Yisrael vehaEnoshut*, p. 241ff.

16. Isaac Abravanel treats this passage as meaning that "The priests shall be the teachers of the law and the redirectors of all men to the worship of the Lord. . . . And also that the priests should be seated within the Sanhedrin . . . and they shall have knowledge of the laws of the Torah and its statutes, and shall endeavor to uphold them" (Abravanel, *Perush al Neviyyim Aharonim* p. 602).

17. David Altschuler—for example—takes the passage from Ezekiel to mean that "On matters of civil law the people shall stand before them for judgement, and they shall judge them in accordance with the laws of the Torah and not according to their personal predilections" (Altschuler, *Metzudat David* on Ezek. 44:24).

18. On the other hand, Malbim qualifies the extent of priestly involvement in the judicial process. Thus, he interprets the passage from Ezekiel as meaning "that they shall

be *among* the Sanhedrin to judge civil matters as well as those involving human life (emphasis added)" (Malbim, *Mikra'ei Kodesh* on Ezek. 44:24).

19. Zvi Hirsch Chajes sums up this idea as follows: "The law and the teaching were given exclusively to the priest and Levite, and the obligation devolves upon them to instruct the people of the Lord with regard to the civil and criminal laws, and to dispense righteous judgement so as to ameliorate the conflicts that break out among them. And to tell them the way of the Lord, and the acts that they should perform in practice with regard to every aspect of the Torah" (Chajes, *Torat Neviyyim*, pp. 12–13).

20. Eliezer Levi writes: "After the death of Moses, the leadership function passed into the hands of Joshua. However, the scroll of the Torah was received by the priests.... The priests became the teachers of the people, and taught them the laws of the Torah. And the judges of the people received their instruction from the priests so that they would be able to render judgement in accordance with the statutes of the Torah" (Levi, *Yesodot haHalakhah*, p. 74).

21. Zacharias Frankel writes: "The teaching of law and practice, to distinguish between the holy and the profane, etc., was in itself, and in accordance with the precepts of the Torah, in the hands of the priests. However, the priests quickly deviated from the path and did not wish to ascend the Holy Mount and deal with matters of the Law and teaching. Therefore, when the last of the Judges arose, that is, Samuel... he established a band of disciples of the prophets, from whom the Law would be disseminated, and who would teach the word of the Lord" (Frankel, *Darkei haMishnah*, p. 4).

22. Maimon, *Hiddush haSanhedrin beMedinatenu haMehudeshet*, p. 24.

23. *Avot* 1:1.

24. See Judah Loew ben Bezalel (MAHARAL), *Derekh Hayyim*, p. 30. Isaac Abravanel bases the preference for Joshua over the high priest on the qualitative differences between the two men. "Even though Eleazar was the high priest, Joshua was more perfect than he in the matter of Torah and in the degree of prophetic insight.... And to make this point, our mishnaic passage states that he 'handed it down to Joshua.' For it was to him that the main transmission of the Torah was directed, and Eleazar was joined to him just as Aaron was to his brother Moses" (Abravanel, *Nahlat Avot*, p. 46).

An alternative approach to dealing with the problem is suggested by Joseph Hiyyun, who—in commenting on the talmudic passage—takes the phrase "Moses received the Torah" as meaning "in my opinion, the Oral Law, because it is in regard to it that it states: 'And handed it down to Joshua.' The written Torah, that was received at Sinai as well, was handed over to the priests the Levites" (Hiyyun, *Millei deAvot* in *Perushei Rishonim leMassekhet Avot*, p. 79). This view is also adopted by the contemporary scholar, Ezra Zion Melamed, who writes: "The 'Torah' that is mentioned in this passage refers to the Oral Law, since the Written Law was transmitted by Moses to the priests" (Melamed, *Mavo leSifrut haTalmud*, p. 1).

25. Frankel, *Darkei haMishnah*, pp. 11–12.

26. Interpreting the clause, "And he shall stand before Eleazar the priest," the Midrash comments: "Since Joshua has need of Eleazar, and Eleazar of Joshua" (*Sifre Bamidbar* 27:21). Considering the same text, Malbim takes notes that the "laying on of hands" connotes the transfer of authority or privilege. However, in Numbers 27, Moses is not told to lay his *hands* upon Joshua, but rather "lay thy *hand* upon him." He then goes on to observe that "after he was commanded to lay upon Joshua only a single hand and to place on him only part of his honor, therefore... with regard to those things that require divine guidance, Eleazar will be the primary one and at his word they will go out [to

war]; that is to say, at Eleazar's word, for Joshua will possess only the external honor of fighting their wars and to lead them" (Malbim, *HaTorah vehaMitzvah*, ad loc.).

27. Malbim, *Mikra'ei Kodesh* on Prov. 29:4.

28. Jer.T. *Horayot* 3:2. Anointment reflects legitimacy.

29. In examining this issue, Nahmanides notes with regard to the relatively short life span of the Hasmonean house: "It is also possible that there was an element of sin inherent in their kingship because they were priests and were commanded to preserve their services for the needs of the altar . . . and that they should not have ruled, but only served in the worship of the Lord. . . . The priests, even though they were in themselves suitable for anointment, are not anointed for the purpose of kingship" (Nahmanides, *Perushei haRAMBAN al haTorah* on Gen. 49:10). See also Bahya ben Asher, *Biur al haTorah* I:382 on Gen. 49:9ff.

8
The Prophetic Institution

"The priests are closely related to the prophets, not only because the two brothers, Moses and Aaron, were chief of the prophets and father of the priests respectively, but mainly because the prophets complement the role of the priest. . . . The role of the priest is to preserve the Torah. . . . The role of the prophet is to relate to the people the word of God that was revealed anew."[1]

The role of the prophet and the function of prophecy within the biblical constitutional constellation reflect the essence of the subtlety of its political theory. The prophetic institution is designed as a delicate mechanism that is employed to maintain a continuous equilibrium between political theory and practice—causing each to adjust to the other, while simultaneously conforming to the divine ethic reflected in the principles and precepts of the Torah. It is to be expected that the successful performance of this important and extremely difficult task would dictate a requirement for extraordinary capability on the part of the prophet. As conceived in rabbinic theory, the prophetic institution is uniquely structured to enable the prophet to both possess and exercise such capability.

The institutionalization of prophecy as a constitutionally mandated element of political society is proclaimed by the Bible: "A prophet will the Lord thy God raise up unto thee, from the midst of thee, of thy brethren, like unto me; unto him ye shall hearken" (Deut. 18:15). This declaration contains five constituent clauses or elements. From the perspective of rabbinic interpretation, each of these elements serves to elucidate one or more of the various aspects of the prophetic institution and to define its function, scope, and authority.

The preliminary question to be dealt with concerns the purpose and function of prophecy within Judaic political society. Saadia Gaon takes the position that the primary purpose of the prophet is to elaborate on the practical application of biblical precepts, in accordance with some ill-defined legislative authority granted to him. He argues that it is imperative there be an authoritative standard accepted by the people as bearing the divine imprimatur, "for if we were to defer in these matters to our own opinions, our views would differ and we would not agree on anything."[2]

This is obviously rather different from a view of the prophet that sees him primarily as a seer relating visions of the future, or as a human transcription machine repeating messages transmitted to him from above. This is not to suggest that, through divine inspiration, the prophets may not prove extraordinarily capable of profound insight into the probable course of events. However, such a capability is never conceived of as an end in itself, but is always used didactically by the prophet in pursuit of the higher moral purpose of redirecting men to the proper moral and political path. Thus—Joseph Albo argues—"The principal purpose of the prophetic institution existing in the human race is not to foretell the future or to regulate particular matters that interest individuals, such as are communicated by diviners and star-gazers, but to enable a whole nation or the entire human race to attain to human perfection."[3]

In the rabbinic view, the course that will lead to human perfection is fully charted in the Torah, and it is through adherence to and observance of the precepts of the Torah that man finds his way along the road. It becomes the mission of the prophet—through employment of his special faculty—to assist the wayward by reorienting them to the appropriate path.[4] The prophet who is true to his responsibility can only be one whose urgings and prescriptions are circumscribed by the Torah: That is, they are in conformity with its fundamental aims and precepts.

One essential characteristic of the prophetic institution is that it is reformist—rather than revolutionary—in character. The prophet does not seek to overturn the government and assume political leadership himself. On the contrary, he seeks to bring about the realization of the good society within the framework of existing legitimate institutions. However, where these institutions are in themselves corrupt, he does not hesitate to raise his voice seditiously, in an effort to bring about the necessary reforms. The prophet does not create an organization around his central leadership. His position and function are unique and personal and are not transferable. In a sense, the prophet may be seen as the forerunner of the modern ombudsman—the champion of the just cause that cannot get an appropriate and responsible hearing. As Abraham Joshua Heschel wrote: "In a sense, the calling of the prophet may be described as that of an advocate or champion, speaking for those who are too weak to plead their own cause. Indeed, the major activity of the prophets was interference, remonstrating about wrongs inflicted on other people, meddling in affairs which were seemingly neither their concern nor their responsibility."[5]

The second element in the text of Deut. 18:15 is viewed as establishing the prophetic institution within a unique territorial context. That is, prophecy is considered to be functionally related to the maintenance of an organized political society in the Land of Israel. The text reads: "A prophet will the Lord thy God raise up unto thee, *from the midst of thee.*" This latter clause is interpreted in the Midrash as meaning "from the midst of thee and not outside the confines of the land."[6]

An obvious difficulty here rests in the fact that the Bible does record prophecy outside the Land of Israel: for example, Moses in Egypt; and Ezekiel in Babylon. The response of the Midrash is that prophecy is indeed essentially restricted to the Land of Israel. However, the apparent exceptions to this rule have occurred because of "the merit of the fathers."[7] That is, these prophets were allowed to prophesy outside the Land of Israel as a mark of special favor, because of the eternal merit of their ancient ancestors—the Patriarchs—who were the first to revolt against paganism and idolatry, and recognize the universal sovereignty of God. An alternate explanation offered by others is to assert that, where a prophet who came after Moses did prophesy outside the Land of Israel, it was only because he was already imbued with the prophetic spirit that came to rest upon him while he was still in the land.[8] Notwithstanding the difficulties inherent in these interpretations, they represent clear testimony to the central importance of the Land of Israel in the rabbinic world view.

Were the biblical text to have concluded with the clause "from the midst of thee," it could be interpreted as suggesting that there would always be prophets in the Land of Israel—irrespective of the nature of the population inhabiting the country. Therefore, a third element is assumed to have been added to indicate that the prophetic institution has definite national implications. The text thus incorporates the phrase "of thy brethren"—which is interpreted in the Midrash as meaning, "of thy brethren and not of any others."[9] The prophetic institution, then, is considered to be uniquely related to the people of Israel on account of their special relationship to the Torah, since the function of prophecy is to uphold the precepts of the Torah. Hence, the prophetic institution becomes a truly national phenomenon, but only when the nation is constituted within its prescribed national territory.

The fourth element in the biblical text establishing the prophetic institution— "like unto me"—is somewhat more problematical. An early Aramaic translation of the Bible renders the phrase as meaning "as I am with respect to divine inspiration."[10] The implication is that the prophet must in some way be comparable to Moses. However, any such comparison is fraught with obstacles in view of the explicit statement in the Bible itself: "And there hath not arisen a prophet since in Israel like unto Moses, whom the Lord knew face to face" (Deut. 34:10). The nature of the relationship between Moses and his prophetic successors becomes critical to the determination of the character and scope of their authority, as well as the criteria for acceptance as a prophet.

Since, in the rabbinic view, the function and mission of the prophet are carefully delineated, the criteria by which the true prophet may be distinguished from the charlatan become highly significant. However, the question of the authentication of the prophet and his prophecy is only of peripheral interest to the central concerns of this study, and will not be examined here. Of far greater immediate relevance are the selection criteria governing recruitment into the prophetic institution—criteria that presumably will serve to emphasize the public role the prophet will play in carrying out his responsibilities.

It should be recalled that the prophetic role is an individual one, even though it has institutional characteristics. It involves the authority and mission of the single prophet. There is no subordinate organization to which he can delegate functions or powers. There are no procedures for succession. Accession to the position of prophet is by divine selection alone. However, since it is an individual that is selected for the office, there must be some basic means by which the public can readily determine his probable legitimacy. This is provided for by Moses' declaration that the successor to the office of prophet shall be "like unto me."

After examining the character of the numerous adjectives used to describe Moses throughout the Bible, the sages of the Talmud derived certain fundamental criteria by which to determine if one in their midst is in fact comparable to Moses. Thus, Rabbi Johanan taught: "The Holy One does not permit His Presence to rest except upon one who is strong, wealthy, wise, and humble, and all [these criteria] are derived from Moses."[11] In another place, we find an anonymous variation on this theme—which states: "The Holy Presence does not rest except upon one who is wise, strong, wealthy and tall."[12] Interestingly, despite the obvious difference between "humble" and "tall," the talmudic dicta appear to be treated as equivalent, within the literature.

At face value, it seems clear from the criteria postulated in the Talmud that the prophet must be capable of exuding charisma, if he is to be able to fulfill his mission. That is, his status and obvious qualities must be such as to command attention and respect. However, there are two rather distinct schools of rabbinic thought on this matter—one interpreting the stated criteria metaphorically; the other school taking them literally.

The metaphorical school bases its interpretation of the criteria on the way in which they are employed by the talmudic sage, Ben Zoma, in his ethical teachings. He said: "Who is wise? He who learns from all men.... Who is strong? He who subdues his passions.... Who is wealthy? He who rejoices in his portion."[13] Maimonides is a powerful advocate of the metaphorical approach. He writes: "The spirit of prophecy does not rest on any other than a wise man, great in wisdom, strong in his attributes, such that his desires do not overpower him in regard to anything in the world, but that he always overcomes his desire by force of his intellect, and maintains comprehensive and highly proper opinions."[14] While there have been attempts to reconcile Maimonides' position with that of the more numerous literalists, it is quite clear that his understanding of the talmudic criteria—to be consistent with his position on the nature of prophecy itself—must entail a nonliteral interpretation of the words of the Talmud.[15]

The metaphorical position is categorically rejected by Joseph Karo, who insists that "where the Talmud speaks of strong, it means the word literally—that he should be a man of physical strength, and the same with wealthy—that he should literally have a large amount of money."[16] This is not to suggest that the literalists reject the values promoted by Maimonides and his followers in the metaphorical interpretation. Indeed, the essence of the literalist position—whose staunchest advocate among the medieval commentators is Nissim Girondi—is that the prophet must literally possess these characteristics in order to gain sufficient credibility with the masses of the people, so that he might also gain acceptance of the message that he brings. This view is predicated on the judgment that the large majority of the people will show greater deference to intellect, wealth, and physical power in their ordinary meanings—qualities that they admire—than to less demonstrable spiritual attributes. It is therefore to be expected that they will pay greater attention to a prophet who reflects these popular aspirations.[17] Only after the prophet has gained the confidence of the people can he proclaim, as did Jeremiah: "Thus saith the Lord, 'Let not the wise man glory in his wisdom, neither let the mighty man glory in his might, let not the rich man glory in his richness: But let him that glorieth glory in this, that he understandeth and knoweth Me' " (Jer. 9:22–23). Only from one who himself possesses wisdom, might, and wealth would such a teaching have the desired credibility. As Nissim explains, the prophet spoke these words to redirect men from their misconceptions as to what attributes have true value in the eyes of the Lord. Therefore—in his opinion—it becomes necessary for the prophet himself to possess these other attributes, in order to get men to acknowledge their relative worthlessness as compared to the moral and spiritual virtues.[18]

Samson Raphael Hirsch takes the literalist position a step further by arguing that the literal interpretation of the criteria applies, not because of the likelihood of greater public acceptance of the prophet—but rather because, without these attributes, he would be unable to properly carry out his mission. "God does not pick out weaklings, simpletons, nor those who are socially dependent on others to be messengers of His Word."[19] Indeed—in Hirsch's view—"only an independent person, who requires nothing for himself and asks nothing for himself, can look on and understand men and things in that complete objectivity, without any, even subconscious, reference to himself, which is so necessary for a messenger of God."[20]

As suggested earlier, one of the basic stumbling blocks in making comparability to Moses a criterion for prophetic selection is the incompatibility of the text that reads, "like unto me" (Deut. 18:15), with "there has not arisen a prophet since in Israel like unto Moses" (Deut. 34:10). Since every prophet is necessarily considered comparable to Moses with regard to his attributes—irrespective of the different interpretations of the metaphoricalists and literalists—the differences between Moses and his prophetic successors cannot be personal ones, and therefore must relate to the very nature of their missions as prophets. Such an approach would permit reconciliation of the conflicting biblical texts—by simultaneously corroborating the validity of the selection criteria established in the Talmud, and basing the mission differentiation between Moses and all other prophets in the explicit statement of Deut. 34:10. This differentiation of prophetic missions is a critical element in the fabric of rabbinic political thought, and is of particular importance in fully understanding the nature of the prophetic institution as conceived in Rabbinic Judaism.

The distinguishing factor of paramount importance between Moses and the other prophets is generally considered to be the unique legislative role of the former. With the establishment of the fundamental Mosaic Law—as reflected in the precepts of the Torah—the superstructure of divine law is considered to be complete. The Bible declares: "These are the commandments which the Lord commanded Moses for the children of Israel on Mount Sinai" (Lev. 27:34). Commenting on the significance of the text, the Midrash notes: "*These* are the commandments; no prophet is authorized to legislate anew from this time on."[21] From this standpoint, the mission of the prophets after Moses must be seen as fundamentally nonlegislative in character. (The term "fundamentally" rather than "absolutely" is deliberately used here, because—as will be shown—the prophets are indeed considered as having a special legislative function and capacity.) As stated in the Midrash, "You should not argue that another Moses has arisen that brings us a new Law from heaven; there remains no other such law in heaven."[22] Furthermore, their mission is seen as entirely derivative from and subordinate to that of Moses.[23]

It would appear from this that the role of the prophet lies primarily in preaching and moralizing to the public, in a sustained effort to raise its ethical and religious awareness. However, the constitutional provision of Deut. 18:15 seems to indicate a responsibility beyond exhorting reform of man and society. Were such intended to be the full extent of the prophetic mission, the fifth and final element of the biblical provision would be both pointless and superfluous. To command a deviant public to obey the exhortations of a prophet when—by definition—they do not obey God would seem to be a rather futile gesture. The biblical insistence that "unto him ye shall hearken"—which announces an unequivocal obligation on the part of society to pay heed to the prophet—clearly implies something more. Consequently, we find the rabbinic theorists ascribing a rather unique political authority to the prophet—one that places the prophet on a par with the other elements of political authority and power in the biblical constitution. This authority—based on the fifth element of the text of Deut. 18:15: "unto him ye shall hearken"—is interpreted in the Talmud to mean that "even if he says to you: Transgress one of the precepts of the Torah . . . in accordance with the needs of the hour, you shall listen to him."[24]

The scope of prophetic authority implied in this talmudic teaching is truly extraordinary. One need but recall that a command by the king to transgress even a minor precept of the Torah justified open resistance on the part of the public. The imputed authority of the prophet in this regard would appear to exceed that of the ruler of the state.

While—as noted above—the prophet is denied legislative authority, it now appears that such denial is only in terms of the authority to amend the law permanently.[25] However, the prophet is granted full authority to abrogate the law temporarily, in accordance with the needs of society at any particular point in its social and political life.[26] The exception to this blanket ad hoc legislative authority concerns matters that could lead to the undermining of the foundations of society. For example, the prophet's authority does not extend to even temporary abrogation of the laws forbidding idolatry, murder, or incest.

The ad hoc legislative authority of the prophet is thus viewed as being circumscribed by the requirement that any deviation from the law be for the exclusive purpose of ultimately strengthening it. Stated in another way, such temporary legislation must be geared toward meeting a particular social or political need that, in the long run, would derogate from the observance and fulfillment of the Torah in greater degree than would take place through a temporary abrogation.[27] Some writers—such as Maimonides and Gersonides—would even extend the obligation to heed the prophet beyond matters pertaining to the observance or nonobservance of Mosaic Law. In their view, there is an obligation to do what the prophet calls for even in matters that are usually considered completely discretionary. What the prophet urges be done is presumed to be in the best interests of both the individual and the society.[28]

There is a general consensus among rabbinic theorists that ascribes ad hoc legislative authority to the prophet with regard to the temporary enactment, amendment, and abrogation of laws—including fundamental precepts, as well as discretionary matters. However—in the view of some—this is all subject to a basic constraint: The prophet must clearly indicate that his legislative acts reflect the divine will, and not his own judgments.[29] On the other hand, the Tosafists ascribe to the recognized prophet the authority to proclaim ad hoc legislation on the basis of his own insights and the fact of his acknowledged status as a prophet.[30] In effect, this places the prophet on a par with the executive power of the polity. The fundamental difference between the two rests primarily on the fact that the ruler will have the means of coercion at his disposal to enforce his commands, whereas the prophet must rely entirely on his moral stature and force of personality.

This significant divergence of views remains unresolved in the rabbinic literature. However, it is interesting to note that the position of the Tosafists lends itself well to the resolution of a different problem mentioned earlier in this study. In discussing the question of civil disobedience, it was pointed out that the tradition was silent about the mechanism by which the decision to mount overt resistance to the government was to be legitimately made. As seen by the Tosafists, the role of the prophet could readily fill that gap. He could be the arbiter who would determine the point at which a government had so far exceeded its legitimate authority as to nullify its legitimacy—thereby meriting the rebellion of its constituents.

The nature of the prophetic mission and the scope of the prophet's authority present a highly complex prospect—a matter dealt with in the literature in a variety of contexts, and perhaps raising more questions than are answered. One of the more difficult problems yet to be addressed concerns the nature of the relationships between the prophet and his political peers—the kings, priests, and judges—in the constitutional scheme. It is particularly difficult to reconstruct the rabbinic view on this question, primarily because the literature hardly deals with it in any significant way. Nonetheless, there are to be found a few teachings that may form a rudimentary basis for a largely unarticulated—yet implicitly held—traditional view on the subject. These statements concern a rather curious passage in the Talmud, which states: "From the day that the Holy Temple was destroyed, prophecy was removed from the prophets and given to the sages.... What does this mean? Even though it was removed from the prophets, it was not removed from the sages."[31]

The inherent difficulty in this passage becomes evident when the text is considered in the light of one of the talmudic criteria for eligibility for prophecy. That criterion specifies that "the spirit of prophecy only rests on one who is wise." What—then—is intended by differentiating the prophecy of the sage from that of the prophet, if the prophet himself is—by definition—supposed to be a sage?

Within the wide-ranging discussions on this question in the literature, there is a tendency to differentiate not only between the prophetic missions of Moses and the other prophets, but also between differing aspects of the nature of prophecy itself. That is, the type of prophecy that is pronounced by the prophet derives from a form of divine revelation, whereas the prophecy of the sage is arrived at through perfection of his intellectual faculties. Conceptually, then, there is a close affinity between the prophet and the sage; the distinction between them being primarily related to the source and nature of their prophecy, rather than on a basic difference in mission. However, recognizing that the sages are primarily concerned with juridical matters, the affinity between the prophet and the sage as suggested here could lead to the overlapping of constitutional authorities, since the roles of both could be performed by a single person. In such an event, there would be no effective way of determining whether, in a particular instance, the prophet-sage was acting in a prophetic or a judicial capacity—thereby obscuring the carefully drawn lines of legislative authority that are intended to circumscribe the prophetic institution.

One approach to resolving this dilemma is predicated on the absolute integrity of the prophet-sage. That is, it would require that the individual in question clearly state whether he were speaking as a prophet or as a sage—bearing in mind the distinction in the source of prophetic knowledge.[32] An alternative thesis is that the prophetic function is actually not coequal with the juridical. This view would argue that prophetic authority is consensually derived from the court—placing the prophet in a subordinate position within the political framework.[33]

As suggested earlier, the determination of the precise nature of the relationship between the judicial and prophetic institutions remains enigmatic. Nonetheless, the principle of separation of powers is reflected in a variety of ways in rabbinic thought. Indeed, in one of the few places in the literature where there is a discussion of the relationship of the prophet to the king, we find the argument that the very nature of the institutions dictates the necessity of separation of powers in order to facilitate the proper performance of their assigned functions.[34]

With regard to the question of the relationship of the prophet to the priest, we refer back to the citation with which this chapter began. It was argued there that the prophet is the complement to the priest, with clearly nonoverlapping functions such that there would be no difficulty in a single person's pursuing both vocations—as occurred among the biblical prophets. However, it is questionable whether the prophet—once elevated to that lofty position—could actually perform priestly functions, as a practical matter.

While it remains evident that an adequate exposition of the place of the prophet within the biblical constitutional scheme is still wanting, it is equally certain that a definitive statement of the nature, function, scope, and relative authority of the prophet cannot be formulated on the basis of the scant clues to be found in the literature—because the nonrational aspects of prophecy are necessarily involved. Nevertheless, the prophet most assuredly is considered as having a distinct political role—the legislative aspects of which appear to involve authorities vested in other components of the constitutional structure, for the most part. However, with the exception of the ambiguity surrounding the relationship of the prophets to the judiciary, the rabbinic views on the prophet's institutional relationships clearly comport with the principle of the separation of powers—as well as with that of checks and balances among the major elements of government.

With regard to the latter, it might be noted from a historical standpoint that the prophets did in fact come into frequent conflict with the other established institutions of government—as might reasonably be expected, in a complex political system. As observed by Abraham Joshua Heschel, "The prophet was not a *primus inter pares*, first among his peers. By his very claim, his was the voice of supreme authority. He not only rivaled the decisions of the king and the counsel of the priest, he defied and even condemned their words and deeds."[35] The prophet appears to have been intended to play a unique counterinstitutional role. He was enabled to offset the abuse of authority and power by any of the other constituent elements of government. It was partly through the creative tension fostered by the presence of the prophet that the promise of the properly ordered polity was to be realized.

NOTES

1. Hoffmann, *Sefer Devarim*, pp. 342–343.
2. Saadia ben Joseph al-Fayyumi, *The Book of Beliefs and Opinions*, pp. 145–147. Abraham Joshua Heschel writes: "The phenomenon of prophecy is predicated upon the assumption that man is both in need of, and entitled to, divine guidance. For God to

reveal His word through the prophet to His people is an act of justice. The purpose of prophecy is to maintain the covenant, to establish the right relationship between God and man" (Heschel, *The Prophets*, p. 202).

3. Albo, *Sefer Ha'Ikkarim* III:107. With regard to the need for prophecy in the first place, Albo's view is almost identical to that of Saadia. "We have made clear that the necessity of prophecy is that men may be guided toward eternal happiness, that they may know through it what is agreeable to God and what is not, and that they may attain to the destiny intended for mankind by doing those things which are agreeable to God" (p. 109).

4. Zvi Hirsch Chajes writes: "The function of the prophet is to admonish the people in order that they should follow the path of the Torah, and that they should at all times pay heed to their teachers, the sages and heads of the community, and not to depart from the Torah to follow an unpaved way; also to give abundant warning that their end will be bad and bitter if they abandon the Law of Moses" (Chajes, *Torat Neviyyim*, p. 13).

5. Heschel, *The Prophets*, p. 205.

6. *Sifre Devarim* 18:68. Nahmanides considers the biblical phrase to "allude to the fact that there is no prophecy except in the land of Israel" (Nahmanides, *Perushei ha RAMBAN al haTorah* on Deut. 18:15).

7. "Before the Land of Israel had been specially chosen, all lands were suitable for divine revelations; after the Land of Israel had been chosen, all other lands were eliminated.... You might argue: I cite the case of those prophets with whom He did speak outside the land of Palestine. True, He did speak with them outside the land, but He did so only because of the merit of the fathers" (*Mekilta De-Rabbi Ishmael* I:4–5).

8. This is the position taken by Meyuhas ben Elijah: "Since the Land of Israel was chosen, there is no longer any prophecy outside the land, and even though we find in the case of Ezekiel [that he did prophesy outside the land], prior to it he had already prophesied in the Land of Israel" (Meyuhas ben Elijah, *Perush al Sefer Devarim*, p. 101).

9. *Sifre Devarim* 18:68.

10. *Targum Yonatan* on Deut. 18:15. Elijah Mizrahi notes: "The intent of this entire passage is nothing other than to cause them to keep away from soothsayers and sorcerers and such as they, and advises them that they have no need of such men" (Mizrahi, *Perush R. Eliyahu Mizrahi* on Deut. 18:15). An identical interpretation is offered by Meshorer in *Siftei Hakhamim* on Deut. 18:15. For alternate interpretations, see Solomon ben Isaac (RASHI), *Perushei RASHI al haTorah* on Deut. 18:15; and Nahmanides, *Perushei haRAMBAN al haTorah* on Deut. 18:15.

11. *Nedarim* 38a.

12. *Shabbat* 92a.

13. *Avot* 4:1.

14. Maimonides, *Hilkhot Yesodei haTorah* 7:1. Elsewhere, Maimonides writes: "When a person enters into a relationship with prophecy ... and will be worthy of it, such as if he were from among the men of wisdom, faith, abstinence, intellect, and pleasantness, attributes that reflect our basic principle that prophecy does not rest on any other than the wise, strong and wealthy" (Maimonides, *Perush haMishnavot*, "Introduction").

Isaac Abravanel similarly advocates a metaphorical interpretation: "In accordance with the Law, if there is need of preparation for prophecy in the attributes and in the intellectual attributes, it may be derived from the saying of our sages: 'The spirit of prophecy does not rest on any other than one who is wise, strong, and wealthy,' for, in saying 'wise,' they give indication of preparation in the contemplative faculties, and their saying 'strong and wealthy,' was intended to indicate the moral attributes" (Abravanel, *Perush Abravanel* pt. 2, p. 67b).

15. Maimonides writes: "As for the principle which I laid down, that preparation and perfection of moral and rational faculties are the sine qua non, our Sages say exactly the same: 'The spirit of prophecy only rests upon persons who are wise, strong, and rich' " (Maimonides, *The Guide for the Perplexed*, p. 220).

16. Karo, *Kesef Mishneh* on *Hilkhot Yesodei haTorah* 7:1.

17. Nissim explains: "A few commentators have offered the interpretation of what is meant when it is said that a man is strong, that is, that the strength of his intellect overcomes all his appetites, and that the wealthy should also have the capacity to be satisfied. They thus compare the strong and wealthy that are mentioned here [*Nedarim* 38a] to those that are cited in the words of Ben Zoma in *Avot*. This explanation cannot be correct, for after the Talmud mentions 'humble,' there is no further need to mention 'strong' and 'wealthy,' since once one has attained to the virtue of humility it is not possible that he should not also possess these other perfections, in accordance with their interpretations. For how could he attain purity and sanctity if he cannot conquer his desire? ... But in order to be the prophet that is to prophesy to the multitude and to inform them of the commandments of the Holy One, such a one must of necessity be acceptable and desired with regard to all his faculties by the lovers of wisdom, the lovers of wealth, and those who choose strength ... and therefore none will be properly qualified for prophecy other than one who has perfected in himself the intellectual virtues, as well as the virtues of the masses, and this is what is meant when the Talmud speaks of one who is tall. For no one besides a man of good appearance is properly fit to admonish many people, because the masses will accept his word more than another's.... Therefore R. Jonathan [Johanan ?] included 'strong' and 'wealthy,' even though these virtues do not perfect the spirit, and are of no lasting benefit, but only because they are the virtues sought after by the masses, and with their possession the prophet will be respected and elevated" (Nissim Girondi, *Shnaim Assar Derushim*, # 5, p. 34).

18. Samuel Eidels (MAHARSHAH) argues that "since all of these virtues were present in Moses, the thread extends to the remaining prophets as well ... because these attributes of the strong, the wise and the wealthy are the greatest virtues in the eyes of man ... it is proper that a prophet, the messenger of the Lord, should not [be] deficient in them, and they added [humility to the talmudic criteria] in order that he should not show pride in these attributes, that he should be as humble with respect to all these as was Moses" (Eidels, *Hiddushei Aggadot* on *Nedarim* 38a).

19. Hirsch, *The Pentateuch* on Ex. 2:11–12.

20. Ibid. on Ex. 6:14–27.

21. *Sifra*, # 120 (13:7), on Lev. 27 (emphasis added). Gersonides comments: "It is known from the words of the Torah that there has not arisen a prophet of the Torah, and there will arise none besides Moses, for no prophet will be trusted to add to or subtract from the Torah in such a manner that he will set forth a law to be followed throughout the generations, much less would he be entrusted to change it and exchange it for another" (Gersonides, *Perush al haTorah al Derekh Biur* II:247b). See also Sforno, *Perush R. Obadiah Sforno* on Deut. 34:10.

22. *Yalkut Shimeoni*, p. 665. Maimonides categorically states: "There is no Torah revealed by the prophets after the first, and there is no adding to it or subtracting from it, as it is written: 'It is not in heaven' [Deut. 30:11]. And the Lord has not authorized

us to learn the law from the prophets, but only from the sages, men of reason and understanding. It does not state: 'And thou shalt come unto the prophet that shall be in those days'—but rather 'And thou shalt come unto the priests the Levites, and unto the judge' " (Maimonides, *Perush haMishnayot*, "Introduction").

23. Maimonides writes: "The history of all our prophets that lived after Moses is well known to you; they performed, as it were, the function of warning the people and exhorting them to keep the law of Moses, threatening evil to those who would neglect it, and announcing blessings to those who would submit to its guidance" (Maimonides, *The Guide for the Perplexed*, p. 231). Expanding on Maimonides, Shem Tov ibn Shem Tov remarks: "All the prophets who came after Moses our teacher are moralists; not that they should originate religion and law as did Moses, but rather that they proclaimed his Torah" (Ibn Shem Tov, *Perush Shem Tov*, pt. 2, p. 83a). See also Malbim, *Hatorah vehaMitzvah* on Lev. 27:34.

24. *Yevamot* 90b. Also cited in *Sifre Devarim* 18:68.

25. Maimonides states: "It is a positive precept that we are commanded to heed each of the prophets, to do all that they bid even if it is contrary to a precept or even all the precepts, under the condition that their bidding is of a temporary nature and not an order for a permanent abrogation or addition [to the Law] (Maimonides, *Sefer haMitzvot*, # 172, pt. 2, p. 18).

26. Aaron HaLevi of Barcelona writes: "The roots of the precept lie in that the highest achievement of man is that of attaining to prophecy, and therefore no man in the world has such a true understanding of things as the truth of understanding through prophecy which is unquestionable knowledge since it derives from the fountain of truth. Few among mankind are worthy of it and ascend to it, for the ladder is very great.... Therefore, the Torah has commanded us that when one man in a generation achieves such heights and is known to us by his vocation and the legitimacy of his actions, that he is to be trusted as a prophet, we should heed him in all that he commands, because it is he who knows the true way and will direct us to it" (Aaron HaLevi of Barcelona, *Sefer haHinukh*, # 499, p. 618).

27. Meiri writes that with regard to one "who prophesied the addition of a precept to the Torah that does not serve to further shield the precepts, or meet the special needs of the hour, or to ensure the fulfillment of the remaining precepts, but claims that he does these things through a new prophetic dispensation . . . even if he performed the greatest of signs such as causing the sun to stand still . . . even if he performed several wonders, he is not to be listened to" (Meiri, *Bet haBehirah al Massekhat Sanhedrin* on Sanhedrin 90a, p. 325).

28. Maimonides states that "if he commands us with regard to matters of discretion, such as to go to a certain place or not to go, to do battle today or not to do so, to build this wall or not to build it, it is a positive precept to heed him, and he who transgresses against his directions is deserving of capital punishment at the hands of Heaven" (Maimonides, *Hilkhot Yesodei haTorah* 9:2).

Gersonides offers a very liberal interpretation of the phrase "unto him ye shall hearken": "This means to say, in all that he will command you in matters of discretion. It is therefore clear that it also indicates that we are obligated to listen to him even with regard to the divine precepts. It is proper that we examine this thesis, and we will argue that if the intent of this phrase is to caution us to heed the commands of the Torah, then it would not be a matter of paying heed to the prophet but rather that of paying heed to the commands of the Torah . . . therefore it creates the obligation for us to heed him in his commands with regard to matters other than the precepts of the Torah so as to leave no doubt [as to the obligation to heed the prophet] in divine matters in accordance with the needs of the hour" (Gersonides, *Perush al haTorah al Derekh Biur* II:225b).

29. Joseph Babad comments: "It appears from the work of Maimonides that the precept to obey the prophet to transgress one of the precepts only holds if he says in the name of the Lord that the Lord so commanded him, but that there is no obligation to pay heed to him if his proclamation proceeds from his own reason" (Babad, *Minhat Hinukh* pt. 3, # 517, p. 148).

30. The Tosafists are even more explicit than Gersonides, in regard to the discretionary authority of the prophet. Commenting on the talmudic passage that establishes the ad hoc legislative authority of the prophet to prescribe for society "in accordance with the needs of the hour" (*Yevamot* 90b), the Tosafists argue: "If it is intended to say [that one should hearken to the prophet because he has been informed] by the divine word, then why specify that it applies 'in accordance with the needs of the hour,' for one is obligated to uphold the commands of Heaven whether or not it is in accordance with the needs of the hour. [A prophet would thus be obeyed under all conditions.] Therefore, the phrase surely refers to the situation where the prophet proclaims in accordance with his own reason" (*Tosafot* on Sanhedrin 89b). See also *Tosafot Yeshanim* on *Yevamot* 90b.

31. Yom Tov ben Abraham Ishbili (RITBA) is cited as interpreting the talmudic teaching as follows: " 'And given to the sages'—this means that they shall ascertain through their reason many things that transcend the powers of comprehension of the natural rational faculty" (Ibn Habib, *Hiddushei haKotev* in *Ein Yaacov* on *Baba Batra* 12a).

Jacob ibn Habib writes: " 'Even though it was removed from the prophets'—where it appeared as an image and vision, the prophecy of the sages, which is effected through the intellect, was not removed' (ibid.).

Hanokh Zundel comments: "The intent [of the talmudic passage] relates to the consideration that there are two varieties of prophecy, real prophecy such as that of Moses and the remaining prophets that heard the law and the precept from the Almighty, and a second form of prophecy whereby he who prophesies does not hear the word directly from the Almighty, but rather through his great wisdom introduces and proclaims laws and ordinances directed toward the truth as if they were transmitted at Mt. Sinai, such as the sages of the Mishnah and the Talmud" (Hanokh Zundel ben Joseph, *Etz Yosef* on *Baba Batra* 12a).

32. Zvi Hirsch Chajes writes: "In the beginning both capacities were encompassed within a single individual who was both prophet and sage, and afterward prophecy was removed but wisdom remained. Therefore it should be understood that even though these capacities were both present in a single individual, he acted in respect of each of them in accordance with the appropriate laws and statutes, and never mixed them. Instead, when he was possessed with the word of the Lord, he said all those things that he received through the Holy Spirit, and when he sat on the seat of judgement, he taught in accordance with the rules of the Mosaic Law without deviating to the left or to the right of the path paved by the Torah" (Chajes, *Torat Neviyyim*, pp. 13–14).

33. This view is based on a midrashic interpretation of Isaiah's statement, "And I heard the voice of the Lord, saying: Whom shall I send, and who will go up for us" (Isa. 6:8). A commentary attributed to Rav notes: " 'Whom shall I send?'—from the Holy One. 'And who will go for us?'—from the high court. Thus, even though they were prophets of the Lord, if the high court were to depart from them they would not have the authority to prophesy" (*Midrash Aggadat Bereshit* 14:4). This passage refers particularly

to the prophets Isaiah and Obadiah. However, J. L. Maimon—apparently using a variant edition of the Midrash as a basis—generalizes the statement to include the prophetic institution as a whole: " 'Everything that the prophets prophesied they did only by means of the high court, and if the high court departed from them they did not have the spirit to prophesy.' . . . And everything that the prophets improved with regard to morality, ethics and good works—everything was stated and proclaimed under the cognizance of the high court of the people" (Maimon, *Hiddush haSanhedrin beMedinatenu haMehudeshet*, pp. 15–16).

34. Abraham Sofer writes: "It was ever so in Israel that the prophet of the Lord and the king of Israel were each one separate unto himself; that is to say, they never existed simultaneously in a single person. It is impossible by its very nature that they should be so united, for the proper role of the king is always to watch over his people with a cautious eye and to lead them in their wars . . . and he is obligated to be deeply involved with his people at all times. However, it is the opposite with the prophet that is sent to Israel as a messenger of the Lord who needs to be free from all worldly engagements, always alone, to sanctify and purify his spirit so that he will be right and worthy of the affairs of the Lord, and through divine revelation to prophesy in the time of need" (Sofer, *Sefer Ktav Sofer al haTorah*, p. 276a).

35. Heschel, *The Prophets*, p. 480.

9
The National Executive

It is a basic tenet of rabbinic political theory that the maintenance of a viable and just policy is in large measure contingent on the existence of a strong central leadership. The precise form that this leadership is to take is a matter of considerable controversy that finds its roots in the dicta of the Bible itself. In the following discussion of this controversy, it will be shown that the essence of the argument concerns a distinction that is drawn (but not well articulated) between the nation per se and the nation conceived as a territorially based political entity—that is, a national state.

The Bible informs us that—in anticipation of his demise, and out of concern for the people (nation) of Israel—Moses "spoke unto the Lord, saying: Let the Lord . . . set a man over the congregation, who may go out before them, and may come in before them, and who may lead them out, and who may bring them in; that the congregation of the Lord be not as sheep which have no shepherd" (Num. 27:15–17). We are subsequently told that this leader was to be Joshua, who appears in the Bible as the first of the judges. It is important to note that, in the cited passage, there is no specification as to the exact form the required leadership is expected to take. More particularly, it does not stipulate the need for a king to serve as leader of the nation. The question of institutional structure and character is left open. Yet, in Deuteronomy, the nation is told by Moses: "When thou art come unto the land which the Lord thy God giveth thee, and shalt possess it, and shalt dwell therein; and shalt say: 'I will set a king over me, like all the nations that are round about me'; thou shalt in any wise set him king over thee, whom the Lord thy God shall choose; one from among thy brethren shalt thou set king over thee; thou mayest not put a foreigner over thee, who is not thy brother" (Deut. 17:14–15).

This text is distinguished from the one cited earlier in at least two important respects. First, the passage speaks of "When thou art come unto the land." The appointment of a king in Israel is thus directly related to the establishment of a national territory, and is predicated on effective occupation and possession of the land by the nation. In the earlier citation, the matter of national leadership is addressed without reference to a national homeland. The implication that may be drawn from this is that the nature of the institution that is to embody the executive functions of government may differ in accordance with whether the nation is constituted as a territorially based political entity.

A second consideration of some significance is that, although the later passage appears to require the appointment of a king, it does not specify his leadership functions—as does the earlier text. The statement that the text of Deuteronomy "appears" to require the establishment of a monarchy in Israel is made advisedly, for it is over the wording of this biblical text that the controversy in the rabbinic literature rages.

The dichotomy of views as to whether monarchy is required in the national state or whether it is merely an optional form of leadership is articulated quite clearly in the Talmud. "R. Judah said: Three commandments were given to Israel when they entered the land: to appoint a king. . . . While R. Nehorai said: This section [Deut. 17:14] was spoken only in anticipation of their future murmurings, as it is written, 'and shalt say, I will set a king over me, etc.' "[1] Thus, according to Rabbi Judah, it is mandatory to set up a king to rule over Israel; while, according to Rabbi Nehorai, it is an option—albeit undesirable—that may be exercised at the nation's discretion.[2]

The controversy over whether the establishment of a monarchy is mandatory or optional has continued as a significant issue in rabbinic political theory since talmudic times, with substantial numbers of rabbinic writers arrayed fairly evenly on both sides of the argument. Maimonides—among many others—considers the establishment of a king to be essential for the proper ordering of society, and counts it as one of the basic precepts of the Torah.[3]

In his attempt to provide a rationale for the precept, Maimonides argues: "It being the will of God that our race should exist and be permanently established, He in His wisdom gave it such properties that men can acquire the capacity of ruling others. Some persons are therefore inspired with theories of legislation, such as prophets and lawgivers; others possess the power of enforcing the dictates of the former, and compelling people to obey them, and to act accordingly. Such are kings, who accept the code of the lawgivers."[4]

The view that considers monarchy as the necessary as well as the most beneficial form of rule over society is one that has been held by many rabbinic theorists throughout the ages. From the eleventh century to the turn of the twentieth, we find this theme constantly repeated in the literature. Thus, at the early part of this period, Samuel ibn Nagdela (Shemuel haNagid) writes in one of his secular poems: "There is no good for the people in the absence of kings."[5] And in modern times, Jehiel Mikhal Epstein remarks: "It should be understood that in the order of perfection [of the nation] the appointment of a king is antecedent to everything else, for without a king there is no people, and therefore a king is fundamental."[6]

An alternate—less absolute—approach stresses the importance of a strong central leader, but does not make the case that the king is the preferred or necessary form such central authority must take. Joseph Albo takes the position that the need for a central leader clearly prevails where societies are governed by "conventional law." However, he leaves open the question as to whether such need obtains in a society governed under Mosaic Law.[7] Malbim goes a step further and argues (in effect) that, while the Torah is unclear as to whether kingship is mandatory or optional, the entire question is only relevant under a given set of sociohistoric conditions—such as when Israel elects to pattern itself after the other nations of the world. Where those conditions do not prevail— as is the case when the divine law is in ascendency and becomes paramount as the keystone of the polity, in place of the conventional or natural law—the very notion of kingship becomes irrelevant.[8] However, the question of whether monarchy is necessary or not does not affect the need for a strong national leadership. In Malbim's view, the need for a central political authority applies to all societies—including one dedicated to the Mosaic Law.

It was indicated earlier that there is another school of rabbinic thought, which strongly supports the Rabbi Nehorai's position that kingship in Israel is not mandatory under any circumstances. By contrast to Maimonides, Saadia Gaon considers the establishment of a monarchy to be optional, and thus omits the requirement for kingship as one of the basic precepts of the Torah.[9]

It is in the work of Isaac Abravanel, however, that we encounter an implacable antimonarchist who frontally challenges the views of the rabbinic advocates of mandatory kingship. Abravanel's argument—in essence—is that there is no historical evidence to support the judgment that a king is necessary to produce cohesion in a political society, or that justice is better served when there is a king. On the contrary, he argues that man and society are better served when the executive power is not held by a single individual—because it is easier to corrupt an individual than a group. Furthermore, it is more reasonable to preclude the potential for arbitrariness in a single ruler by having the executives of the society appointed for specific terms of office, and held subsequently accountable—once out of power—for transgressions against the public committed while holding office.[10] Abravanel summarizes his argument with the comment that "it is clear that the king is not necessary for a people, neither for the improvement of the polity nor for the purpose of bringing about harmony, continuity, or ultimate authority. And therefore I think that, at first, kings were not made by the choice of the people, but were imposed by force and by whoever was the most powerful."[11]

Abravanel's antimonarchist arguments reflect his perception of the relative beneficence of the republican forms of government that he found in the Italian republics. Coming to Italy in the wake of the expulsion of the Jews from Spain, Abravanel found in Venice a state free from the excesses of the monarchies that he had served in Portugal and Spain as statesman and financier. Thus, his biblical commentaries—completed in the relative tranquility of Venice, toward the end of his turbulent career—contain sharp comparisons between the republican and monarchical systems of government.[12]

Obadiah Sforno takes the position that not only is monarchy not required by the Torah, it is actually undesirable even as a permissible option. He argues that "the permission to appoint a king is the same as the permission to marry a 'woman of goodly form' [yefat toar] which suggests that the end will be to hate her and give birth through her to a rebellious son, such as happened to David in the matter of Absalom."[13] Sforno is alluding to Deut. 21:11, which discusses the question of marrying a "woman of goodly form" who is taken captive in war. This was the case with David, who married such a captive and produced Absalom as the offspring of the union—who turned out to be a rebel and attempted to overthrow his father. By drawing this analogy, Sforno is suggesting that, even though it is permissible under biblical law to establish a monarchy, it is not desirable. Once in power, the king may and probably will tend to use his authority for purposes other than those originally intended. Thus, the king is compared to a beautiful captive who appears most desirable at first glance, but whose allure may obscure other features that promise eventual incompatibility and regret. Naftali Zvi Berlin argues that it is inconceivable there should be a biblical requirement for the establishment of a monarchy, since such an unequivocal command might well prove inconsistent with the nature of the people who are to be governed.[14]

This basic cleavage in rabbinic thought regarding the question of the necessity of establishing a monarchy as the form of government through which the polity is to be organized and governed remains unresolved. However, even the most vociferous of the antimonarchists will concede that—although there may be no necessity for a king in the first instance—once a monarchy is in fact established, the king's appointment and consequent rights and obligations must be in accordance with the dictates and requirements of the Torah.

It was observed earlier that the question of kingship is pertinent only when the nation is constituted as a territorially based political entity. This is not a relevant issue when considering the intrinsic leadership needs of the nation, as such. For the latter, the Torah decrees a national political and military leader (Num. 27:17), and not a king. This raises the question as to how these two categories of political office and authority are differentiated. The differences between the king and the leader may perhaps be best considered through an examination of the character of Moses' role as political leader, since it is with Moses that the nation of Israel first takes distinctive form.

Although the Bible nowhere specifies precisely the type of leadership authority exercised by Moses, a passage that is generally assumed to be referring to Moses states: "And there was a king in Jeshurun" (Deut. 33:5).[15] This would suggest that—notwithstanding the absence of any direct attribution of the title to him—Moses had the status of a monarch. However, in a statement that appears to contradict this inference, the Talmud informs us that "Moses requested kingship but it was not given to him."[16]

Abraham ibn Ezra attempts to reconcile the apparent difficulty, by explaining that the "king" spoken of in the biblical text is indeed Moses "from whose lips the chiefs of the people heard the Law explained; and the reason [for the use of the term 'king'] is because Moses was like a king and all the chiefs of the tribes gathered to him."[17] Josiah Pinto takes the position that Moses was indeed a king, and that the request for kingship that the Talmud refers to as having been denied to him was for kingship in perpetuity. That is—according to Pinto—Moses sought to establish a dynasty for his sons and their descendants. It was this request that was refused.[18] The implication is that one of the distinguishing features of kingship—as opposed to nonmonarchic leadership—is that monarchy (by definition) includes hereditary succession.

While the matter is not explored in the traditional literature to any great extent, there is some evidence of a tendency in rabbinic thought to equate the biblical judges (the title given to the nonmonarchic national political and military leaders) to kings. In this regard, it should be noted that, in four places in the Book of Judges (17:6, 18:1, 19:1, and 21:25) where periods of anarchy and crisis are described, the wording—with slight variation—reads: "In those days there was no king in Israel." Since the Book of Judges is supposed to relate the history of the period between Joshua and the establishment of the monarchy under Saul (related in the First Book of Samuel), the repeated reference to the absence of a king during this premonarchy period clearly begs for some explanation. While the explanations offered in the literature vary widely, they all involve a central notion that equates the judge with a king.

For example, Maimonides implies that Joshua—the first of the judges—was a king, as well.[19] Gersonides explains the biblical texts by suggesting that they refer to the period between the death of Joshua and the rule of Othniel—the first judge mentioned in the Book of Judges.[20] Evidently, the implication here is that the texts refer to an interregnum between two judges who were the equivalent of kings. Similarly, David Kimhi explains the absence of a king as referring to the period "between Samson and Eli, when there was no judge for Israel."[21] A third variation on the theme is offered by Isaac Abravanel, who considers the references to the absence of a king to refer to the period when Samson the Judge was in captivity. "Thus, there was no king in Israel, because, though Israel had a judge, he was not among them because he was in the hands of the Philistines."[22]

It would seem, then, that there is really no substantive difference between the judge—as national political and military leader—and the king, except insofar as it concerns the subject of their rule—the nation or the national state. One procedural distinction between the two categories of leaders—as we have seen—involves the matter of hereditary succession. There are several other such distinctions suggested in the literature, as well.

Abravanel—alone among the major commentators—has written extended remarks on this particular subject. In his treatment of the question, Abravanel provides a comparative analysis of kingship and judgeship, and enumerates five points of similarity and five of dissimilarity—which also serve to define the constitutional character of the two forms of governmental leadership. The five points of convergence are:

1. Both kings and judges are appointed by the court, and must be acceptable to the public.
2. Both are charged with responsibility for leading the army in war, and for dispensing justice.
3. Both are empowered to enforce rules that are inconsistent with the requirements of the Torah, but that are required to meet the exigencies of the hour.
4. Both represent lawful authority, and rebellion against them is a capital crime.
5. Both are links in a chain of legitimate authority—each succeeding, and succeeded by, another judge or king.

The points of divergence are as follows:

1. Only the king is anointed, symbolizing his legitimacy as one chosen by God.
2. "The powers of the king and his appointees do not extend to matters of law and to the adjudication of disputes between man and his neighbor in accordance with the Torah. He stands solely for the improvement of the political society, to save the people from their enemies and to decide the law temporarily and in accordance with the needs of the period, and not in the manner of dispensing righteous judgement [which is the province of the judge]."
3. There are specific biblical precepts that the king is obligated to observe for as long as he wears the crown—precepts that do not apply to judges.
4. According to the Torah, the king is entitled to certain privileges and benefits in matters of honor and property—privileges that are not accorded to the judges.
5. For the *anointed* king, the crown is hereditary, and the succession is assured to his descendants in perpetuity.[23]

From Abravanel's analysis, it would appear reasonable to conclude that the fundamental distinctions between king and judge rest more on the question of political status than on political function. This is made explicit in Abravanel's comment on the biblical passage that relates how "all the men of Shechem assembled themselves together . . . and went and made Abimelech king" (Judges 9:6). Abravanel writes: "It is appropriate to understand that, even though it states here that they made Abimelech king, in truth he was not a king and is not reckoned among the kings of Israel. The text states: 'And Abimelech was prince over Israel three years' (Judges 9:22), because his concern was with government and rulership, not kingship. And this is because, in truth, the term 'kingship' is not applied where there is no anointment, and the first anointed king in Israel was Saul. However, the usage here and in the Book of Judges of the title 'king' is as an expression for every judge, officer and ruler."[24] Abravanel's emphasis is thus on the king's divine selection, anointment, privileges, and hereditary succession—as compared to the more prosaic functional description of the judge or national leader. However, the very similarity of the political functions of the two offices raises a very difficult question. Why does the establishment of the nation as a territorially based entity call for a different category of leadership than that required by the nation under other conditions?

Unfortunately, this question does not appear to be dealt with to any extent in the literature. Yet, a partial answer may be inferred from Gersonides' commentary on Judges 18:7, which describes the city of Laish as being ruled in the "manner of the Zidonians... for there was none in the land, possessing authority." Discussing the implications of the word "authority" in the context of the succeeding passages, Gersonides observes that "it was the intent of the text to indicate that this government did not pass from father to son, and that this is the factor that would prevent their leader from placing himself in danger for the sake of protecting a nation that is not his patrimony."[25]

The implication here is that a leader cannot be depended on to take great risks for the people unless he has a significant personal stake in their protection. Gersonides seems to be saying that, if the leadership or government were hereditary, such a stake would exist. Applying this notion to the differentiation between king and judge, it could be argued that, where the nation is not yet established in a permanent territory, the very absence of real property enforces a rough equality among all—regardless of the degree of responsibility that some may have for the national welfare. Under these conditions, one who assumes the mantle of leadership will most likely do so out of a sense of personal responsibility and readiness for self-sacrifice for his people, since he has little to gain materially from the position. However, under the conditions of a territorial state and the consequent possibility of acquiring property and wealth, the commitment and fidelity of the ruler to the nation becomes questionable, unless he has a tangible and significant stake in its welfare. In other words, why should he risk his life to protect the property and wealth of others? The obvious solution to this dilemma is to give special status and privileges to the leader, and to ensure his fidelity by making his position hereditary—giving him a permanent and important stake in preserving the state from its enemies, both external as well as internal. The endemic succession crises in states that do not have a hereditary monarchy or very strong democratic traditions and processes seem to lend additional credence to this idea.

NOTES

1. *Sanhedrin* 20b. In the Midrash, we find an alternate version of the disagreement between the two sages: "R. Nehorai says that the text speaks to the shame of Israel [in that they request a king].... R. Judah said: But it is a precept of the Torah to request a king as it is written: 'Thou shalt in any wise set him king over thee' " (*Sifre Devarim*

17:28). The "murmurings" referred to by Rabbi Nehorai reflect the desire of the nation to be constituted in a manner comparable to the nations that surround them.

2. Malbim explains the issue between the sages as follows: "According to R. Judah it is a commandment, [as though to say] I command you that you shall say to the prophet and the Sanhedrin: I will set a king over me; for the phrase 'and shalt say' is not to be interpreted as meaning, '*if* you should say,' for it is written: 'thou shalt in any wise set him [king over thee].' They are thus commanded to establish a king. . . . R. Nehorai's understanding is that where it is written: 'I will set a king over me,' it is not a commandment to do so. It is rather in reference to the shame of Israel that the text speaks, as if to say, that you will in the future murmur and speak in such a manner" (Malbim, *HaTorah vehaMitzvah* on Deut. 17:14).

3. Maimonides, *Sefer haMitzvot*, pt. 2, p. 35. Jacob Anatoli writes: "Because the natures of men differ from one another, and the will of one is opposed to that of another, except for a single ruling authority over them there would be no agreement concluded between them and conflict would be rife. Therefore we have the precepts regarding judges and officers, and the establishment of a king over the people to rule them and guide them in the straight path" (Anatoli, *Malmad haTalmidim*, p. 167a).

Similarly, in explanation of the inclusion of establishing a king as one of the basic precepts, Aaron HaLevi of Barcelona writes: "It is impossible for mankind to form a civilization without making one among them a chief over the rest, to do his bidding and to keep his regulations; for the opinions of men differ from one to the other and they will never agree to a single understanding in order to accomplish a single thing" (Aaron HaLevi of Barcelona, *Sefer haHinukh*, # 97, p. 130). Thus—he continues in another place—"We are commanded to appoint a king over us from among the people of Israel that will gather us all and will lead us according to his will . . . [because] of the benefit that accrues to the people by having over them a single person as chief and commander, because otherwise civilization could not be maintained in peace" (ibid., # 493, p. 608).

4. Maimonides, *The Guide for the Perplexed* II:40.

5. Ibn Nagdela, *Ben Mishlei*, # 828, p. 238. Other later medieval apologists for monarchy include Nissim Girondi, who writes: "We find that the appointment of a king in Israel is as necessary as among all other nations that require political order" (Nissim Girondi, *Shnaim Assar Derushim*, p. 75). Abraham Shalom writes: "Man, by nature, has need of political existence, and to gather with his kind to form a political civilization, and to be perfected through the strength of a just king" (Shalom, *Nevei Shalom*, p. 108).

6. J. M. Epstein, *Arukh haShulhan heAtid*, "Hilkhot Melakhim" 71:3, p. 67).

7. Albo writes: "Conventional law cannot exist unless there is a ruler, or a judge, or a king, placed at the head of the group or city, who compels the people to repress wrong and observe the law so as to secure the welfare of the group. It follows therefore that the establishment of a king or ruler or a judge is almost imperative for the continuance of the human species, seeing that man is political by nature" (Albo, *Sefer Ha'Ikkarim* I:73).

8. Malbim writes: "As those who have investigated the matter have said, the relationship of the king to political society is as the relationship of the heart to the living being whose body has a heart, and as the relationship of matter to the first cause; and they say that the kingdom will fulfill three things: 1) harmony and the order of [political] participation; 2) continuity and the order of [political] change; 3) the power of ultimate decision [see note 10 below]. Indeed, all this is so with regard to all the peoples that are on the face of the earth that conduct themselves in accordance with the processes

of nature, and so also Israel in the time when the 'image' departed from them and their conduct was under the sway of chance and nature. Then it became necessary that they should raise up a king over them to fight their battles.... It was only after they inherited and settled the land that there were periods when they left the Lord of Hosts and became as all other peoples under the rule of nature; then it was either a commandment or they were given permission to establish a king as had all the nations that surrounded them" (Malbim, *Mikra'ei Kodesh* on 1 Sam. 8:6). See also Malbim's *HaTorah vehaMitzvah* on Deut. 17:14.

David Zvi Hoffmann argues: "The Holy One, blessed be He, did not command unconditionally and absolutely that Israel should appoint a king over themselves, except when the people feel that they have the need for such.... In the event that the people should feel weak... [then] it is not only permissible but mandatory to appoint a king over them" (Hoffman, *Sefer Devarim*, p. 333).

9. Saadia ben Joseph al-Fayyumi, *Perushei Rabbenu Saadia Gaon al haTorah*, p. 144. See also Ibn Ezra, *Perushei haTorah leR. Abraham ibn Ezra* on Deut. 17:15. For comparative tabulation of variant listings of the precepts, see Rabinowitz, TARYAG, pp. 146–166.

10. Abravanel writes: "It is fitting that we should understand if the king is a necessary thing and self-obligatory upon a people, or whether it is possible to manage without one. And the philosophers have already considered... that the monarchy will realize three things: first—harmony and political participation; second—continuity and political change; third—the power of ultimate decision. We will see that in truth their views regarding the obligation to have a king as well the necessity for one are fallacious, because they do not preclude there being among the people numerous leaders to organize and unify and to agree upon a common course, and that through them there should [be] leadership as well as justice, and this applies to the first consideration. And why should their leadership not be on an annual basis or for three years... or for less, and when their turn arrives, different judges and officers will take their places and examine the transgressions of their predecessors, and those who are condemned for their acts will pay compensation for their misdeeds, and this will apply to the second consideration. And should not the power of decision be delimited and structured in accordance with the laws and legal precepts which state that in the case of a minority and a majority, the law is as seen by the majority? For it is more likely that an individual will transgress the law... than that many people within a single entity will commit evil... and by their tenure being temporary, they will fear because they will be called to account in a short while. But why do we have to bring rational argument to this issue? Experience provides greater evidence. Look and see those lands that are ruled by kings. We have seen several lands that are governed by temporary judges and rulers, selected from among themselves ... and still today, the rulership of Venice, mistress of nations and chief among states, and the government of Florence, an example to all other lands and governments, both small and large, have no king among them, and they are led by leaders who are selected for an allocated time.... All this demonstrates that the presence of a king in a nation is not necessary" (Abravanel, *Perush haTorah*), "Devarim," pp. 26a–36b). For critique of Abravanel's position, see Alsheikh, *Torat Moshe*, "Devarim," pp. 124–125.

11. Abravanel, *Perush al Neviyyim Rishonim*, p. 147.

12. See Netanyahu, *Don Isaac Abravanel: Statesman and Philosopher*, pp. 173–180.

13. Sforno, *Perush R. Obadiah Sforno* on Deut. 17:14. For additional support for this position, see Rapa, *Minhah Belulah*; and Ibn Attar, *Or haHayyim*—both ad loc.

14. "There are states that cannot tolerate the idea of monarchy, and there are states

which, in the absence of a king, are like a ship without a captain. And in this regard, it is impossible to [impose a monarchy] through the requirement of a positive commandment. For in matters that relate to the governing of the society, it is comparable to matters concerning the 'preservation of life' [*pikuah nefesh*] which take precedence over the positive commandments. Thus it is not possible to command absolutely the appointment of a king so long as the people have not agreed to accept the yoke of kingship on the basis of the observation that surrounding states are conducted in a more proper order thereby. In that event, it becomes a positive commandment for the Sanhedrin to appoint a king" (Berlin, *HaAmek Davar* on Deut. 17:14).

15. *Zevahim* 102b.

16. The source for the talmudic statement is the biblical text that relates the story of the Burning Bush, where the Lord "called unto him out of the midst of the bush and said: 'Moses, Moses.' And he said: 'Here am I.' And He said: 'Draw not nigh hither' " (Ex. 3:4–5). This passage is interpreted in the Midrash as follows: " 'And he said: Here am I.' . . . Here am I to receive priesthood and kingship. . . . Moses requested that priests and kings should descend from him. Thereupon the Lord said to him: 'Draw not nigh hither.' This means to say: Your sons will not perform sacrifices because the priesthood is already assigned to your brother Aaron. The word 'nigh' refers to kingship. . . . The Lord said to him: The monarchy is already assigned to David. Even so, Moses attained to both of them. The priesthood, because he served in it in the interim period. The monarchy, because it is written: 'And there was a king in Jeshurun' " (*Exodus Rabbah* 2:13).

17. Ibn Ezra, *Perushei haTorah leR. Abraham ibn Ezra* on Deut. 33:5. In similar manner, Gersonides—in his commentary on the passage in Exodus that describes how Jethro, Moses' father-in-law, gave to Moses an advance warning of his coming—remarks: "This means to say that if Jethro had come and Israel were to have no prior knowledge of it in order to conduct themselves with proper deference towards him, it would be an embarrassment for Moses. In what way? Because Moses was at the level of kingship, and it is proper that the people conduct themselves deferentially toward the relatives of the king for the sake of his honor" (Gersonides, *Perush al haTorah al Derekh Biur* I:73b).

18. "Moses requested kingship, but it was not given to him as it is written: 'Draw not nigh hither.' This relates to the fact that he requested [kingship] in perpetuity; because Moses was king of Israel, as it is written: 'And there was a king in Jeshurun.' If so, what is the meaning of 'Draw not nigh hither'? This relates to his progeny, forever" (Pinto, *Meor Einayim* on *Zevahim* 102b).

19. In a passage dealing with the method of establishing a monarchy, Maimonides states: "A king is not established, at first, except by a court of seventy elders and a prophet: such as Joshua who was appointed by Moses and his court" (Maimonides, *Hilkhot Melakhim* 1:3).

20. Gersonides, *Perush haRALBAG* on Judges 17:6.

21. Kimhi, *Perush haRADAK* on Judges 18:1.

22. Abravanel, *Perush al Neviyyim Rishonim*, p. 143.

23. Ibid., pp. 93–95.

24. Ibid., p. 123.

25. Gersonides, *Perush haRALBAG* on Judges 18:17.

10
The Monarchy

Defining the authority and powers of the monarchy in the Judaic polity—as understood in rabbinic political theory—presents a particularly formidable problem. While the fundamental constitutional provisions establishing the monarchy are set forth in Deuteronomy, the nature of kingship is dealt with in the First Book of Samuel. The section of the Book of Samuel that discusses the subject is taken as amplifying the provisions of Deuteronomy, and—as such—has provided the ground for a lingering controversy paralleling that over the necessity for establishing a monarchy, in the first place.

As cited previously in Chapter 9, the relevant section of Deuteronomy states: "When thou art come unto the land . . . and shalt say: I will set a king over me, like all the nations that are round about me; thou shalt in any wise set him king over thee, whom the Lord . . . shall choose." Yet, in Samuel, we read: "And it came to pass, when Samuel was old . . . all the elders of Israel gathered themselves together and came to Samuel. . . . And said unto him . . . now make us a king to judge us like all the nations. But the thing displeased Samuel, when they said, Give us a king to judge us. And Samuel prayed unto the Lord. And the Lord said unto Samuel, Hearken unto the voice of the people in all that they say unto thee. . . . Nevertheless protest solemnly unto them, and shew them the manner of the king that shall reign over them" (1 Sam. 8:1–9).

Samuel then proceeds to describe the "manner of the king" in its most negative aspects—presumably to discourage the people from their clamor for a monarchy.

And he said, This will be the manner of the king that shall reign over you: He will take your sons, and appoint them for himself, for his chariots, and to be his horsemen . . . and will set them to plow his ground, and to reap his harvest, and to make his instruments of war. . . . And he will take your daughters to be confectionaries, and to be cooks, and to be bakers. And he will take your fields, and your vineyards, and your oliveyards, even the best of them, and give them to his servants. And he will take your menservants, and your maidservants, and your goodliest young men, and your asses, and put them to his work. He will take the tenth of your sheep; and ye shall be his servants. And ye shall cry out in that day because of your king which ye shall have chosen you; and the Lord will not hear you in that day. (1 Sam. 8:10–18)

Samuel's dark picture of what awaited them should they persist in demanding a king failed to dissuade them from the course they had chosen. "Nevertheless the people refused to obey the voice of Samuel; and they said, Nay; but we will have a king over us; That we also may be like all the nations; and that our king may judge us, and go out before us, and fight our battles.... And the Lord said unto Samuel, Hearken unto their voice, and make them a king" (1 Sam. 8:19–22).

The interpretation of these passages from the Book of Samuel has been the subject of continuing controversy in the literature. The rabbinic theories of monarchy derive primarily from the interpretation of the cited biblical texts, and may be segregated into two distinct thematic strains—the differences between them lying in the approach to constitutional construction. At issue is the distinction between a broad and a narrow construction of the scope and applicability of the statements found in the Book of Samuel, and their relation to the constitutional provisions of Deuteronomy.

The controversy in the literature begins with the talmudic passage referring to the section of the Book of Samuel that deals with the "manner of the king that shall reign over you": "R. Jose said: All that is set out in the chapter [relating to the king], the king is permitted to do. R. Judah said: That section was stated only to inspire them with awe, for it is written: 'Thou shalt in any wise set him king over thee' [Deut. 17:15], that his awe should be over thee."[1]

According to Rabbi Jose—who evidently takes the prophet's declamation literally—the text provides the king with a very wide range of authority (bordering on tyranny), as well as broad confiscatory powers. By legitimating the various practices enumerated by Samuel, Rabbi Jose would seriously restrict the limits of acceptable opposition to the arbitrary acts of the king—straining the concept of effective public control over the actions of its political leaders. Thus—as understood by Reuven Margaliot—Samuel issued his caveat "because they were giving unlimited power into the hands of a single person," and would come to regret it after it was too late.[2] On the other hand, Rabbi Judah—who interprets Samuel's words figuratively—would deny to the king the legitimate authority to carry out the enumerated acts, which are considered to be abuses of royal power.[3] Not surprisingly, proponents of the position taken by Rabbi Jose have generally been those who maintain that the establishment of the monarchy is mandatory under Mosaic law.

In his legal code, Maimonides categorically states: "The king has the authority to levy taxes on the nation for his needs or for the wars.... Everything that is stated in the chapter relating to the king, the king is entitled to do."[4] Commenting on this dictum, Joseph Karo notes that Maimonides "ruled that all that is stated in the chapter relating to kings, the king is entitled to because . . . in a controversy between the sages, R. Judah and R. Jose, the law is decided according to R. Jose."[5] It is important to observe that Karo attributes Maimonides' stance to the traditional procedural rule for resolving controversies among the sages, for the purpose of practical application. That is, where the two talmudic authorities—Rabbi Judah and Rabbi Jose—are in conflict, the views of the latter are taken to be governing.[6] The fact that Maimonides himself makes no reference to the application of the procedural rule—as well as the obvious point that the whole question was theoretical even in talmudic times, let alone in the medieval period—suggests that Karo (the preeminent codifier of *halakhah* after Maimonides) may not be supportive of R. Jose's position on its own merits. As will be shown shortly, other writers who would undoubtedly follow the procedural rule in application do nonetheless directly challenge the position of Rabbi Jose as an incorrect interpretation of the biblical text.

In essence, the literalist approach to the issue reflects the implicit conviction that effective kingship requires the monarch to have extensive legitimate powers, even though they have the potential for leading to tyranny. Abraham Sofer goes so far as to attribute this view to Moses.[7] However, this need not and should not imply that the king is intended to be a law unto himself. Quite the contrary: according to the requirements of the Torah, the king is to "turn not aside from the commandment, to the right hand, or to the left" (Deut. 17:20). It is in the context of this biblical dictum that Maimonides concludes his discussion of the powers of the king with the statement: "In all these things, his law is the law, and all his actions should be for the sake of Heaven, and his purpose and thought should be to elevate the true law, and to fill the world with righteousness, and to break the power of the wicked and to wage the battles of the Lord."[8]

However, if—as it is argued by Rabbi Jose and those who adopt his position—the extensive powers that they would grant to the king come within the scope of the king's legitimate authority, why does the prophet forewarn the people of the extent of the king's powers? Indeed, why is Samuel upset over the request made to him to appoint a king, if the establishment of the monarchy is mandated by the Torah? A possible answer to the first question rests in the consideration that the mere establishment of bounds on the legitimacy of the powers of the monarchy does not of itself preclude their trespass by the king. While the king who abuses his authority is answerable to Heaven for his violation of the biblical injunction to observe the Law, he is not readily answerable to the people for his actions. The power of the king may thus tend to become arbitrary and tyrannical. In effect, as a practical matter, he may choose to act as if he were above the law.

This idea is expressed in a talmudic passage that succinctly and explicitly describes the royal prerogative, through the use of a Greek epigram. Introduced in an argument to exemplify the distinction between conventional and divine law, this passage states: "R. Eleazar said, *para basileus o nomos agraphos* [for the king the law is unwritten]: in the conduct of the world in which a human king legislates an enactment. If the king chooses to observe it, he does so. However, he demands that everyone else shall observe it."[9] Stated differently, this pronouncement affirms that the king is in fact sovereign, in the conventional sense—in that he represents the final authority in law, even to the extent that he may choose to place himself above and beyond its reach. However, from a biblical and rabbinic perspective, the king always remains subject to the higher law of the Torah—notwithstanding the difficulty, if not the impossibility, of compelling his compliance by any means short of the overt threat of rebellion.

Concern over how to prevent the king from becoming a tyrant seems to be the underlying primary concern of those who argue for a figurative interpretation of Samuel's description of "the manner of the king"—as reflected in the position taken in the Talmud by Rabbi Judah. Thus, they maintain that the extensive powers that Samuel describes are not in fact to be exercised by the king; those powers are merely enumerated to portray to the people the tyranny that awaits them, once they do establish a monarchy. Implicit in this position is the corollary argument that, although the king may only exercise such powers in violation of the norms of the Torah, he may nonetheless elect to do so—in which case, the people will have no ready means of redress for their grievances. This argument is made explicit by Gersonides, who writes: "It is my opinion that the king is not permitted those things that are enumerated, but rather that Samuel wished to frighten and alarm the people; to advise them of what the king would do once he became powerful and oppressed them in a manner that would be impermissible for him from the standpoint of the laws of the Torah."[10]

As might be anticipated—because of his strong antimonarchist views—Isaac Abravanel wholeheartedly adopts and supports this latter position.[11] He adduces further support for this view, by drawing attention to the wording of two different but related texts in the Book of Samuel. He notes that the text under discussion here speaks of the "manner of the *king*" (1 Sam. 8:9). However—after the prophet finally accedes to the wishes of the people, and grants them the king they had demanded of him—he proceeds to advise them of the "manner of the *kingdom*" (1 Sam. 10:25). Abravanel argues that—while the "manner of the king" was calculated to dissuade the people from their demand for a monarchy, by painting the worst-case scenario of a despotic monarch—it is the "manner of the kingdom" that is operative in actuality. And the "manner of the kingdom" mandates compliance by the monarch with the specific constraints specified in Deuteronomy.[12]

The textual differentiation drawn by Abravanel appears to have been neglected or ignored by those writers who adhere to the literalist approach to the issue. However, those who follow the figurative approach of Rabbi Judah—as amplified by Abravanel—seem to have seized on it as a major point in support of their opinion. David Altschuler—for example—defines the "manner of the king" as meaning "that which recommends itself to the king without reference to the laws of the Torah."[13] On the other hand, he defines the "manner of the kingdom" to mean "statutes of the kingdom that are proper in accordance with the Torah and the commandment that his awe should spread over the people and that they should not raise their voice in rebellion."[14] Similarly, Malbim considers the "manner of the kingdom" to refer to "those things that are merited by the monarchy from the standpoint of law and religion," and defines the "manner of the king" as "the law and the statute that he will establish by himself, arbitrarily and illegitimately."[15]

From the standpoint of those who maintain that the appointment of a king is optional, the explanation of why "the thing displeased Samuel, when they said, Give us a king to judge us" seems self-evident. For any number of possible reasons, Samuel was opposed to the establishment of a monarchy. However, from the standpoint of those who maintain that the establishment of the monarchy is a positive requirement of the Torah, Samuel's position seems untenable. As the prophet of Israel, he could hardly be opposed to implementing a basic requirement of the Torah.[16]

One approach to the resolution of this problem may be inferred from a singularly difficult talmudic passage dealing with this question—a passsage that has in itself stirred considerable controversy. "R. Eliezer said: The elders of the generation made a fit request, as it is written, 'Give us a king to judge us [1 Sam. 8:6]. But the common people acted unworthily, as it is written, 'that we may also be like all the nations; and that our king may judge us, and go out before us' [1Sam. 8:20]."[17] Taken at face value, Rabbi Eliezer's statement suggests that Samuel was not upset by the request for a king made by the elders. What disturbed him was the translation of that request by the popular spokesmen for the masses of the people into a desire to emulate the surrounding societies— thereby threatening the surrender of Israel's uniqueness as a nation. However, the elders are also recorded as having said to Samuel, "Now make us a king to judge us like all the nations" (1 Sam. 8:5)—a request that would appear to explicitly contradict the teaching of Rabbi Eliezer.

Josiah Pinto attempts to resolve the problem by suggesting that what was being asked for by the common folk—though not by the elders—was nothing less than the abandonment of divine law, in favor of the conventional.[18] In a modified version of Pinto's thesis, David Altschuler takes the position that Samuel was displeased because the elders wished to have a king judge them according to the principles of conventional law—in place of the judges, who adjudicated according to the laws of the Torah.[19] This view—while arriving at the same end point—starts out from a rather different premise than that of Rabbi Eliezer. Rabbi Eliezer and Josiah Pinto both assume that, were the king to comply with the standards of justice of the Torah, he would be acceptable as a judge. By contrast—and as will be further explored later in this study—

Altschuler and others insist on a more rigid separation of powers in the constitution of the state. They would deny the king any legitimate judicial functions or powers other than on a temporary and emergency basis.

A rather different approach to dealing with the question at hand is that taken by Ephraim Solomon of Luntshits. He draws attention to subtle distinctions in the biblical texts—which tend to be ignored by other commentators. He notes that, in Deuteronomy, the request for a king is phrased, "I will set a king *over me*"; whereas, in the Book of Samuel, the request is, "Give *us* a king." He then suggests that this distinction explains Samuel's displeasure. The implication in asking for a king "over me" is an acknowledgment that society is in such a state that it has need of a ruler plenipotentiary, who will impose order to prevent its disintegration into anarchy and social chaos. The request for a king is thus deemed justified and appropriate; and, therefore, God instructs: "Thou shalt in any wise set him king *over thee*" (Deut. 17:5). However, in the days of Samuel, the situation appears to have been quite different. Here, the request for a king comes as a reaction to government by judges in accordance with the laws of the Torah. The request to "give *us* a king" was a demand to set up a government under popular control and responsive to the elders who would, in effect, rule through the king—who would be under their control. In this case, the king would not be *over them*. This—in Samuel's view—was improper, and not in accord with the biblical prescription. Therefore, he was opposed to such a demand.[20]

Ephraim Solomon of Luntshits goes on to argue that Samuel then warns the people: "This will be the manner of the king that shall reign *over* you" (1 Sam. 8:11). Regardless of their plans, they will not be able to control the king that they appoint. Once enthroned, he will usurp their power, and will turn out to be a tyrannical despot—instead of the benign and compliant figurehead that they desired.[21] Indeed, this was bound to happen as a punishment for demanding a king not in accordance with the stipulations of Deuteronomy. It is then— only after they realize the import of Samuel's warning—that they modify their demand (in order to placate Samuel), and state: "Nay, but we will have a king *over* us" (1 Sam. 8:19).[22] Ephraim Solomon of Luntshits thus presents a cogent argument explaining Samuel's position on the issue of monarchy. It clearly implies that the king does not have the legitimate authority to do those things enumerated by Samuel—while, at the same time, challenging the legitimacy of even a conditional or constitutional monarchy delimited by any constraints other than the laws of the Torah.

Since the text of Deuteronomy does not specify what the executive functions of the king entail, rabbinic theorists turned to the Book of Samuel for guidance in this regard. Particular reference is made to the text that describes the people's demand for a king—"That we may also be like all the nations; that our king may judge us, and go out before us, and fight our battles" (1 Sam. 8:20). On the basis of this text, Maimonides declares that "a king is not enthroned in the first instance except to do justice and battles."[23] The character of the justice to be applied by the king, the complex nature of his juridical status, and his relationship to the judiciary—as understood in rabbinic thought—will be explored in the following chapter.

NOTES

1. *Sanhedrin* 20b.
2. Margaliot, *Margaliot haYam* I:48, # 18.
3. As understood by RASHI, Rabbi Judah's view is "that the section in the Book of Samuel was not stated except to inspire them with awe, that the awe of the king they would have should be upon them, but not that the king was permitted to do those things" (Solomon ben Isaac, *Perush RASHI* [T], ad loc. note 1 above).
4. Maimonides, *Hilkhot Melakhim* 4:1. Expanding on the matter of the king's entitlements, Meiri notes that "it is forbidden to rob from him anything that he carries off or lays aside, for according to law he is entitled to all these things. And he may establish duties and it is forbidden for anyone to avoid or flee from them" (Meiri, *Bet haBehirah al Massekhet Sanhedrin*, p. 70, on *Sanhedrin* 20b).
5. Karo, *Kesef Mishneh* on Maimonides, *Hilkhot Melakhim* 4:1. See also Ibn Zimra, *Perush haRADBAZ*, ad loc.
6. See Malakhi ben Jacob haKohen, *Yad Malakhi*, # 231.
7. Commenting on the text of Num. 27:17, which establishes the need for a national leader, Sofer writes: "This passage should be interpreted as saying that upon occasion members of a state accept a king over them at whose word they will 'go out and come in'; however, they place before him a set of conventional laws that were legislated by their wise men and chiefs, and they follow according to these laws. Hence the king cannot do as he wills or desires except through the [agreement of] the great men of the nation. But Moses did not wish the leader of Israel to be such, but rather that he should be able to do as he sees fit. For if the leader has to go according to their ways, they lead him and take him out and lead him in. Therefore, Moses said: 'Who may go out before them,' but not at their command. Instead, he should lead them out and bring them in— he himself should be the leader and not merely act in accordance with the consensus of the generation" (Sofer, *Sefer Ktav Sofer al haTorah*, p. 227b).
8. Maimonides, *Hilkhot Melakhim* 4:10.
9. *Jer. T. Rosh haShannah* 1:3.
10. Gersonides, *Perush haRALBAG* on 1 Sam. 8:11.
11. Abravanel notes that Maimonides "ruled that the law conforms to the view of R. Jose. However, the simple sense of the texts does not indicate support for that position, but demonstrates rather that, in truth, the proper interpretation of the law is in accordance with the words of R. Judah who stated that it was merely meant to inspire them with awe, because the Torah does not mention anything in this regard in the portion relating to the king [in Deuteronomy] which would have been the proper place for it, but does state instead, 'that his heart be not lifted up above his brethren, and that he turn not aside from the commandment, to the right hand, or to the left [Deut. 17:10].' And it is this latter statement which indicates that according to the law and the Torah the king was not permitted to do those things that are enumerated in the chapter relating to the king here [in the Book of Samuel]" (Abravanel, *Perush al Neviyyim Rishonim*, p. 209).

12. Abravanel writes: "Then Samuel told the people of the 'manner of the kingdom,' and that is . . . the power that the king possesses over his people and the fitting punishment for anyone who would raise his voice in opposition, and those things that he is obligated to observe as commanded in the Torah. And this [the manner of the kingdom] is not the same as in the earlier chapter [regarding the 'manner of the king'] that the Lord stated in order to awe and frighten them" (ibid., p. 223).

13. Altschuler, *Metzudat David* on 1 Sam. 8:11.

14. Ibid. on 1 Sam. 10:25.

15. Malbim notes further that "the ruler who is subordinate to the laws of the Torah will not endeavor to by-pass the Law and take that which does not legally belong to him, for he too must observe the Torah and the law" (Malbim, *Mikra'ei Kodesh* on 1 Sam. 8:9).

16. Manasseh ben Israel, in *The Conciliator*, pp. 285–289, examines nine different explanations of Samuel's displeasure—including his own views on the matter.

17. *Sanhedrin* 20b.

18. Pinto writes: "In my view, it appears that when the elders asked, 'Make us a king to judge us,' and later said, 'like all the nations,' the meaning of 'to judge us' concerns true judgement in accordance with the requirements of the Torah; but the vulgar said: 'That we also may be like all the nations,' that is, they wanted to be like all the nations in their worship and then to be judged according to their conventions" (Pinto, *Meor Einayim* on *Sanhedrin* 20b).

19. Altschuler argues that Samuel is upset "because [the dispensation of] justice was the assigned responsibility of the judiciary, to adjudicate in accordance with the Torah, and not of the king to render judgement in accordance with his own understanding" (Altschuler, *Metzudat David* on 1 Sam. 8:6).

20. Ephraim Solomon of Luntshits writes: "It is my opinion that it was the divine will that for the sake of justice they should have a king rule over them, in order to spread his awe over them all, as our sages said: 'Pray for the welfare of the government, for if not for fear of the government, a man would swallow up his neighbor alive' [*Avot* 3:2]. The king was not needed for judicial purposes, because there were permanent courts in every city, but only for the needs of political society and its improvement . . . because after they inherit and settle the land . . . and each man will do as is right in his own eyes, because there is no king over them, then certainly those that remain will conclude that it is time to request a king 'and shalt say: I will set a king over me, like all the nations that are round about me' [Deut. 17:14], so that his awe may be over me, for that is the meaning of the phrase 'over me,' that he should be above me and rule and dominate me with a strong hand as among all the nations that are around me, where among the most advanced of them they do not despise the king's authority but instead accept it. . . . Therefore it is said: 'Thou shalt in any wise set him king over thee' [Deut. 17:15], because this request is a proper one, that there should be over you a king. . . . However, in the days of Samuel they did not speak properly because they said: 'Give us a king.' They did not say 'over us a king,' only 'to us,' since they did not wish to accept his authority, that his awe should be over them, but that he should be 'to us,' that is, placed in our hands to enthrone or dethrone at our pleasure. And the result of this for us will be that he will of necessity show favoritism to us. Therefore they said, 'to judge us like all the nations' [1 Sam. 8:5], for the major concern with favoritism is in connection with judicial matters as is the custom in those lands where they accept a rabbi for a specific period so that his awe should not be over them. On the contrary, their awe is

over him and therefore he must cater to them so that they do not cast him aside" (Ephraim Solomon of Luntshits, *Kli Yakkar* on Deut. 17:15). See also Alsheikh, *Torat Moshe*, "Devarim," p. 118. Alsheikh makes a similar argument with regard to the requirement of Deut. 16:18 to appoint judges.

21. Isaac Abravanel writes: "The philosopher [Aristotle], in the *Politics*, mentioned that there are two types of leaders, one who fears sin and one who is a violent transgressor. By definition, he who fears sin is a leader by consent of the led and on the basis of law, and the violent transgressor is one who imposes his rule over them by force and in accordance with his will; and how can the reason suffer it that people, both wise and understanding, should request an officer, ruler or king that should lead them in a poor manner and run away from the bounds of righteousness? And if on many occasions it is found that there are sinful kings that are called tyrants, note that they have become so after they had control of their kingdoms, and not that they were enthroned on that basis" (Abravanel, *Perush al Neviyyim Rishonim*, p. 205).

22. Malbim writes: "This means to say, not in accordance with your words that he will be a tyrant, not subject to the law of the Torah and its rules, for such a one is not called a king at all, but rather by the name of tyrant (for by definition [paraphrasing Abravanel] the king is chosen by the people and the tyrant is one who tyrannizes over them by force); and the ruler that we desire will not be a tyrant but a king. We will not be subjected to him as slaves. On the contrary, he will be devoted to us in that he will lead us in accordance with law and justice" (Malbim, *Mikra'ei Kodesh* on 1 Sam. 8:19).

23. Maimonides, *Hilkhot Melakhim* 4:10. Malbim describes the primary functions of the king as follows: "He will be obligated to arrange our affairs in two respects: a) 'That our king may judge,' meaning in accordance with the law of the Torah . . . b) 'and go out before us, and fight our battles,' that he should battle against our adversaries, and the text was careful to specify 'our battles,' so that he should not be like a tyrant that relates the battles to himself, and who will fight wars for the sake of dominion and glory, and who will call the lands he may conquer by his name; rather, he should wage our battles for our needs, and that which he conquers should be ours. For this reason the constraint is placed on the king that is established in accordance with law and justice, that his every intent should be for the prosperity of the nation and to improve their affairs both within the state as well as against the troublesome enemy" (Malbim, *Mikra'ei Kodesh* on 1 Sam. 8:20). Malbim's explanation of the first function—that of "judging in accordance with the law of the Torah"—is problematic in that it appears to violate the basic separation of powers (as written into the biblical constitution), by assignment to the king of powers specifically granted to the priests and judges.

11
The King and the Law

In rabbinic political theory, the juridical status of the king is addressed in two distinct but related contexts: one dealing with the monarchy as a legitimate political institution; and the other, with the king's personal status relative to the institutions and processes of law within the polity.

As discussed earlier, the monarchy is conceived as performing two fundamental functions: leadership, and the dispensation of justice. This latter function is somewhat problematic, since it appears to overlap considerably with the basic mission of the judicial institution—and to negate, thereby, the basic concept of a constitutional separation of powers. However, on closer examination of the rabbinic writings, it becomes clear that the essential integrity of both the monarchy and the judiciary as separate constitutionally established institutions in rabbinic political theory is defended and maintained unimpaired.

The king's justice is conceived in terms of the extraordinary legislative and judicial authority needed for the monarch to safeguard the Judaic character of the polity. Starting from the fundamental premise that the Torah is the embodiment of divine law—and provides, through its principles and precepts, for the establishment of societal relations on the basis of true justice—the king's justice is considered as a necessary counterpart of that law. Not seen as an inherently viable alternative to divine law as the basis for the polity, the king's justice is intended—rather—to ensure the preservation of the integral character of the Judaic polity, in the face of circumstances that might otherwise lead to a breakdown of the social tranquility necessary for the absolute justice of the Torah to be applied in practice. The king's justice is thus conceived as serving to prepare the ground for the effective implementation of the justice of the Torah.

An example of the supportive function performed by application of the king's justice concerns the matter of capital crimes. It is an established principle of Judaic jurisprudence that, in cases where a judgment of guilt invokes a biblical penalty of capital punishment, the Torah requires exceptionally stringent safeguards to protect the indicted from death through procedural error.[1] Accordingly, capital punishment may be exacted only where the evidence presented meets the exacting criteria of the Torah and where the indicted had been clearly forewarned not to commit the act in question, in full recognition of the penalty by which it would be punishable.[2] Under the rules of Torah law as understood in rabbinic jurisprudence, conviction of a capital offense became virtually impossible, as a practical matter. However, in a less than perfect world, the exclusive application of such principles of absolute justice may have disastrous consequences for the society. As Nissim Girondi points out (reflecting a traditionally conservative position on the matter), failure to punish the perpetrator might result in a significant increase of capital crimes, to the detriment of the polity as a whole. Therefore, "the king may judge without forewarning in accordance with his view of what is required for the [well-being of] society."[3]

The king's justice is not restricted to matters of capital punishment. It is considered applicable to any threat to the stability and well-being of the polity, if it cannot be dealt with decisively and effectively within the normal processes of the legal system based on the principles and precepts of the Torah. Since a failure to act against such threats could have dire consequences for the broader interests of the polity, the king is permitted to take such steps as he deems necessary to meet the challenges of the hour. To be sure, such extralegal authority is intended to be employed only in an instance where the essential interests of the polity are in jeopardy. It is not to be considered the personal prerogative of the king to be exercised at his discretion for private reasons or benefit.[4] This places a very high premium on the person who can sit on the throne without becoming ensnared in the temptations of power that go with the crown. Some commentators see this reflected in the biblical teaching, "The king by justice establisheth the land; But he that exacteth gifts overthroweth it" (Prov. 29:4).

Meiri—for example—considers this biblical passage as an admonition to kings, "to lead the nation in equity, and to dispense righteous judgement to the people."[5] Similarly, Gersonides takes it as meaning that "the king will establish the land through justice, for this will be the cause of the completing of the perfection of the state, so that there should be no oppression between groups. But, if the ruler should subvert justice for the gifts that will be set aside for him ... he will overturn the land and devastate it because everyone will turn to exploitation and will be certain of being absolved because of the bribes that he will give the ruler. Such a person will not be called a king, because one such as he is not fit to be a king."[6]

Thus, the king's justice is essentially conceived to be an ad hoc extralegal authority, invoked because of the need to be capable of responding to the challenges of the moment that confront the polity. Without such a capability—

available to be called into play as the need emerges—it is considered questionable whether the polity could persist solely on the basis of the absolute justice of the divine jurisprudence promulgated by the Torah. Stated differently: in order to be operational in the polity, the true justice of the Torah demands a society characterized by a high degree of observance of the Torah's ethical standards. To bring such a truly ethical polity into being, the ideal jurisprudence of Torah must be supplemented by the king's justice. As a practical matter, the emergence of such a polity would in itself eliminate the basis—and therefore the legitimacy—of the continuing use of the extraordinary extralegal powers of the king.

It is this extraordinary juridical role of the king that constitutes the fundamental distinction between the king and the national leader or judge, in terms of political function. While both equally fulfill the functions of political and military leader, only the king—by invoking his extraordinary authority—can (much like the prophet) temporarily abrogate the laws of the Torah, and emend them in accordance with the needs of the hour. On the other hand—as will be discussed shortly—the king in his public role as monarch is considered to be constrained in his participation in the regular judicial process that operates under the normative rules of the Torah.[7]

However, it is one thing to assert that the king has extraordinary ad hoc authority and power ascribed to him. It is quite another matter to establish their legitimacy in accordance with the Torah. The problem is as follows: Starting from the premise that the Torah embodies the divine law, if the king's authority to go outside the bounds of that law is itself prescribed by the law, then—in effect—the king is above the law. But if this is so, then the king's law—which is conventional law—is higher than divine law. This is clearly a contradiction in terms, and is in opposition to the very foundations of rabbinic political theory. This problem does not appear to be discussed to any extent in the literature—leaving us to speculate on how the paradox posed by the extralegal authority of the king is rationalized in rabbinic thinking.

Nonetheless, it appears to be a universally held view among the classical rabbinic theorists that all political authority—including the extralegal authority of the monarch—is ultimately derived from divine dispensation. As owner and master of the universe, the Lord cannot but be the ultimate source for any authority exercised in His domains. A primary source for this concept is the biblical text that reads: "Thine, O Lord, is the greatness, and the power, and the glory, and the victory, and the majesty: for all that is in the heaven and in the earth is thine; thine is the kingdom, O Lord, and Thou art exalted as head above all" (1 Chron. 29:11). The Talmud goes so far as to state that "even the well-keeper [*resh garguta*] is established by Heaven."[8] That is, the authority of even the most pedestrian position of public responsibility within the polity derives ultimately from God, as master of the universe. This thesis is repeated throughout rabbinic literature.[9]

In a somewhat awkward formulation, RASHI essentially argues that political sovereignty in the world of man is indivisible—in the sense that, if one is sovereign, he cannot at the same time be subordinate to another. However, in respect to Heaven, there is no true sovereignty on earth. All derive their sovereign authority from Heaven and are consequently subordinate to the divine law, which is paramount.[10] Thus, where the king has the authority to deviate from the divine law as embodied in the Torah, that authority is severely circumscribed and is not to be considered as abrogating the Torah in favor of conventional law. The king's justice must serve to further and uphold the divine law, and not supplant it—except under the most limited of conditions, and then only temporarily. In the final analysis, the king must also answer to a higher authority for any of his actions that go beyond the pale of the law.

This concept of the nexus between divine and earthly authority is further reflected in rabbinic discussions of the manner in which the kingdom is established. Abraham ibn Ezra notes that the appointment of the king is contingent on his being chosen by a prophet, and not through popular selection.[11] Clearly—in his view and that of other commentators—the establishment of the kingdom requires divine intervention, even if only through the medium of prophecy.[12] The emphasis given by this school of thought to the nominating role of the prophet in the process of appointing the king would substantially enhance the public stature of the prophet as a significant actor within the political system. On the other hand, Nahmanides tends to discount those views that hinge the choice of the king on prophetic selection. He places emphasis on the role played by the high court in the political process.[13]

Another somewhat different approach to the question of who selects the king is found in the Talmud, where it is argued: " 'Thou shalt in any wise set him king over thee'; it is not written, 'I will set.' but rather that 'thou shalt,' to indicate that it is dependent upon you."[14] This citation is generally construed as an argument against the mandatory establishment of a kingdom.[15] The implication of this passage also seems to be that, since the actual appointment of the king is to be by those who requested one—that is, the elders of the people, rather than the prophet—what is sought from the prophet (in this interpretation, Samuel received the request of the people as a prophet, and not as a judge) is sanction for appointing a king, and not the nomination of one. Presumably, once approved in principle, the people's choice will be acceptable to God.[16]

This interpretation appears to lend some support to the singular position maintained by Zvi Hirsch Chajes in regard to the character of the king's justice. Essentially, Chajes' argument is that there is no conclusive evidence in the literature on which to base the avowed legitimacy of any deviation by the king from the law of the Torah. However, since it is evident that the king—to properly perform his assigned functions—must have such legitimate authority in order to meet the demands of the hour, Chajes concludes that the legitimate basis for the king's justice rests entirely with the consent of the governed.[17] While there are traces of social contract theory to be found in the nooks and crannies of rabbinic literature, there is probably not to be found anything else quite so explicit in this regard as the position argued by Chajes.

In any case—irrespective of how the legitimacy of the king's justice is established—it is evident that the king is severely constrained by the laws of the Torah, under those conditions where the exercise of his extraordinary legislative and executive powers is not applicable. The king's powers may therefore be likened to emergency powers—the abuse of which cannot readily be curtailed, since it is the king who determines when those powers should be called into effect. This situation only further emphasizes the great concern that the king be a righteous and inherently just person—because he does truly have access to almost limitless political powers, should he choose to violate the precepts of the Torah. The only sanction that can effectively be brought against him by the people is rebellion—which, while legitimate in the face of royal abuse of the Torah, is nonetheless extremely difficult to carry out successfully, in practice. To limit the king's capacity for the arbitrary exercise of his power, a series of constitutional safeguards were conceived. The violation of these safeguards would serve as warning signals to the public about the propensity of their king to violate the norms of the Torah.

Surely, the primary safeguard rests in the monarch's scrupulous observance of the biblical injunction, "that he turn not aside from the commandment, to the right hand, or to the left" (Deut. 17:20).[18] The rabbinic perspective on this injunction against the king is perhaps best articulated by Zvi Hirsch Chajes, who argues: "It is certain from the standpoint of the law that the king too is forbidden to put himself at a distance from the Mosaic Law even by so much as a hairbreadth . . . and there is no difference between the king and the people except with regard to financial matters as well as those matters that touch upon the life of the nation. These are acquiesced in because of the general welfare realized through the improvement of the state. However, in the absence of this circumstance, the law of the Torah reassumes its position of primacy."[19]

In the preceding discussion, we have concerned ourselves with the nature of the king's justice and its relationship to the law of the Torah. Throughout the discussion, the king has been considered from the standpoint of his public role as monarch. To complete our examination of kingship in rabbinic political theory and our review of the constitutional safeguards provided by the Torah, it is necessary to turn to a consideration of the king from the standpoint of his private capacity—both with respect to the law, as well as to the other constituent elements of the government.

There is a consensus that the king's functions in his public role do not include the dispensation of justice in accordance with the principles of absolute justice reflected in the Torah—which is the special province of the judiciary. A question of some interest in the literature is whether the king—acting in his private capacity as a member of the polity—may serve as a member of the judiciary. As will be seen, this question raises numerous complexities that preclude a simple affirmative or negative answer. The matter is treated as a procedural issue, and the Talmud renders the definitive judgment that "The king may neither judge nor be judged, testify nor be testified against."[20] However, this apparently straightforward dictum is interpreted quite differently in the Babylonian and Jerusalem Talmuds.

In the Babylonian Talmud, a sharp distinction—in respect of this injunction—is made between the kings of the House of David and all others. "R. Joseph said: This refers only to the Kings of Israel, but the kings of the House of David may judge and be judged, as it is written: 'O, House of David, thus saith the Lord, execute justice in the morning' [Jer. 21:12]; and if they may not be judged, how could they judge?"[21] The Talmud goes on to explain that the reason for this injunction against non-Davidic kings—such as the Hasmoneans—is the consequence of an incident in which King Jannai (103–76 b.c.e.) was called to testify before the high court in a criminal proceeding. The king appeared, but then used his position to intimidate the court and subvert the judicial process. Consequently, an injunction that excluded kings from the judicial process in any capacity was enacted. The inherent assumption here is that the Davidic kings—presumably because of the weight of dynastic tradition—would not make such improper use of their powers and would adhere to the procedures of the court, like any other citizen.

One curious facet of the literature is that the story about King Jannai—related in the Babylonian Talmud—is entirely omitted from the Jerusalem Talmud, which is generally considered to more authoritatively reflect the Palestinian rabbinic tradition. Moreover, the Jerusalem Talmud adopts a significantly different interpretation of the talmudic injunction against royal participation in the judicial process. In a terse treatment of the question, it states: "[The king] may not judge. However, it is written: 'And David executed judgement and justice unto all his people' [2 Sam. 8:15], yet the text says [that the king may not judge]. The text should be [understood] to say, from this time on."[22] The phrase "from this time on" is generally taken to mean from the time of David on.[23] This would then mean that the injunction against participation by the king in the judicial process applies to all kings (Davidic and non-Davidic alike), with the single exception of David himself—which is a clear rejection of the distinction drawn in the Babylonian Talmud. In commenting on the injunction that the king may not be judged, the Jerusalem Talmud merely cites the biblical text attributed to David: "Let my sentence come forth from Thy presence."[24] This is interpreted as implying that *only* the Lord could judge the king.[25]

From a critical standpoint, there are substantial difficulties to be overcome with respect to both talmudic approaches, and there is a considerable body of commentary devoted to the matter. However, it is neither possible nor necessary to deal with these issues within the scope of this study. For the purpose at hand, it should be sufficient merely to give some indication of the rationales that the literature applies to the dictum.

In his commentary on the talmudic passage under discussion, Maimonides explains why a distinction is drawn between the kings of Israel in general and those stemming from the House of David. In his view, it is "because they [the non-Davidic kings of Israel] were transgressors [of the Torah] in their rule; they did not value humility and they did not subordinate themselves to the commandments of the Torah. However, the kings of the House of David judge and may be judged, because they have knowledge of the Torah and humility, and their subordination to the commandments of the Torah did not appear inappropriate in their eyes since their kingdom was based on the Torah."[26]

Maimonides' explanation of the issue may be seen as supporting the position taken in the Babylonian Talmud, which—as a general rule—is considered as taking precedence over the Jerusalem Talmud in the event of a difference of opinion between the two in matters of law.[27] However, the nature of the argument offered in explanation of the same dictum by a contemporary of Maimonides—Jonathan ben David of Lunel—may be viewed as lending greater support to the position taken by the Jerusalem Talmud. Without referring to any distinctions between the kings of Israel and those of the House of David—which is comparable to the approach taken in the Jerusalem Talmud—he argues that the king may not be judged because "it would be degrading for him to appear before a court lower in stature than himself . . . and since he may not be judged, he is not qualified to judge others."[28]

In the two interpretations just cited, the fundamental difference in approach transcends the question of the royal house to which the talmudic rule applies. On the one hand, Maimonides argues that the basic criterion is whether or not the king considers himself above or subordinate to the laws of the Torah. The presumption of the school of thought that supports the position of the Babylonian Talmud is that—for historical reasons—the House of David is far more likely to willingly subordinate itself to the dictates of the higher law. Thus, the basic criterion to be applied is acknowledged subordination to the Torah.[29]

On the other hand, Jonathan of Lunel seems to be arguing that the fundamental consideration involved is the preservation of the status of the monarch as a vital element in maintaining order in the state. From this standpoint, it may be suggested in support of the position of the Jerusalem Talmud—which dates the applicability of the talmudic dictum from the time of David onward—that perhaps only a king as popular as David is reputed to have been could afford to subject himself to the give-and-take of the judicial process, without seriously eroding his public image and credibility. In any case, Jonathan of Lunel's argument could be similarly derived from a kindred passage in the Babylonian Talmud, which states: "If a king foregoes his honor, it is not accepted; for it is written: 'Thou shalt in any wise set him king over thee,' intimating that his authority should remain over you."[30]

A related constraint placed on the king with respect to his active participation in the judicial process concerns his serving as a member of the court. (This constraint has no relevance for the position presented in the Jerusalem Talmud. However, as noted earlier, it is the Babylonian Talmud that constitutes the primary authoritative source for the rabbinic legal tradition.) In this regard, the Talmud states: "The king may not be given a seat on the Sanhedrin."[31] Here, no distinction is made with regard to which ruling house is in power. Thus, in his legal code, Maimonides declares: "A king of Israel is not given a seat on the Sanhedrin because it is forbidden to disagree with him and to contradict his words.... Kings of the House of Judah, even though they are not to be seated on the Sanhedrin, may sit and judge the people."[32] Nissim Girondi deduces an even more stringent constraint on the king—which is calculated to reduce to a minimum any influence that the king might exercise over the courts. In his view, not only may the king not be a member of the court, he may not even be an observer in a capital proceeding.[33]

In addition to the constraints placed on the king to limit his direct interference with the judicial process, the king is also subjected by the Torah to a set of personal disabilities that are designed to impede any tendency on his part to confuse his public responsibilities with his private ambitions and interests. These additional constraints are explicitly enumerated in the constitutional code of Deuteronomy, as follows: "Only he shall not multiply horses to himself.... Neither shall he multiply wives to himself, that his heart turn not away; neither shall he greatly multiply to himself silver and gold" (Deut. 17:16–17). In respect to the first of these three negative injunctions, the Talmud states: "Our Rabbis taught: He shall not multiply horses to *himself*: I might think not even such as are required for his horsemen and chariots. Scripture therefore states: 'to himself': for himself he may not multiply, but he may multiply as many as are required for his chariots and horsemen."[34] The implication here is that, while it is acceptable that the king build a mobile army as large as he deems necessary to serve the national needs, he may not use his authority to build such forces that only serve to enhance his personal vanity. Indeed, the king is required to portray a modesty in this regard that is not required of wealthy private citizens.[35]

In principle, the injunction relates not only to horses. The dictum is phrased in terms of horses because, in the context of biblical times, horses represented both wealth and military power. In contemporary times, the same injunction would apply to vehicles and aircraft.[36] In the rabbinic view, then, the king is constrained to remain constantly aware of the purpose for which he is enthroned; and that purpose is decidedly not self-aggrandizement, but rather to attend to the needs of the nation—to the exclusion of personal desires and ambitions. Toward this end, the injunctions applied to the king far exceed those that apply to the people at large—who are not enjoined to possess but one horse, nor are they cautioned about reckoning any such possessions among their wealth.

The personal disabilities of the king are perhaps best exemplified by the injunction, "Neither shall he multiply wives to himself, that his heart turn not away." Once again, this restriction is not placed by the Torah on the people at large, but only on the king. It is he above all others who must be wary of submitting to a life of licentiousness and profligacy. His personal morality must be exemplary. As Samson Raphael Hirsch notes, the passage does not say that the king should not have many wives because "they will turn his heart away"— but rather that "his heart turn not away." The intent of the passage is that "even without any direct corrupting influence, his heart will become estranged from the spiritually high seriousness of the life of duty of a king."[37] This view finds expression—albeit somewhat cryptically—in the oft-repeated fable concerning King Solomon's penchant for collecting spouses. The Talmud relates: "R. Isaac said: When Solomon married Pharaoh's daughter, Gabriel descended and stuck a reed in the sea, which gathered a sandbank around it, on which was built the great city of Rome."[38] By his act—which contributed to his violation of the biblical injunction against having many wives—Solomon is considered to have precipitated a series of events that ultimately led to the destruction of the Second Hebrew Commonwealth by the Romans.[39] Maimonides goes even further than the literal understanding of the biblical injunction by arguing that, even if the king had but one wife, he must refrain from frequenting the company of women—which will lead to moral corruption. "Since his heart is the heart of the entire community of Israel, the dictum of the Torah applies more strongly to him than to the rest of the nation."[40]

With regard to the third of the biblical injunctions directed at the king—concerning the accumulation of wealth—the Talmud states: "Our Rabbis taught: And silver and gold he shall not greatly multiply 'to himself'; I might think [this applied] even for *aspanya* [supply and pay for the army]. Therefore Scripture writes: 'to himself'; only for himself he may not multiply silver and gold, but he may do so for *aspanya*."[41] Some see this restriction as a disincentive for the king to levy extortionary taxes on the public or to engage in remunerative but illegitimate financial practices.[42] In the Jerusalem Talmud, it is suggested that even the accumulation of funds for the army should be restricted to an annual appropriation,[43] without reserves being set aside for the following year.[44] The king would thus be limited to obtaining only sufficient revenue to meet the needs of his administration on a single-year budget basis. This procedure would surely tend to constrain the monarch's ability to divert any significant portion of the revenue for his personal use, without undermining the security of the state.[45] However, it would also leave the state in an awkward financial position, if it were to face a long-term crisis that required the ready availability of resources in order to successfully cope with it. Accordingly, Maimonides attempts to modify the definition of the scope of the injunction, to provide for accumulating the necessary financial reserves.[46]

These views on the relative status of the king in his private capacity are clear evidence that the rabbinic writers were only too well aware of how easily a monarchy can be perverted and corrupted into a tyranny. The three primary injunctions placed on the king in Deuteronomy—injunctions that, if obeyed, would tend to make the crown a far less enticing prospect for the politically ambitious—are clearly designed to establish a kind of autolimitation on the king, once he assumes power.[47]

Despite the potential hazard of the monarchy transforming into a tyranny, the good king who obeys the laws of the Torah and properly administers the king's justice offers—in the general rabbinic view—the ideal form of national executive leadership, in conformity with the constitutional provisions of Deuteronomy. The monarch is widely considered as essential to the practical success of the biblical constitutional scheme.[48]

Throughout the preceding discussion, great emphasis has been placed on the relationship of the king—as the national leader—to the judge, as well as to the king's place within the polity's overall system of justice. This has been necessary because—as will become evident in the next chapter of this study—the judiciary (understood in the rather special rabbinic sense) provides the thread of tradition that ties the nation together in the absence of a king, and continues in this role (in appropriately modified form) to this day.

Before leaving the subject of the monarchy, it is important to take note of the rather interesting relationship between the king and the priesthood. In Chapter 7, the close relationship between the priests and the national executive was indicated. When that executive is a king, the relationship takes on some additional unique aspects. In this connection, it should be noted as a point of reference that the section of the biblical constitution dealing with the priests and the Levites follows immediately after the section dealing with the king. This contiguity has not gone without comment in the literature. The Midrash explains: "This section is adjacent to the chapter relating to kings in order to teach that if there is no king there is no priest; and if there is no priest there is no king."[49]

From the historical standpoint, the interplay of king and high priest—especially throughout the period of the Second Commonwealth—seems to lend support to the idea expressed in the Midrash: namely, that both king and priest are required to complement one another, and that one cannot survive without the other. The argument implicit here is that neither institution can individually fulfill the political mission assigned to it independently of the other.[50] This dual leadership of the priest and king is considered necessary for the proper ordering of society. These institutions converge on the common goal of giving effect to the precepts of the Torah.[51] Malbim argues that there is a necessary complementarity between the two institutions: The king is responsible for maintaining social peace—in terms of the relations between man and man—through his system of applied justice; while the priest is responsible for seeing to the proper adjustment and orientation of man's relationships to Heaven, and the inculcation of the precepts of the Torah among the public. Both are deemed essential.[52] Malbim seems to be restating the fundamental thesis that predicates the stable well-ordered polity on the faithful observance of the precepts of the Torah—particularly by those entrusted with public responsibilities. Failure to do so—on their part—will undermine the entire foundation of the society.

In this chapter on kings and in the earlier one on the priesthood, the relationships between these institutions and to the judiciary have been considered from a standpoint that assumes the monarchy and priesthood to be existing and viable institutions. However, there is one other aspect of these relationships that is of concern here, and that relates to the method or means by which one becomes a king or a high priest. Of particular interest in this regard is the talmudic dictum: "Neither a king nor a high priest may be placed in the position except by a court of seventy-one."[53] As will be discussed in the following chapters, rabbinic political theory conceives of the monarchy, the high priesthood, and the judiciary as interlocked in a "checks and balances" arrangement designed to reduce the capacity—particularly of the king—to treat the state as a private domain for exploitation.

NOTES

1. Some writers have taken the position that—for all practical purposes—it is impossible to meet the biblical criteria for capital punishment, and that this reflects the intent of the Torah to eliminate capital punishment de facto—if not de jure. See Hen, BeMalkhut haYahadut I:263.

2. In support of this principle, Nissim Girondi writes: "There is no doubt that this is proper according to the true Law, for why should a man be put to death without having the full knowledge that he had involved himself in an action subject to the infliction of the death penalty.... And this is the true justice, intrinsically absolute, that has been given into the charge of the judges" (Nissim Girondi, Shnaim Assar Derushim, # 11, p. 74).

3. Ibid. Maimonides expounds this view in a terse dictum: "Every manslayer, against whom there is no clear evidence, or who was not given a forewarning... the king has the authority to put him to death and thereby improve the world in accordance with what the hour demands" (Maimonides, Hilkhot Melakhim 3:10). Similarly, in another place, Maimonides declares: "All these slayers, and those analogous to them, that do not merit capital punishment at the hands of the court, if the king desires to put them to death in accordance with the law of the kingdom and the improvement of society, the authority is his" (Maimonides Hilkhot Rotzeah 2:4). Meir Simha haKohen of Dvinsk qualifies Maimonides' statement to restrict the actions of the king exclusively to matters that affect state interests, but not matters between man and Heaven—which remain the jurisdiction of the courts. See Meir Simhah haKohen, Or Sameah on Maimonides, Hilkhot Melakhim 3.10.

4. David ibn Zimra suggests that "the king should direct his attention to the strengthening of the Torah and the correction of the crooked and not [to take such measures] for the sake of his honor" (Ibn Zimra, Perush haRADBAZ on Maimonides, Hilkhot Melakhim 3:10).

5. Meiri, Perush haMeiri al Sefer Mishlei, p. 271b.

6. Gersonides, Perush haRALBAG on Prov. 29:4.

7. This functional distinction between the king and the judge is discussed by Nissim Girondi, as follows: "It will be found that the appointment of judges was in order to dispense the justice of the Torah alone.... The appointment of the king was to complete the perfection of the political order, and all that was required for the demands of the hour.... In the period when there would be in Israel a Sanhedrin and a king, the Sanhedrin was to judge the people with righteous judgement alone, and not to correct their affairs in excess of this, unless they were so empowered by the king. However, when there will be no king in Israel, then the judge will encompass both powers, that of the judge and the power of the king" (Nissim Girondi, Shnaim Assar Derushim, # 11,

p. 75). It is interesting to note that Nissim would allow the king to delegate some of his extralegal powers to the judiciary.

While denying the fundamental necessity for a monarchy in the first place, Isaac Abravanel adopts an almost identical position as Nissim with regard to the distinctions between the judge and the king—which, in his view, rest in that "the powers of the king and his appointees do not extend to matters of law and to the adjudication between man and his neighbor in accordance with the Torah; he stands solely for the improvement of the political society, to save the people from their enemies and to decide the law in matters temporarily and in accordance with the needs of the time, and not in the manner of dispensing righteous judgement. And, the judges have this difference, that they are appointed for the specific purpose of adjudicating between man and his fellow in accordance with the Torah.... Therefore their leadership function was first and foremost to judge in accordance with the true principles of law, and for this reason they are designated as judges. And if we find that the judges that are mentioned in this book [the Book of Judges] used to lead the people out to war, and were in receipt of the ultimate authority to decide the law in accordance with the needs of the hour and not in accordance with the Torah, it was not attributed to them because of the fact that they were judges, but rather because there was not yet a king in Israel, and they therefore possessed the powers of the judge as well as those of the king" (Abravanel, *Perush al Neviyyim Rishonim*, p. 94).

8. *Baba Batra* 91b. The implication of this passage for the understanding of the biblical text is explained by Samuel ben Meir (RASHBAM) as follows: " 'Resh Garguta'— an officer appointed over the wells to decide who would draw water today to irrigate his fields, and who would do so tomorrow. It is a minor position of authority. However, from the text, 'Thine is the kingdom, O Lord, and Thou art exalted as head,' one is to be instructed as if to say: through You who are exalted above everything, even the appointment of a well keeper is by Your word" (Samuel ben Meir, *Perush haRASHBAM haIkkari*, ad loc.).

Samuel Eidels (MAHARSHAH) writes: "It would certainly have been more novel and a greater affirmation of greatness to state that His power is such that even great kings are established from Heaven. However, in the matter of supervision, the passage states that the guidance of the Lord extends even to the lowly, in contrast to the arguments of the wicked that the Lord is dissociated from the earth because of its lowness. We may also derive from this the moral principle that since all are appointed from Heaven, each wielder of authority, within his own sphere, must oversee the people of his domain to direct them in the right path and to admonish them for the sake of Heaven" (Eidels, *Hiddushei Aggadot*, ad loc.).

9. David Kimhi interprets the biblical passage "as if to say, with regard to the chiefs and kings, it is You who are exalted above them all, and the use of the term 'head' is to indicate 'above all who are appointed as heads' " (Kimhi, *Perush RADAK al haTorah* on 1 Chron. 29:11). Similar interpretations are suggested by Gersonides, *Perush haRALBAG*, ad loc., and David Altschuler, *Metzudat David*, ad loc.

Others derive this same idea from the text: "Thou shalt in any wise set him king over thee, whom the Lord ... shall choose" (Deut. 17:15). Nahmanides writes: "It is my view that, by means of literal interpretation, the meaning of 'shall choose' is that every king of the nations is chosen by the Lord" (Nahmanides, *Perushei haRAMBAN al haTorah*, ad loc.). Similarly, Bahya ben Asher interprets the phrase "shall choose" as intending "to teach that kingship as well as all the rest of the high positions are all derived from Heaven, and the choice rests on high" (Bahya ben Asher, *Biur al haTorah* III:355).

10. RASHI writes: "If a human king gave one of his servants dominion and rule in a different kingdom, he remains the king's servant no matter where and his kingdom is not that of a king. Where the kingdom is his, [that is, where the servant becomes a king in his own right] the ruling servant is not his [that is, is no longer a servant of the appointing monarch]. However, in so far as the Lord is concerned, the servant that is appointed to rule is His as well as his kingdom" (Solomon ben Isaac, *Perush RASHI [M]*, on 1 Chron. 29:11).

11. Ibn Ezra, *Perush haTorah leR. Abraham ibn Ezra* on Deut. 17:15.

12. See Meyuhas ben Elijah, *Perush al Sefer Devarim*, p. 90; and Gersonides, *Perush al haTorah al Derekh Biur* II:224a.

13. Nahmanides, *Perushei haRAMBAN al haTorah* on Deut. 17:14. Nahmanides argues that, when the Bible states "And shalt say: I will set a king over me" (Deut. 17:14), it emphasizes "and shalt say"—" because it is a commandment that they should come before the priests the Levites and to the judges and they shall say to them: It is our wish that you should set a king over us." He notes that, when the elders came to Samuel and requested that he give them a king, he was acting in his capacity as judge—and not as prophet.

14. Jer.T. *Sanhedrin* 2:6.

15. See Margoliot, *Pnei Moshe*, ad loc. note 14 above; and Epstein, *Torah Temimah* on Deut. 17:14.

16. An anonymous sixteenth-century commentary on this passage states: "It is not written, 'I will set'—this means that if it had been so stated it would imply that [the selection of the king] had to be by means of a prophet, at the word of the Lord. However, since it states, 'thou shalt,' it implies that whoever is chosen by Israel will also be the choice of the Lord" (*Perush* on Jer.T. *Sanhedrin* 2:6, in the Cracow edition of 1609, reprinted in *Talmud Bavli veYerushalmi*).

17. Chajes writes: "It appears to me ... that the laws of the kingdom are merely a matter of a bond between the king and the nation, and on this set of conditions the various sides consent; the people consent to surrender their wealth and property for the general welfare ... and not necessarily only their property and wealth do they renounce for the needs of the king and for the benefits that will accrue from his rule, but also at the very risk of their lives have they undertaken that anyone who raises his voice in rebellion against the king, the king has the authority to put to death. All the people agreed to this at the time they placed a king over them" (Chajes, *Torat Neviyyim*, pp. 46–47).

18. RASHI takes this injunction to apply to "even a minor commandment of a prophet" (Solomon ben Isaac, *Perushei RASHI al haTorah* on Deut. 17:20). RASHI bases his view on the events depicted in 1 Sam. 13. It is related there that Saul was directed by Samuel to await him, but that Saul failed to do so—and, as a consequence of his disobedience, he forfeited perpetual possession of the crown by his heirs.

19. Chajes, *Torat Neviyyim*, p. 48.

20. *Sanhedrin* 18a.

21. *Sanhedrin* 19a–19b.

22. Jer.T. *Sanhedrin* 2:3.

23. Moses Margoliot takes this phrase as implying that "David was unique in that he

would dispense justice to one and charity to the other, and is not comparable to the rest of the kings" (Margoliot, *Mar'eh haPanim*, ad loc. note 22 above).

24. Jer. T. *Sanhedrin* 2:3.

25. Margoliot explains the use of the biblical reference as implying that "there are no others that may judge him" (Margoliot, *Pnei Moshe*, ad loc. note 24 above).

26. Maimonides, *Perush haMishnayot* on *Sanhedrin*, ch. 2.

27. See Alfasi, *Hilkhot haRIF* on *Eruvin* 35b.

28. Jonathan of Lunel, *Perush Rabbenu Yehonatan haKohen miLunel al haMishnah vehaRIF le Massekhet Sanhedrin*, "Sanhedrin" 2:4, p. 24.

29. Joseph Karo points out that "the dictum does not rest on whether it is the House of David or the House of Israel, but is instead dependent on whether they are righteous or wicked; for until the time of Jannai they [both houses] judged and were judged, and if this were not the case, then how is it that they judged him [Jannai, in the first place, since he was not of the House of David]" (Karo, *Kesef Mishneh* on Maimonides, *Hilkhot Melakhim* 3:7).

30. *Sanhedrin* 19b.

31. *Sanhedrin* 18b.

32. Maimonides, *Hilkhot Sanhedrin* 2:4–5.

33. Nissim writes: "A king may not be given a seat on the Sanhedrin—that is to say, it is not proper that the king should sit with the Sanhedrin while they judge a capital case, even though he is not a member of the Sanhedrin; for if it referred only to being a member of the Sanhedrin, we have learned that a king may not judge nor may he be judged. Even kings of the House of David that do judge, and who may be judged, are nonetheless not seated on the Sanhedrin. From where do we derive that he should not be a member of the court? The reason for the dictum has been explained [in the Talmud] as being due to [the biblical injunction] 'Thou shalt not speak *al riv* [in a legal proceeding (Ex. 23:2)].' [Note: This translation deviates from the standard one, which is not serviceable in terms of its use in this discussion by the Talmud and the commentators.] This is to say that if the king were to express his view no one in the Sanhedrin would be able to disagree with him. . . . However, where he is not a member of the Sanhedrin, [but is present at its proceedings], upon occasion he may desire to voice his disagreement with a member of the court, [and this too comes under] the injunction of 'Thou shalt not speak *al riv*' " (Nissim Girondi, *Hiddushei haRAN al Sanhedrin*, p. 6b).

34. *Sanhedrin* 21b (emphasis added).

35. Maimonides explains the point as follows: "It is permissible for the king to multiply horses as much as he wishes in order to mount his troops and to display many mounts in his wars in order to frighten the enemy. However, what the Torah has forbidden is that he should possess idle horses in his stables that stand by in readiness for him to ride on any day that he chooses, or to have them precede him [in a procession] as all the other kings do; he is not permitted to possess [for his personal use] but a single horse for him to ride on as one of the people" (Maimonides, *Perush haMishnayot* on *Sanhedrin*, ch. 2). Maimonides also includes this injunction as one of the basic precepts of the Torah: "The king is cautioned about multiplying horses . . . and the limit is that he should have no horse run before him, and that he should not possess any horses other than the one that he himself rides, or those that he places in stables to be ready for war and for his cavalry to mount" (Maimonides, *Sefer haMitzvot*, pt. 2, p. 112).

36. Bahya ben Asher writes: " 'Only he shall not multiply horses to himself'—This means to say, even though you may have a king like the kings of other nations, he shall

display the minimum of the characteristics of the other kings, as there are kings that strive for the multiplication of horses and chariots. But a king of Israel may multiply to himself neither horses, nor wives, nor silver and gold. There are kings who make a principle of attaining these things. However, a king of Israel will be deficient in this and will instead make a principle of the Torah and the fear of Heaven" (Bahya ben Asher, *Biur al haTorah* III:356, on Deut. 17:16).

Samson Raphael Hirsch addresses the same point in more modern terms: "The 'Only' [of the biblical text] limits the capacity of [the precept, 'Thou shalt in any wise set him king over thee'] whereby the nation is commanded to grant the king considerable powers over them.... To that then comes 'Only' and imposes on the king the duty of himself limiting these powers, and primarily with regards to just those factors which, according to the experience of all ages have been the rocks on which the virtue of rulers has come to grief and the happiness of their people shattered. These are: the passion for military glory and renown, women and possessions" (Hirsch, *The Pentateuch* on Deut. 17:16).

37. Ibid. on Deut. 17:17.

38. *Sanhedrin* 21b.

39. Judah J. Slotki aptly summarizes the significance of this fable in the rabbinic tradition. He writes: "By this, his moral weakness, he laid the foundations of a hostile world, symbolized by the Talmud as Rome, which overthrew Israel" (commentary in *The Babylonian Talmud: Sanhedrin*, I:117, n. 11).

40. Maimonides, *Hilkhot Melakhim* 3:6.

41. *Sanhedrin* 21b. The rationale behind the injunction is explained as follows by Aaron of Barcelona: "The king that transgresses this precept and sets as his goal the filling of treasure houses in order to fulfill his personal desires, and whose intention is not for the benefit of the people and their protection... his punishment is great because all the people are dependent upon the king. Therefore, it is necessary that he direct all his attention to the well-being of his people and not for his self-glorification and the satisfaction of his appetites" (Aaron HaLevi of Barcelona, *Sefer haHinukh*, # 515, p. 636). See also the discussion in Rosenberg, *Beer Shemuel al haTorah* II:194.

42. In a succinct commentary, Abraham ibn Ezra notes that the basis for the biblical injunction is "so that [the king] should not punish Israel" (Ibn Ezra, *Perushei haTorah leR. Abraham ibn Ezra* on Deut. 17:17). Gersonides writes: "The reason for this is that his demands for increasing amounts of silver and gold will bring him to take it illegally and he will deviate from the Torah" (Gersonides, *Perush al haTorah al Derekh Biur* II:224a).

43. "R. Joshua ben Levi said: 'Only as much as is required for *aspanya*'—for this year alone" (*Jer. T. Sanhedrin* 2:6).

44. Moses Margoliot explains this as meaning that "in each year the king accumulates silver and gold in order to supply and pay for the army for that year, but not for a succeeding year" (Margoliot, *Pnei Moshe*, ad loc. note 43 above).

45. The position of the Jerusalem Talmud is echoed by RASHI in his commentary on the Babylonian, where he defines *aspanya* as "the pay of the army, on an annual basis, for those that come in and go out with him all the year [a complement of 'full-time' troops]" (Solomon ben Isaac, *Perush RASHI* [T], on *Sanhedrin* 21b). Similarly, Jonathan of Lunel writes: "This means to say, in order to pay his troops on an annual basis.... However, he is not to accumulate more so that his heart should not become elevated, and that he should not become exalted over his brethren" (Jonathan of Lunel,

Perush Rabbenu Yehonatan haKohen miLunel al haMishnah vehaRIF leMassekhet Sanhedrin, "Sanhedrin" 2:8, p. 28).

46. Maimonides writes as follows: "He is not to multiply unto himself silver and gold to place in his storehouses, to take pride in it or to enjoy it. [He may do so] only in order to issue it to his troops, servants and attendants. However, [with regard to] all the silver and gold that he might accumulate for the treasury of the House of the Lord, to be there ready for the needs of the public and for their wars, it is an obligation that he should accumulate it" (Maimonides, *Hilkhot Melakhim* 3:4). In another place, he states: "The king is cautioned against multiplying wealth especially for himself... and the limit [of the biblical injunction] is that it should not exceed the amount required for his chariot and personal servants. However, it is permitted for him to gather money for the benefit of all Israel" (Maimonides, *Sefer haMitzvot*, pt. 2, p. 112).

47. Meiri observes: "These things are all so that the king should not be overly arrogant in his reign" (Meiri, *Bet haBehirah al Massekhet Sanhedrin*, p. 58, on *Sanhedrin* 18a). Ben-Zion Firer argues that these injunctions all have a single aim: to deter the king from adopting "a culture alien to the spirit of Israel and the diversion of his heart from the Mosaic Law" (Firer, *Hegyonah shel Torah* V:147).

48. Zvi Hirsch Chajes writes: "The king encompasses all the nation and on him depends the well-being of the state; and even in that which touches only his honor, this too is in the interest of the general well-being of the people.... And if his reign is adorned with all kinds of glory and honor, from this too will sprout general well-being and very great benefit, because the inhabitants of the extremities of the land will have fear and dread of him, and his throne will thereby be more stable, dynamic and awe-inspiring than those of the surrounding neighbors" (Chajes, *Torat Neviyyim*, p. 47).

49. *Yalkut Shimeoni* I:624.

50. Meiri writes: "The leadership is generally transmitted to two persons, one from the standpoint of Torah which is the high priest, and one for the leadership of the world which is the king" (Meiri, *Bet haBehirah al Massekhet Sanhedrin*, p. 58, on *Sanhedrin* 18a).

51. Eliezer Levi notes that "the participation of the king or his representative at the side of the president of the High Court (as usual, the High Priest) is acknowledged throughout the entire period of the kings" (Levi, *Yesodot haHalakhah*, p. 75). However, from a theoretical standpoint, such a presence on the high court would be subject to the vagaries of the earlier discussion of the rabbinic perspectives on this matter.

52. Commenting on the biblical statement: "The king by justice establisheth the land; But he that exacteth gifts overthroweth it" (Prov. 29:4), Malbim writes: "The king and the high priest are established for the purposes of justice and righteousness; that is to say, the king was set up to bring about justice in the land between man and his fellow. The high priest was responsible for the House of the Lord, and the teaching of the Torah, and the precepts governing the relationship between man and Heaven. When both of them travel in the path of the Lord, they will establish the land.... If the high priest and the priests subordinate to him do not labor to straighten the people, but only strive to receive gifts [that is, the priestly offerings] and to wax rich, they will overturn that which the king will erect, for without the worship of the Lord, and faith and righteousness, justice itself will also prove unstable" (Malbim, *Mikra'ei Kodesh* on Prov. 29:4).

53. *Tosefta*, "Sanhedrin" 3:2.

12
The Judiciary

The judiciary is differentiated from the other organs of the polity—the prophetic, sacerdotal, and monarchic institutions—both from the standpoint of its fundamental functions, as well as its structure. As has been shown, the other institutions are basically—by their very natures—highly centralized. The prophetic and monarchic institutions are essentially singular or personalized; the priesthood is focused on the central religious shrine, from which even the pedagogic functions of the priests and Levites draw authority and strength. The judicial institution—however—is constitutionally decentralized, and this factor will be seen to exercise a decisive influence on the political structure of the Judaic polity.

The basic constitutional dictum that establishes the judiciary declares: "Judges and officers shalt thou make thee in all thy gates, which the Lord thy God giveth thee, tribe by tribe; and they shall judge the people with righteous judgement" (Deut. 16:18). In Chapter 6, it was pointed out that there is a divergence of views with respect to the nature of the relationship between the judges and the officers—the point of contention being whether the officer's authority is dependent on or independent of that of the judge. The dominant rabbinic view held that the executive powers of the officer are derivative from the fundamental authority of the judiciary. However, note was made of the unanimous agreement that, unless supported by the power of enforcement, the effectiveness of the judge in discharging his responsibilities is highly problematical. Dispensation of justice in society is seen as requiring the ultimate sanction of coercion, to overcome the inevitable challenges to the authority of the judges. Hence, the concern is to clearly specify the mandatory requirement that the judiciary be complemented with officers who enforce the decisions of the court.[1] In addition to establishing the judicial system and the system of officers, this same biblical text is also considered to provide that both are to be decentralized to the tribes and cities (where justice is traditionally rendered in the gates).[2]

To fully explore the rabbinic theory of the structure of the judicial institution and its place in the basic political organization of the state, it is necessary to refer to another biblical section, where the groundwork for the constitutional dictum and its interpretation in rabbinic thought is laid. The key to the rabbinic scheme for the organization of political society and its perhaps most significant institution—the judiciary—is to be found in Ex. 18:13–26, where the structural needs of political society are dealt with in the following manner:

And it came to pass on the morrow, that Moses sat to judge the people; and the people stood about Moses from the morning unto the evening. And when Moses' father-in-law saw all that he did to the people, he said: "What is this thing that thou doest to the people? Why sittest thou thyself alone, and all the people stand about thee from morning unto even?" And Moses said unto his father-in-law: "Because the people come unto me to inquire of God; when they have a matter, it cometh unto me; and I judge between a man and his neighbor, and I make them know the statutes of God, and his laws." And Moses' father-in-law said unto him: "The thing that thou doest is not good. Thou wilt surely wear away, both thou, and this people that is with thee; for the thing is too heavy for thee; thou art not able to perform it thyself alone. Hearken now unto my voice, I will give thee counsel... thou shalt teach them the statutes and the laws, and shalt show them the way wherein they must walk, and the work that they must do. Moreover, thou shalt provide out of all the people able men, such as fear god, men of truth, hating unjust gain; and place such over them, to be rulers of thousands, rulers of hundreds, rulers of fifties, and rulers of tens. And let them judge the people at all seasons; and it shall be, that every great matter they shall bring unto thee, but every small matter they shall judge themselves; so shall they make it easier for thee and bear the burden with thee. If thou shalt do this thing... then thou shalt be able to endure, and all this people also shall go to their place in peace." So Moses hearkened to the voice of his father-in-law, and did all that he had said. And Moses chose able men out of all Israel, and made them heads over the people, rulers of thousands, rulers of hundreds, rulers of fifties, and rulers of tens. And they judged the people at all seasons: the hard causes they brought unto Moses, but every small matter they judged themselves.

This rather long citation contains several implied concepts that are of critical importance to our subject. First, the only aspect of Moses' multifaceted political functions discussed in this biblical section is his role as supreme judge of the people. Thus, when he makes administrative divisions within the people and appoints various levels of "rulers" over them, he is considered to be doing so in his judicial capacity. Consequently, the rulers of thousands, hundreds, fifties, and tens are delegated the indicated judicial functions.[3] In effect, they become magistrates. That is, they are considered as encompassing and wielding both the judicial and the political leadership functions and authority. It is with respect to the latter functions that they are "rulers." It is evident that the underlying concern is with the problem of span of control. Irrespective of charters, constitutional authority, or even autocratic arrogation of authority, there is a finite limit to the capacity of one person to interact with numerous others. Beyond a given number, order begins to turn into disorder, and—if unchecked—may result in anarchy and chaos.[4] It is basic to the rabbinic perspective that the maintenance of social peace—and the antecedent preservation of the kind of society necessary to the fulfillment of this essential aim—is contingent on the adequacy of the judicial institutions for the resolution of any social conflicts that may arise—expeditiously and with deliberate attention to the requirements of true justice. These needs can only be effectively met through the medium of a judicial system sufficiently decentralized as to allow for the prompt and proper resolution of any disputes that may arise within the communities and other subdivisions of the polity.[5]

Second, by reserving the authority to deal with "every great matter" and with "hard causes" to himself, Moses establishes a judicial hierarchy—which encompasses an appeals system for matters over which the lower courts may be assigned original jurisdiction, and culminates in a final central authority.[6] The latter retains original jurisdiction in matters of vital national interest and scope—presumably including the trial and judgment of capital offenses—in addition to serving as court of last appeal. Initially, this central judicial authority is Moses. However, it is thereafter considered to repose in a collective successor—the high court or Great Sanhedrin.[7]

Finally, this biblical section in conjunction with the text of Deut. 16:18 (cited at the beginning of this chapter) provides a basis for a concept of federation as the appropriate structure of the state. In Scripture, this concept is related to a society that is primarily tribal in character. Nonetheless, the underlying principles of governmental decentralization would be equally applicable to a nontribal society. Since—with the exception of Jerusalem, which was a border city—all municipalities in ancient Israel were located within tribal boundaries, the literature contains a good deal of discussion of this federal structure—particularly with regard to the relations between the tribes and their urban centers.

In some respects, the relation of a municipality to the tribe within whose borders it is situated is typical of federal systems as we know them today. The citizen of a city was also simultaneously subject to the jurisdiction of the tribe. Nahmanides points out that "no litigant can compel another to appear for judgement in a city other than his own.... However, the tribal court can compel all the members of the tribe to appear before it. Even if they were already judged in their city, one may say: Let us go before the tribal high court.... If the court finds it necessary to correct or enact something for its tribe, it proceeds to do so."[8]

The tribal high court—like the Great Sanhedrin at the national level—is seen as having primary responsibility for the affairs of the tribe as a composite political entity. The tribal high court embodies both the judicial and political leadership functions at the subnational level. With regard to overlapping tribal jurisdictions—as observed by one group of commentators—"if there is found in a single city residents from two tribes, they establish two [municipal] courts."[9] Thus, the requirement to provide judges for every city is not taken as implying any intrinsically autonomous political status for the municipality. Instead, the city is viewed as a composite element within the tribal jurisdiction; and, where the population of a city is not tribally homogeneous, municipal courts are to be established along tribal lines. In effect, this position would give one tribe extraterritorial rights in the lands of another. In the instance where litigants in a single proceeding were from two different tribes, the case would presumably come under the jurisdiction of the national court, unless one of the tribes waived its jurisdiction.[10]

The prevailing view in the rabbinic literature is that there is a biblically mandated hierarchical judicial system consisting of three tiers: a national jurisdiction (the Great Sanhedrin), provincial jurisdictions (the tribal high courts), and the municipal courts. A notable exception to the general consensus is Isaac Abravanel, who registers a strong dissent.

Abravanel takes issue with the ascribed validity of a tribal jurisdiction. He asserts that the words "tribe by tribe" in the text of Deuteronomy cannot justifiably be construed as implying a requirement to establish courts at the tribal level. In his view, those words have a rather different implication. He calls attention to the fact that, in the account of Moses' organization of the tribes according to the recommendations of Jethro, Moses personally selected the rulers of thousands, hundreds, fifties, and tens. Similarly—in other texts—it is Moses who personally selects the leaders of the nation. Based on these observations, Abravanel argues that, in presenting the requirement to establish judges "tribe by tribe," Moses is simply informing the elders that—whereas he is choosing the leaders of the nation in his capacity as a prophet—there will come a time when there will be no prophets to follow him in this task. Therefore, it is necessary that the people themselves learn to choose their own judges, and this responsibility is assigned to the tribes: not that there should be tribal jurisdictions, but that the tribal leadership should select the judges.[11]

Abravanel does not explain what he means when he says that the judges are appointed by the tribes, and therefore leaves the reader in somewhat of a quandary. There is an implication in his argument that, for the tribes to appoint the judges, there must be some tribal structure that would facilitate the selection and appointment process. However, if we assume a tribal political structure that has no judicial functions other than the selection of judges—at the same time that the municipalities do have such functions—the requisite interjurisdictional relationships become quite complex and the politics highly sensitive. What is of particular interest in Abravanel's position is the implied notion of local political autonomy—a point to be brought up again later in this study.

Recapitulating, we find the general trend of rabbinic theory as considering the judiciary to be constitutionally decentralized in a three-level hierarchical configuration. Within this structure, each level is seen as having a distinct area of original jurisdiction—corresponding to the national, provincial or tribal (recognizing that the territory of Israel was originally divided on a tribal basis), and municipal. In addition, the institutional structure of the judicial system provides for an appellate process, which culminates in the Great Sanhedrin— the supreme judicial authority. It is also clear that the judicial structure as outlined is predicated on the existence of a territorial state. Consequently, no insuperable difficulty should be inferred from the fact that the three-level system provided for by the constitutional provisions of Deuteronomy does not tally with the five-level hierarchical structure described in Exodus—a structure designed for the period before the nation became a state. However, while the constitutional basis for the tribal and municipal courts is considered to be clearly derivative from the text of Deut. 16:18, it is not at all clear that a similar derivation of the authority for the Great Sanhedrin can be inferred from the same source.

The existence of a national high court is assumed to be implied by the Deuteronomy passage that states: "If there arise a matter too hard for thee in judgement . . . even matters of controversy within thy gates; thou shalt arise. . . . And thou shalt come unto the priests the Levites, and unto the judge that shall be in those days; and thou shalt inquire; and they shall declare unto thee the sentence of judgement. And thou shalt do according to the tenor of the sentence, which they shall declare unto thee . . . and thou shalt observe to do according to all that they shall teach thee. According to the law which they shall teach thee, and according to the judgement which they shall tell thee, thou shalt do; thou shalt not turn aside from the sentence which they shall declare unto thee, to the right hand, nor to the left" (17:8–11).

Support for the assumption that this passage implies a national high court is seen by some writers as provided by the description of the actions of King Jehoshaphat on his return to Jerusalem, as related in 2 Chronicles: "And he set judges in the land throughout all the fortified cities of Judah, city by city. . . . Moreover in Jerusalem did Jehoshaphat set of the Levites and the priests, and of the heads of the father's houses of Israel, for the judgement of the Lord, and for controversies. . . . And he charged them, saying . . . whensoever any controversy shall come to you from your brethren that dwell in their cities . . . between law and commandment, statutes and ordinances, ye shall warn them, that they be not guilty towards the Lord" (19:5–11).[12]

The establishment by Jehoshaphat of a supreme judicial body "for the judgement of the Lord, and for controversies" would seem to provide for original jurisdiction, as well as a high court of appeals. However, the notion of an appeals process is not clearly articulated in rabbinic literature, and there is some doubt as to whether it is considered to refer to an appeal against the judgment of a lower court. Thus, David Z. Hoffmann argues that "the High Court is not an appeals court; its role is to instruct the municipal courts."[13] That is, the high court is an appeals court in the special sense that the lower courts appeal to it when they have difficulty arriving at a judgment, but it does not sit in review of the rulings of the other courts on the basis of an appeal by a party to an adjudicated dispute. The high court thus serves as the final arbiter of the meaning and proper application of the law, to ensure uniformity of justice throughout the land. Its purpose is to limit inconsistencies in judicial interpretation. The basic problem that it must deal with—according to Nahmanides—is that, since "general agreement on anything is rare, disagreements will multiply and the Torah will be transformed into a multiplicity of Torahs. Therefore Scripture determined that we should pay heed to the High Court... with regard to all that it may dictate to us concerning the interpretation of the Torah."[14]

The high court is thus seen to constitute not only the highest national judicial entity, but also the ultimate repository of the authoritative interpretation of the Torah—both written and oral. As Samson Raphael Hirsch put it, Israel's supreme judicial body is intended to be "the ultimate authority on whose shoulders rests the responsibility for the authentic tradition and interpretation of the Torah, as well as making all arrangements for it being kept correctly. It has the power to make final decisions which the people in general as well as the officials appointed to teach them the Law have to accept and put into practice without contradiction."[15]

Reflecting on the primacy of the Torah in rabbinic political theory, it is evident that the high court becomes the central institution of government in the state. It is this crucial role that gave to the Sanhedrin—in its various manifestations—the capacity to survive the destruction of the Second Commonwealth, and remain a viable institution of government for some time—even in the absence of the state.

It would lead far beyond the scope of this study to undertake an examination of the operation of the judicial system, as it is conceived in traditional Jewish thought. It must be recognized that the Torah—as the embodiment of the divine law—is not restricted in applicability to a particular territorial state, although it does clearly provide for the specific structure of the Judaic state when such a state should in fact come into being. Because of this, a full study of the court structure and its procedures would have to take under its purview the vast legal history of the rabbinic courts over the past nineteen centuries.

However, it is abundantly evident that, in the rabbinic view, the Torah is the critical factor in establishing the proper political order. Within that framework, it is the judiciary that has the responsibility for the interpretation of the precepts and laws of the Torah, as well as that of dispensing justice in accordance with its principles of jurisprudence. Thus, the judiciary becomes the organ of government that holds the key to the proper achievement of the fundamental purpose of the Judaic state.

Considering the central importance attributed to the judicial institution in rabbinic political theory, it appears evident that what we are describing here far transcends the usual role of the judiciary in other systems of government. In addition to its juridical functions, the high court is considered to also possess certain legislative authority. The character of this legislative authority must be explored in the context of the interrelationships of the judiciary and the other constitutionally mandated elements of the polity, nationally as well as locally. However, before we direct our attention to an examination of these jurisdictional relationships, it will be helpful to gain some perspective as to what sort of men were to be assigned the awesome responsibilities of the judicial-political leadership roles discussed above.

NOTES

1. As Barukh Epstein notes: "In order to extract ill-gotten gains from the extortionist there is need of officers. For as long as the officers do not perform their duty, in that they do not extract the extortion, justice will not be fulfilled for practical purposes. . . . Hence, the containment of the oppressor is a branch grafted onto the very root of justice" (B. Epstein, *Tosefet Berakhah* V:129).

2. The Talmud states: "Our Rabbis taught: Whence do we know that judges are to be set up for Israel?—From the verse, 'Judges . . . shalt thou make thee.' . . . Whence the appointment of judges for each tribe?—From the words, 'Judges . . . tribe by tribe.' . . . Whence the appointment of judges for each town?—From the words, 'Judges . . . in all thy gates.' . . . Rabban Simeon b. Gamaliel said: [The contiguity] of 'they shall judge' and 'tribe by tribe' indicates that the tribal court must judge only those of its own tribe" (*Sanhedrin* 16b).

3. There is some controversy among commentators with regard to the relationships between the rulers of thousands, hundreds, and so on—as well as to precisely what is meant by these subdivisions. The resolution of these issues is entirely peripheral to the subject under discussion, and is therefore not addressed in this study. Suffice it to note that, if we assume that the text is to be taken at face value—and given that some 600,000 men are included, at a minimum—the indicated apportionment would result in 78,600 "rulers"—all ostensibly chosen and appointed by Moses. A rather formidable task.

4. Reflecting on the organizational principles underlying Jethro's recommendation to Moses, Isaac Abravanel writes: "The correct understanding, as I see it, is that in the matter of justice and in the matter of wars, which are things of great concern to the people, Jethro, in his wisdom, and our lord Moses as well, saw that with regard to an appointment [to a position of authority], the more all-encompassing it is the more disorderly it will prove to be. Therefore they did not consider the appointment of rulers of ten thousands or rulers of hundred thousands and others such as these; for the oversight of many people will confuse the leadership. Thus it is sufficient that the most extensive appointment be over a thousand people. For in the matter of justice it will suffice that one person judge one thousand, and in the matter of wars it is even clearer that at best a strong person could be found to lead and command a thousand men . . . in a proper manner" (Abravanel, *Perush haTorah*, "Shemot," p. 31b).

5. Gersonides writes: "The matter is, according to my view, that Moses selected from them [the able men] for the tribe, each one individually from among the most respected, and placed them as rulers of thousands so that they should be firm and powerful in order to compel the people to accept their legal edicts, and beneath them he placed other respected judges whom he appointed as rulers of hundreds. He did it in this manner so that the judges should be able to adjudicate between a man and his neighbor with a minimum of difficulty" (Gersonides, *Perush al haTorah al Derekh Biur* I:73a).

6. Obadiah Sforno observes that "there will be these four levels [of magistrates], each

one higher than the next; the lowest will judge first and he who would protest against the judgement rendered will appeal to the next highest court. And so from the second to the third and from the third to the fourth" (Sforno, *Perush R. Obadiah Sforno* on Ex. 18:21).

7. The idea of a judicial hierarchy is broached in the Talmud with the teaching of Rabbi Judah, that "one is set over all the others" (*Sanhedrin* 16b). RASHI considers this as referring to "the Great Sanhedrin," and notes further that, "by the advice of Jethro, Moses was judge and referee in respect of the divine word and was equal in weight to the Great Sanhedrin that sits in Jerusalem" (Solomon ben Isaac, *Perush RASHI* [T], ad loc.).

8. Nahmanides, *Perushei haRAMBAN al haTorah* on Deut. 16:18.

9. *Tosafot* on *Sanhedrin* 16b. See also Asher ben Jehiel, *Tosafot haROSH al Sanhedrin*, p. 18. Barukh Epstein writes: "It therefore appears to be the case that, aside from the court that is appointed for every city, a court is also appointed for every tribe irrespective of location, and its members are the supervisors of the affairs of their tribe even though the tribe is spread out among several cities. And we find, accordingly, that every person of Israel has two judges, one from his city and the second from his tribe" (B. Epstein, *Torah Temimah* on Deut. 16:18).

10. Jacob Emden writes: "It appears to me that a general court is appointed over the tribe so that if conflicts should develop within the gates of the cities, between one city and another, with regard to either the criminal or the civil law, where the citizen of one city causes damages to the resident of another from a single tribe, either to his person or his property; and similarly with regard to those matters which are the general concern of municipalities such as its boundaries, fields, hamlets and suburbs; these matters should all be adjudicated by the general court of the concerned tribe.... And if such matters should arise between tribes, they would come for judgement before the high court in Jerusalem" (Emden, *Hiddushim veHagahot* on *Sanhedrin* 16b).

11. Abravanel considers this system to be necessary "in order that Israel should not think that it will always be so, that is to say, that the prophet that will be in each generation will appoint the judges that are to be in each city by virtue of the fact that it is he who would know by means of his prophetic powers who is suitable to be a judge. Therefore Moses informed them that this is not to be, but that they themselves will be the ones to appoint the judges, because the appointment of judges was assigned by the Lord to the tribes and not to the prophet of the generation. The issue of Moses' involvement in the appointment of the judges was a matter of 'the need of the hour.' It was not desired that it should be the permanent responsibility of the prophet; for it would be a great burden for him to appoint judges for all the cities of Israel. And, in addition, at such time that prophecy departs from Israel there will not remain any longer anyone to appoint the judge, and therefore it was given over to the tribes" (Abravanel, *Perush haTorah*, "Devarim," p. 33b).

12. See Gersonides, *Perush haRALBAG* on 2 Chron. 19:10; Hoffmann, *Sefer Devarim*, p. 305; Israel W. Slotki's commentary in the Soncino edition of the Bible, p. 246.

13. Hoffmann, *Sefer Devarim*, p. 305.

14. Nahmanides, *Perushei haRAMBAN al haTorah* on Deut. 17:11. See also Maimonides, *Sefer haMitzvot*, pt. 2, p. 36; Sforno, *Perush R. Obadiah Sforno* on Deut. 17:8; Malbim, *HaTorah vehaMitzvah* on Deut. 17:8; Berlin, *HaAmek Davar* on Deut. 17:8; and B. Epstein, *Torah Temimah* on Deut. 17:8, and *Tosefet Berakhah*, ad loc.

15. Hirsch, *The Pentateuch* on Deut. 17:8–13.

13
The Magistrates

In considering the judicial-political position of the magistrate in the Judaic polity, there are several questions of primary importance that merit examination. The first concerns the recruitment or eligibility criteria for such office. What sort of man was to be selected to fill the role of magistrate? A second question concerns how the selection and appointment of the magistrates were to be carried out, and by whom. A third issue to be examined concerns the means by which the independence of the magistrates was to be assured—an independence that was clearly necessary if the courts were to be unimpeded in the dispensation of true justice. How were the magistrates to become independent of those who brought about their appointment in the first place?

As with all other facets of rabbinic political theory, here too the primary source is Scripture. An examination of our first question above requires us to turn back to the Book of Exodus. There we find Jethro counseling Moses as to how best to organize the nation and its leadership cadre. He sets forth the basic criteria for the magistrate's vocation: "Moreover, thou shalt provide out of all the people able men, such as fear God, men of truth, hating unjust gain; and place such over them, to be rulers. . . . And let them judge the people at all seasons" (Ex. 18:21).

The criterion of most immediate relevance to our subject is that of "able men." What are the implications of this term? In what respects are the men who are to become magistrates to be "able"? Actually, the use of the term "able men" by the Bible translator is most appropriate—in spite of its ambiguity—since the original Hebrew term is equally obscure. This latter is *anshei hayil*, meaning "men of ----." The blank space, which should be filled by an equivalent to the word *hayil*, could be occupied by any of the following terms—all valid translations of the word in question: strength, power, efficiency, wealth, force, army, host, vigor, or health.

Behind the several rabbinic interpretations placed on this vague term may be seen a rather substantial polarization of viewpoints. On the one hand, there is a school of thought that appears to hold that the most beneficial and pragmatic arrangement for the government of the state at all levels is that of a limited plutocracy: that is, rule by the rich. Under this notion, the magistrates would be wealthy, but wealth alone would be insufficient qualification for office. As this school sees it, men who are both wealthy and wise are those best suited for a career of disinterested public service. By contrast, a second school of thought disregards wealth as a necessary qualifying condition for public office. Instead, it seeks the establishment of a true aristocracy—the rule of the best, determined on the basis of personal merit—as the means whereby the functions of the magistrate may best be carried out.

The locus classicus for the advocates of plutocracy is the position of the sage Rabbi Joshua, who takes the term *anshei hayil* to mean "wealthy people, people of means."[1] In his commentary on the biblical text, RASHI elaborates on the definition of Rabbi Joshua: "The wealthy have no need to fawn [upon the rich and powerful] and to favor [them in the adjudication of disputes]."[2] The implication here is that only the wealthy are immune to the blandishments of wealth, and are therefore incorruptible to a greater extent than other men. However, RASHI elsewhere imposes a limiting qualification on the plutocracy, by noting that the biblical intent is to "appoint judges who are experts as well as righteous so that they may render righteous judgement."[3] These qualities— in conjunction with wealth—are seen to be crucial to the well-ordered regime.

RASHI finds further support for his position regarding the desirability of a limited plutocracy in the interpretation by the sage Rabbi Nahman of this biblical text: "The king by justice establisheth the land; But he that exacteth gifts overthroweth it" (Prov. 29:4). Rabbi Nahman taught: "If the judge is similar to the king who needs nothing, the land will be established, and if he is like the priest who goes about the threshing floors to collect that which is due to him, he will overthrow it."[4] Once again, the fundamental point here is that independence in the face of powerful contending forces can only be achieved and assured by a countervailing factor. In the case at hand, wealth is considered to be the necessary attribute of the independent, disinterested, and just public servant—beyond all the other necessary qualifications for service as a magistrate.

A corollary to the position expounded by RASHI is the opinion that non-plutocratic rule will result in a potentially greater tyranny over the poor and the weak. David Altschuler suggests that the poor man turned ruler will probably oppress the poor more than the rich, "because the rich man will not permit him to rob him of his wealth since [by virtue of his wealth] he is the more powerful."[5] From this perspective—all other things being equal—the weak will be better served by rulers and judges who have no incentive for using their positions of political power as a means of attaining wealth, at the further expense of the poor.

A primary source for the view that disregards tangible wealth as a basic criterion for public office—and, instead, seeks to establish a true aristocracy based on personal merit—is the view of the sage Rabbi Eleazar of Modi'in. He considers the biblical term *anshei hayil* to mean "people of trust."[6] Trustworthiness—rather than financial status—becomes the guarantor of incorruptibility. Elsewhere in the midrashic literature, *anshei hayil* is interpreted to mean "mighty men of the Torah."[7] This latter interpretation seems to be the source text for Maimonides, who takes the biblical term as meaning "those who are mighty men in the performance of the precepts and are exacting with themselves, who conquer their desires so that they should bear no shame or evil name, that their reputation should be without blemish. Generally speaking, *anshei hayil* means that they should have the strength of heart to retrieve the extortion from the hand of the oppressor."[8] In this perspective, it is only men of exceptional personal merit that should rule or judge—the measure of their merit being their unflinching devotion to the Torah, which makes them fearless with regard to the machinations of men. Only such can be trusted to be just—to withstand the pressures and temptations that will be brought to bear on them. Abraham ibn Ezra suggests that the major characteristic of such men may be their capacity for suffering.[9]

While generally adhering to the view of the aristocratic school, Isaac Abravanel places his greatest emphasis on the element of power—in explicit disagreement with the position maintained by RASHI. Thus, in regard to the meaning of *anshei hayil*, Abravanel argues that "they are not the wealthy, as RASHI states, but rather men of battle."[10] He explains this point by stating that the biblical phrase means "powerful men, and men of heart, that will fear no man in matters of the law."[11] An even stronger expression of this view is offered by Ephraim of Luntshits who takes the phrase to refer to "those men of strength who have the capacity, then as now, to smash the arms of those who claim the upper hand."[12]

Finally—as noted earlier—the argument that rule by other than the wealthy will result in potentially greater tyranny over the weak and the poor was grounded in the text of Prov. 28:3, which taught: "A poor man that oppresseth the weak is like a sweeping rain which leaveth no food." Meiri interprets this same passage in a manner that lends support to the contrary position held by Maimonides and the "aristocratic" school. In his view, the terms "poor" and "wealthy" should be understood in the sense of self-control and satisfaction. One who is wealthy is one who is content with what he has. Similarly, one who is poor—in the sense intended by the author of the Book of Proverbs—is one who wants more, regardless of how much he already has. Consequently, wealth in the fiscal sense is no guarantor of independence and justice on the part of a wealthy jurist. He can be just as corrupt as a poor man seeking to better his situation at the expense of the weak.[13]

It seems clear that Meiri uses the term "wealthy" in a companion sense to Maimonides' use of "mighty," in his interpretation of the phrase *anshei hayil*. Both usages are derived from the sage Ben Zoma, who taught: "Who is strong?

He who conquers his passions. . . . Who is rich? He who rejoices in his portion."[14] Maimonides and the school that takes its lead from him may be seen as arguing—in effect—that actual wealth should not in itself be a criterion for selection to become a magistrate. If the candidate has the qualities of the true aristocrat, he will be wealthy in the ethical sense, and this will serve to ensure his incorruptibility.

This same divergence of views between proponents of the plutocratic and aristocratic schools of thought is also to be found—albeit in less explicit fashion—within the Talmud. There, we find the following dictum: "The blood-letter [barber-surgeon], and the bath-attendant, and the tanner may not be appointed to the position of king or high priest. What is the reason for this? Not because they are [personally] unfit but rather because their trade is held in low esteem."[15] However, in another place, this dictum is modified in a rather significant manner, and reads: "R. Jose Taba said . . . the blood-letter, and the tanner, and the builder are not appointed officer over the public."[16] This latter formulation is more encompassing than the former, in that it clearly excludes the very poorest (those who would undertake work of such low esteem) from all public office—let alone the highest in the land. This position would comport with the stance taken by RASHI—not because there is anything inherently wrong with the people who pursue such low esteem occupations, but rather because in order for the public official to be effective he must command the respect of those over whom he is to exercise authority. Such grant of respect is generally not the lot of the poor, who would continually be under suspicion of having sought office as a means to improve their economic status—and therefore of being particularly susceptible to bribery.

Not surprisingly, Maimonides bases his restatement of the rule of law in this regard on the former talmudic text, rather than the latter—although in slightly modified form. He states: "We do not appoint as king or high priest, the butcher, nor the barber, nor the bath-attendant, nor the tanner; not because they are unfit, but since their trades are held in low esteem, the people forever have contempt for them, and whoever performs any of these tasks for a single day is disqualified."[17] In this formulation, there is no restriction against practitioners of any of the enumerated menial trades becoming magistrates, officers, or other public officials—even though they are clearly precluded from the monarchy and the high priesthood.

However, even though there is no formal restriction against even the poorest—if otherwise deemed qualified—from becoming magistrates, there is a general recognition that the evidence of poverty in a public official will inevitably bring about low esteem and disrespect, to the ultimate detriment of the public order. To offset this possibility, the Talmud imposes certain restrictions on the freedom of behavior of public officials. The sage Samuel states: "As soon as a man becomes appointed an official over the public it is forbidden for him to perform manual labor in front of three people."[18] RASHI—consistently maintaining his position—treats Samuel's dictum as implying that "it is a disgrace and a humiliation to a generation that is subject to one that has no one to perform his labor for him."[19] On the basis of this same dictum, Maimonides goes on to derive an extension of the rule, and similarly forbids an official from overindulgence in food and drink in public—actions that would presumably cause loss of respect on the part of observers.[20] In adopting the talmudic dictum as the basic rule, Maimonides amends it in a manner that evidently reflects his concern for personal merit as the overriding criterion for public service.

Interestingly enough, despite the general recognition that a public official must have some minimum of wealth in order to meet the condition forbidding him to perform manual labor in public, what that minimum should consist of is nowhere specified. David ibn Zimra would make appointment to public office conditional on the candidate's having sufficient wealth to meet his needs, without having to work in a demeaning fashion in public after his appointment.[21] Nonetheless, beyond such limited financial qualification, the overwhelming weight of rabbinic opinion clearly favors the concept of rule by a true aristocracy—one of the mind and the spirit. Isaac Abravanel goes so far as to note specifically that familial lineage is irrelevant in this regard. For him, the primary need is for men who are wise—"who are full of knowledge of the Torah and the sciences and . . . are full of the knowledge of political behavior."[22]

The second issue posed at the outset of this chapter concerned the process by which magistrates are selected and appointed. The source text for the literature's examination of this matter is Moses' instruction to the elders of Israel: "Get you, from each of your tribes, wise men, and understanding, and full of knowledge, and I will make them heads over you" (Deut. 1:13). However, once again, the standard translation of the biblical text as cited here—while conforming to what is considered by some to be the simple meaning of the passage[23]—nonetheless represents but one particular point of view. It may also be rendered in a manner that would alter its significance somewhat—becoming of special interest in regard to the issue under discussion. Thus—as suggested by the Midrash—by translating the text in strict conformity with the Hebrew word order, the following rendering would result: "Get you men who are wise and understanding, and known to your tribes, and I will make them heads over you."[24]

The implication of this rendition of the text is that the candidate's qualifications are to be affirmed by his native constituency—which, in the case at hand, would give the tribes a significant role in the candidate selection process. This implication is seconded by RASHI. In commenting on the biblical text, he adopts the midrashic rendering, but interpolates the notion that only the tribe that raised the candidate can stipulate as to his worthiness for office.[25] This further suggests that the local constituency not only needs to be consulted in the nomination and selection process, but may also exercise an effective veto over executive selections—through its nonendorsement of the candidate. As put by Rabbi Isaac in the Talmud, "We must not appoint a leader over a community without first consulting it, as it states: 'See, the Lord hath called by name Bezalel, the son of Uri' [Ex. 35:30]. The Holy One, blessed be He, said to Moses: Do you consider Bezalel suitable? He replied: Sovereign of the Universe, if Thou thinkest him suitable, surely I must also! Said [the Lord] to him: All the same, go and consult them."[26] This passage suggests that, even where selection of a public official is ordained by Heaven, he must nonetheless be judged acceptable to the community over which he is to be placed, before his appointment may be put into effect.

Furthermore—in accordance with rabbinic tradition—in the period following the deaths of the literary prophets Haggai, Zechariah, and Malachi at the beginning of the Second Commonwealth, there was no longer any authoritative prophecy in Israel. Without a prophet, it was no longer possible to determine by divine inspiration who should be appointed from the rosters prepared by the tribal or local authorities. However, since the authority of the prophets is considered to have been transferred to the sages, only those determined to be qualified for such office within the framework of a local determination process could then be appointed by the sages to be judges and magistrates. This point will soon be considered further.

As seen earlier, the qualifications for the office of magistrate stipulated in the Bible are couched in rather general terms—such as men of wisdom, men of understanding, and men of knowledge. Obviously, these terms are too broad to serve as criteria for determining whether a particular person is in fact competent and suitable for such an office, with its attendant important public responsibilities. Accordingly, the Talmud attempts to provide additional criteria that are somewhat more definitive. "R. Johanan said: None are to be appointed members of the Sanhedrin, but men of stature, wisdom, good appearance, mature age, with a knowledge of sorcery, and who are conversant with all the seventy languages of mankind, in order that the court should have no need of an interpreter."[27]

There is an interesting discussion in the Talmud regarding the requirement that the jurists be polyglots. From the standpoint of jurisprudence, a knowledge of languages is considered essential so as to ensure that the judge's view of a matter under litigation or under review is not swayed in one direction or another as a result of nuances introduced in the translation from one language to another. It is taken as a given that all translation involves interpretation, which can prejudice one's perception and understanding of the matter at hand. However, some of the discussants of the issue in the Talmud feel that it is too unrealistic to demand that all the jurists on a court possess such extraordinary linguistic ability, and they therefore attempt to limit the requirement to a minimum of three members of the court.[28]

The Talmud also adds some additional criteria, designed to ensure that those who sit in judgment will be compassionate. Thus, "it has been taught: 'We do not appoint as members of the Sanhedrin, an aged man, a eunuch or one who is childless.' R. Judah includes also a cruel man."[29] In providing a rationale for these teachings, Maimonides argues: "We do not appoint as members of any court an aged man or a eunuch because there is in them an element of cruelty, or one who is childless, so that he shall be compassionate."[30]

In addition to these criteria—which relate primarily to the juridical aspects of the judge's responsibility—there are also the political qualifications. Primary among the latter is that the judges also be "elders." This derives from the biblical passage where the Lord instructs Moses: "Gather unto Me seventy men of the elders of Israel, whom thou knowest to be the elders of the people" (Num. 11:16). Isaac Abravanel takes "elders" as meaning men who have the accumulated wisdom of long experience in leadership roles.[31]

To recapitulate, the judiciary is a complex institution, both judicial and political in nature, and requiring competence in both fields in order to gain the necessary public trust that must be maintained. The fact that the Talmud and the codes of law—the *halakhic* literature—tend to consider the magistrate in terms of his judicial functions and requirements should not be construed as implying fundamental disagreement with the Bible commentators who place greater emphasis on the political aspects of the position. The distinction that may be discerned between the two categories of literature—insofar as this matter is concerned—is primarily the result of differing literary purposes: the codes providing insight into the requirements of the Torah, as they apply under the prevailing circumstances of a particular historical situation; the commentaries attempting to reflect the full essence and intent of the biblical legislation, irrespective of time or place or historical conditions. Thus, it is quite reasonable—and fully consistent with the traditional rabbinic approach—to blend the two sets of general criteria into a single comprehensive notion of what law and tradition consider to be the criteria against which the magistrates—the fundamental bearers of the public trust, and the cornerstone of the polity envisioned in rabbinic political theory—should be measured.

Returning to the fundamental question concerning the selection and appointment process for magistrates, it was suggested earlier that—as inheritors of the authority of Moses and the prophets—the sages of the Sanhedrin retained the authority to appoint judges, but that this grant of authority was constrained by their need to limit their choices to those determined to be eligible by the local jurisdictions. This procedure is considered to extend to the selection and appointment of the members of the Great Sanhedrin, as well.[32]

The actual selection process for membership in the Great Sanhedrin is described in the Talmud in the following terms: "From there [the Chamber of Hewn Stones] documents were written and sent to all of Israel, appointing men of wisdom and humility and who were esteemed by their fellow men as local judges. From there [the local courts] they were promoted to the Temple Mount, then to the court in the Temple courtyard, and then to the Chamber of Hewn Stones."[33] When a vacancy occurred on the Great Sanhedrin as a result of the death or incapacity of a member, jurists recruited from the local courts went through a promotion program that took them successively through the higher courts, until they might reach the highest judicial body.[34] It remains unclear, however, how the members of the Great Sanhedrin were appointed in the first place. Abravanel suggests that "at such time that there was a king, he would appoint them. And when there was no king, the chief judge would appoint each member of the Sanhedrin in consultation with it. . . . And with the death of the chief judge, the entire Sanhedrin would appoint one of them as head and judge over them."[35]

Finally, we turn to the third question raised at the outset of this discussion— namely, the means by which the magistrates were to become, in fact, independent of those who brought about their appointment in the first place.[36]

The preceding discussion of the promotion process actually presents the essential elements of the answer to the question at hand, as well. For it was noted that the judge remained at a single judicial level until a vacancy occurred in a higher court as a result of the death of a member. The clear implication of this is that the normal tenure of the judge was for life, although it is nowhere so stipulated. Furthermore, there are those who maintain that all appointed positions in Israel are for life—and may be inherited by their sons in perpetuity, if they be qualified for the position.[37]

The matter of the inheritance of public offices involves numerous complexities that require extensive treatment, and cannot be explored within the context of the present study. However, it should be noted that, although there is broad agreement that such positions are hereditary—subject to a host of qualifications and constraints—the generally held rabbinic view would not support the notion that judicial position and authority may similarly be inherited. The reasoning behind this exception is simply that the position of judge—alone among public offices—is primarily based on knowledge and understanding (especially with regard to the Torah), and that such matters are not transmissible through inheritance.[38]

However, there would be general agreement among rabbinic authorities with regard to the proposition that the judge normally has life tenure—a factor that, in ancient times as well as today, is one of the few guarantees of judicial independence.

NOTES

1. *Mekilta de-Rabbi Ishmael* II:183.
2. Solomon ben Isaac, *Perushei RASHI al haTorah* on Ex. 18:21. See also Samuel ben Meir (RASHBAM), *Perush haTorah asher Katav haRASHBAM*, on Ex. 18:21.
3. Ibid. on Deut. 16:18.
4. *Yalkut Shimeoni* II, # 999. RASHI adds: "If the judge is like the king who has no need to purchase favors and to take graft, he will establish the land" (Solomon ben Isaac, *Perush RASHI* [M], on Prov. 29:4).
5. Altschuler, *Metzudat David* on Prov. 28:3. See also Malbim, *Mikra'ei Kodesh* on Prov. 28:3.
6. *Mekilta de-Rabbi Ishmael* II:183.

7. *Midrash Tanhumah*, "Yitro" 2, p. 272. While interpreted here consistently with the general tradition, this passage could be read as implying a far greater focus on physical rather than moral strength—as the term is taken by another sage, Rabbi Tanhum bar Hanilai. See *Yalkut Shimeoni* II, # 860. A comparable focus on *anshei hayil* as meaning simply men of strength—without further qualification—may be seen in the Aramaic translations of *Targum Onkelos* and *Targum Yonatan* on Ex. 18:21.

8. Maimonides, *Hilkhot Sanhedrin* 2:7. See also Bahya ben Asher, *Biur al haTorah* II:165, on Ex. 18:21; Gersonides, *Perush al haTorah al Derekh Biur* I:73a; Rapa, *Minhah Belulah*, p. 78b; and Malbim, *HaTorah vehaMitzvah* on Ex. 18:21.

9. Ibn Ezra, *Perush haKatzar leSefer Shemot* on Ex. 18:21.

10. Abravanel, *Perush haTorah*, "Devarim," p. 3b.

11. Ibid., "Shemot," p. 31b.

12. Ephraim Solomon of Luntshits, *Kli Yakkar* on Ex. 18:21.

13. Meiri, *Perush HaMeiri al Sefer Mishlei*, p. 263.

14. *Avot* 4:1.

15. *Kiddushin* 82a.

16. *Derekh Eretz Zuta* 10.

17. Maimonides, *Hilkhot Melakhim* 1:6.

18. *Kiddushin* 70a.

19. Solomon ben Isaac, *Perush RASHI* [T], ad loc. note 18 above. See also Maimonides, *Hilkhot Sanhedrin* 24:4; and Moses of Coucy, *Sefer Mitzvot Gadol*, "Lo Taaseh," # 208, p. 65b.

20. Maimonides, *Hilkhot Sanhedrin* 25:4.

21. Ibn Zimra, *Perush haRADBAZ* on Maimonides, *Hilkhot Sanhedrin* 25:3.

22. Abravanel, *Perush haTorah*, "Devarim," p. 3b.

23. See Nahmanides, *Perushei haRAMBAN al haTorah* on Deut. 1:13.

24. *Sifre Devarim* 1:13.

25. Solomon ben Isaac, *Perushei RASHI al haTorah* on Deut. 1:13.

26. *Berakhot* 55a. See also Jacob ben Asher, *Perush Baal haTurim al haTorah* on Ex. 35:30; Abravanel, *Perush haTorah*, "Devarim," p. 3b, 34a; and Malbim, *HaTorah vehaMitzvah* on Deut. 1:13.

27. *Sanhedrin* 17a. Presumably, the need for a knowledge of sorcery is to enable the members of the court to understand the influences of the esoteric doctrines that flourished at the time of the Talmud. The statement regarding 70 languages is not to be taken literally, but rather as a linguistic formalism conveying the idea that the judges should have the competence to deal directly with matters involving the use of one or more of the languages common throughout the region.

28. See also Maimonides, *Hilkhot Sanhedrin* 2:1, who omits the requirement entirely.

29. *Sanhedrin* 36b.

30. Maimonides, *Hilkhot Sanhedrin* 2:3.

31. Abravanel, *Perush haTorah*, "BaMidbar," p. 10a. See also Gersonides, *Perush al haTorah al Derekh Biur*, "To'elet," # 12, II:185b; and Malbim, *HaTorah vehaMitzvah* on Num. 11:16. For a discussion of the essential political role of the elders prior to selection for the judiciary, see Hirsch, *The Pentateuch* on Num. 11:16.

32. See Levi, *Yesodot haHalakhah*, p. 55.

33. *Sanhedrin* 88b.

34. See Solomon ben Isaac, *Perush RASHI* [T], on *Sanhedrin* 88b; and Maimonides, *Hilkhot Sanhedrin* 2:8.

35. Abravanel, *Perush haTorah*, "Devarim," p. 34b.
36. See Alsheikh, *Torat Moshe*, "Devarim," p. 118.
37. See Abravanel, *Perush haTorah*, "Devarim," p. 34a.
38. See J. Epstein, *Arukh haShulhan heAtid*, "Melakhim," 71:12, p. 69.

14
Priest, Prophet, King, and Judge

In the examination of the several key institutions that make up the Judaic political constellation derived from the constitutional provisions of Deuteronomy, it has been shown that the fundamental point of contiguity connecting the priest, the prophet, the king, and the judge is the Torah. From the rabbinic perspective, it is quite natural that this should be so, for the Torah is the very basis of Judaic society and is the standard against which all social and political activities are measured and evaluated.

We saw that the priesthood served two essential functions: the sacerdotal and the pedagogic—the latter bringing it into the sphere of law. It was the responsibility of the priesthood to serve as the educated elite and as teacher of the Torah to the people. Because of its special status and pedagogic responsibility, the priesthood was considered to be the prime source of recruitment for the high court. But—as shown—priests who were judges were considered to be serving in their capacity as sages of the Torah, rather than because they were members of the priesthood.

With regard to the prophet, it has been shown that the fulfillment of the prophetic mission was predicated on the capacity of the prophet to abrogate the law on an ad hoc basis for the temporary needs of society at a given time and place. As with the priests, the prophet could also judge—as is evidenced by Samuel, who was both prophet and judge. Yet, here too, the prophet served as judge in a capacity other than when he acted as prophet.

In our examination of the monarchy, it has been shown that the king and judge performed identical executive leadership functions, with the single exception being related to their roles in the dispensation of justice. The king—much like the prophet—was considered to be invested with extralegislative authority and could administer justice on an ad hoc basis in accordance with the demands of the time and place, so as to assure the preservation of order in society.

Viewing the extraordinary ad hoc powers of the prophet and the king as being validated under emergency or special contingency conditions, they may further be considered as complementing the exclusive juridical competence of the judges in matters of law under normal circumstances—that is, at times when the relative tranquility of the polity is assured and the emergency powers of the state do not warrant invocation. However, the maintenance of such a view is problematic, in that it appears to make the judiciary subordinate to both prophet and king—since the latter seem able to exercise their extraordinary powers whenever they determine that the prevailing circumstances justify such measures. As a result, the judiciary could be rendered ineffectual—or even superfluous—at the discretion of those who bear the authority to supersede the normal judicial processes and invoke their ad hoc powers. Consequently, it is difficult to reconcile this consideration with the view propounded earlier that held the judiciary to be the political institution of central importance in rabbinic political theory. Furthermore, it raises a basic challenge to the validity of the separation-of-powers concept, as applied to the biblical constitution.

Perhaps because of these problems—and to strengthen the position of the judiciary within the rabbinic constitutional framework—the sages undertook to extend to the courts the ad hoc authorities already granted to both prophet and king. Thus, the Talmud contains the following statement: "R. Eliezer b. Jacob said: I have heard that the court may impose flagellation and pronounce sentences [of capital punishment] even where not warranted by the Torah; yet not with the intention of disregarding the Torah but in order to safeguard it."[1] RASHI and Nissim Girondi would constrain this authority by precluding its being applied to a violation of one of the court's own legislated rules. That is, the court might inflict excessive punishment on a perpetrator for violating one of the laws of the Torah, because of the exigencies of the period—but not for violation of a rule established by that court, in the first place.[2]

It would appear that there is a substantial basis for consensus among rabbinic writers with regard to the ascription of ad hoc legislative authority to the judiciary in addition to the prophet and king. As discussed earlier in this study, the possession of the ad hoc extralegislative powers by the judiciary is not considered to be a usurpation of the distinctive authority of the king in this field. Both Nissim Girondi and Isaac Abravanel—antagonists on the question of monarchy—appear to agree that the court can only exercise its extraordinary ad hoc authority when deputized by the king. When there is no king—in which case, the political responsibility for maintaining public order falls on the judges—the judge might properly assume the functions of the king, but not his prerogatives. While eliminating the most obvious problems of overlapping jurisdictions between king and court, this view nonetheless leaves the judiciary—in effect—as a potentially coequal organ of government, but not as an actual coequal. This is because even its potential exercise of extraordinary authority would be contingent on the will of the king, or—at a minimum—on the existence of a power vacuum resulting from the absence of a monarch.

However, there is another approach to the issue—exemplified by Zvi Hirsch Chajes—which overcomes the question of overlapping jurisdictions between king and court without subordinating the court, in practice. This approach is based on the view that all judicial matters—whether relating to the laws of the Torah, which clearly fall within the exclusive jurisdictional domain of the court, or to the ad hoc legislative domain of the king—come under the direct cognizance of the court alone. The king himself does not become directly involved in the judicial process, at all. According to Chajes: "It seems to me that the king does not judge the king's law by himself, but must rely upon proceedings in the Sanhedrin; and the Sanhedrin will judge the rebellious not in accordance with the law of the Torah but only in accordance with the laws of the kingdom."[3] This approach suggests that the courts have available to them more than a single legal corpus, and adjudicate a case in accordance with the requirements of the appropriate jurisdictional domain.

This position does not necessarily come into conflict with the views of Nissim and Abravanel, as summarized above. It may be considered as complementing those views, which do not specifically deal with—as does Chajes—the process by which the king's law is adjudicated. However, there is one apparent difficulty with Chajes' position. If his view is carried to its logical conclusion, the king would—in turn—become subordinate to the court, since he would have to rely on it to give effect to his ad hoc authority. This problem is resolved by Eliezer Levi, who describes the actual procedure to be as follows: "All political matters were removed from the jurisdiction of the high court and remained the king's concern. The *Nagid haBayit* (*major domus*) was the representative of the king that took his place in the trial (the king himself did not attend court) . . . and [the proceeding] was conducted in the name of the king."[4] Presumably, by augmenting the court with a special representative of the king, the latter was able to allow the court to deal with "political" cases, while he still retained some coordinate jurisdiction over them.

Recapitulating the fragmentary views expressed by the several rabbinic authorities cited above, the following synthesis may be suggested: The fundamental distinction between king and judge remains that the king alone—when there is in fact a king—has the ad hoc extralegislative authority to exceed the laws of the Torah; however, the king may delegate this authority to the court, to legislate on his behalf in accordance with the demands of the time and place. Where there is no king, the ad hoc extralegislative authority of the king reverts entirely to the court. However, all issues determined to be justiciable—that is, nonpolitical in nature—came under the competence and cognizance of the court, as matters of original jurisdiction. It was incumbent on the court to apply the appropriate law in its deliberations—the law of the Torah, where applicable, or the king's law, when required. Hence, in terms of the ad hoc extralegislative authority of the king and the judge, the authority granted to each institution is identical; what precludes—or at the least reduces—conflict or overlap of these authorities, in practice, is the institutional arrangement whereby they cannot be exercised by both institutions simultaneously.

In examining the relationship between the ad hoc extralegislative powers of the king or the judge and that of the prophet, we encounter an extremely complex problem in rabbinic theory. The complexity of the matter is reflected in what seems to be the diametrically opposed positions taken by Chajes and Malbim on the nature of the judge-prophet relationship. Chajes writes: "We have an undisputed legal principle that it is not necessarily only the acknowledged prophet who may nullify precepts of the Torah temporarily for the purpose of safeguarding it, but that this power has been transmitted to the sages of each generation and the chiefs of the elders of the court, those who sit in the seats of judgement, as well."[5]

From Chajes' statement, it could be concluded that the authority of the prophet and judge is also identical. Malbim—on the other hand—explicitly denies this. He bases his view on a strict construction of the relevant biblical constitutional texts. Thus, the text that establishes the authority of the court states: "According to the law which they shall teach thee ... thou shalt do." However, the text establishing the authority of the prophet is stated in somewhat different terms, and it is on this distinction that Malbim builds his argument. This latter text reads: "A prophet will the Lord ... raise up unto thee ... unto him ye shall hearken." Focusing on the last clause of this passage, Malbim writes: "The word 'unto him' implies 'only unto him'; yet Israel is admonished to pay heed to the sages and especially the court as well. However, there is a special factor involved in the paying of heed to the words of the prophet if he commands the transgression of any of the precepts of the Torah (except for the one concerning idolatry) at a particular point in time, for in this one does not listen to the court, because it is written: Only 'according to the Torah which they shall teach thee.' However, to the prophet you shall absolutely pay heed, even to violate religious precepts."[6]

Malbim's argument appears not only to contradict Chajes, but the Talmud and rabbinic tradition as well—since it has been clearly established that the court is considered to have the same ad hoc authority as the king, to dispense justice in contravention of the precepts of the Torah when this is deemed justified by prevailing circumstances. However, it would be unwarranted—if not presumptuous—to simply dismiss Malbim's position as an aberration on the basis of a superficial examination of his argument.

A clue to Malbim's intent may be derived from the view categorically stated some 200 years earlier by Josiah Pinto, who wrote: "A court is not granted the authority to uproot a commandment of the Torah to lighten the burden of the law, but only in order to intensify it and to establish a safeguard."[7] Seen from the perspective implied by this statement, Malbim's argument takes on a different complexion.

Applying Pinto's principle to Malbim's statement, we find Malbim arguing—

in effect—(as was discussed earlier with respect to Nissim and Abravanel) that the court has no intrinsic ad hoc extralegislative authority. Where it appears to be exercising such authority, it does so only on behalf of the king—either by delegation or by assumption of his authority in his absence. However, even though the court may at times exercise the authority of the king, that authority is in itself qualitatively different from the extralegislative authority of the prophet—for it is the prophet alone who may command one to violate established precepts of the religion, through an apparent lessening of the severity of the law.

The assumption of such a viewpoint is in itself somewhat problematic; it is clear that the authority granted to the prophet is also for the sole purpose of providing a safeguard for the Torah, in accordance with the particular needs of the time and place. Yet, the suggested distinction between the judge and the prophet would tend to negate that intent—by implying that the prophet might undertake to weaken the law, rather than strengthen it.

Indirectly, this problem is addressed by Chajes, who—interestingly—provides a resolution of the difficulty just raised, while at the same time insisting that there are no qualitative distinctions among the ad hoc authorities of the judge, the king, or the prophet. For Chajes, the distinctions among the three institutions—in regard to the authority to legislate on an ad hoc basis in order to safeguard the Torah as the blueprint for the ideal society—is to be found not in the scope of their authorities, but rather in the specified conditions under which their authorities are to be accepted and obeyed. Chajes argues that "the difference between the sage and the prophet is that, with regard to the uprooting of a law of the Torah, the sage's prescription is not honored until its benefit is revealed to the eyes of all, which is not the case with the prophet who is trusted implicitly and from whose uprooting of the law the general welfare will be promoted. And now, in my view, the king of Israel has the same legal status as the acknowledged prophet in all that the king says. For, in accordance with the situation and the condition of the generation, an uprooting of the law may be urgently required, and in the king's view very great benefit may be derived from such an uprooting, since heeding the commands of the king in that which he requires for the administration of the state is at all times of significant benefit, even with regard to matters that merely concern his honor."[8]

In Chajes's view—then—the position stated by Pinto should not be construed as implying that, whereas the sage was precluded from lightening the burden of the law, the prophet is at liberty to do so. On the contrary, both may exercise their ad hoc authority only for the purpose of strengthening the law. However, since the prophet commands allegiance through faith, an apparent lightening of the law at the present time may actually result in great positive benefits that will strengthen the law at some time in the future—at a time beyond that where immediate benefits may be convincingly portrayed to the public. Consequently— as Malbim puts it—the prophet must be obeyed, even if he commands violation of the precepts of Judaism. Insofar as the sage or judge is concerned—since his prescriptions are not accepted on faith alone, but require clear evidence of the benefit to accrue—he may not abrogate the law in such a manner as to weaken it, even if only momentarily. The rationale behind this position may simply be that it is impossible to conclusively demonstrate in advance the benefit to be derived in safeguarding the law by means of a temporary abrogation of it.

Chajes places the king in the same category as the prophet, in respect to the obligation on the part of the public to accept his ad hoc decisions as legitimate—not because he stands in a comparable relation to God, but rather because the king bears the burden of the state, and a properly ordered state is essential for the general welfare. Chajes does not give any specific indication as to whether the king would have the same authority as the prophet with regard to a lessening of the burden of the laws of the Torah. An assumption that this is implied by his statement that the king possesses the same legal competence as the prophet would create additional difficulties, since the king—not being under divine guidance, as is the prophet—could undermine the entire Torah-oriented structure of the society, if he were to be obeyed without question in this regard. A thorough examination of this complex issue with all its attendant ramifications would lead far beyond the immediate focus of this study, and must be deferred to another work.

While the resolution of the issue discussed above would be of great concern to an understanding of the theoretically ideal biblical state, the relative status of the judiciary is of greater immediate concern in the exploration of rabbinic political theory. As noted earlier, the judiciary alone of all the constitutional elements of government has continuity in the absence of a territorial state (without which there is no king) or central shrine—the Holy Temple (without which there is no functioning priesthood and—since the destruction of the First Commonwealth—no longer any prophecy as such, either). It is in this sense that the judicial institution is central to the rabbinic political scheme.

The relative status of the judiciary can only be fully appreciated if it is viewed in the context of an institution having both political as well as judicial functions and authority. Zacharias Frankel places the courts in their appropriate context, when he notes retrospectively: "At that time there stood at the head of the community, the Sanhedrin; and this term is, in its signification, one with assembly, and according to the Greek writers the Council of Elders in Rome was also so called, and this is the name accorded to every assembly of municipal and state judges."[9]

If we view the High Court as a senate in the classical sense of the term, the political significance of the following authority assigned to the court by the Talmud becomes self-evident: "A tribe, a false prophet and a High Priest can only be tried by a court of seventy-one. War of free choice can be waged only by the authority of a court of seventy-one. No addition to the city of Jerusalem or the Temple can be sanctioned except by a court of seventy-one."[10]

In the context of the first clause of this statement of law, the court is clearly depicted in the role of the supreme national tribunal—which alone has the competence to impeach the prophet or high priest, as well as to try the major political subdivision of the state as an entity. The final clause may be seen as giving to the high court the ultimate voice over the status of the capital of the state—serving as a potential restraint on the king (who might be tempted to enlarge the city for personal political advantage), as well as a restraint on the priests (who might attempt to enhance their status as guardians and functionaries of the central religious shrine in the capital).

It is the middle clause that particularly merits further examination because it—perhaps more than any other—exemplifies the special legislative nature of the Sanhedrin. In this regard, the matter of a "war of free choice" is presented in another place in the Talmud, where it is mentioned in the context of the authorities of the king. It states there: "He may lead forth [the army] to a voluntary war on the decision of a court of seventy-one."[11] This is tantamount to a stipulation that the king cannot issue a declaration of war on his own authority—a procedure not uncommon under contemporary constitutions, which may require that the decision to go to war be ratified by the national legislative body. However, the talmudic rule goes beyond the matter of declarations; it restricts the king's authority to take effective action, as well. It is concerned with both the de jure and de facto aspects of a decision to make war. As will be seen, this is intended as part of a deliberate effort to ensure that political decisions having major effects on the people as a whole are determined beforehand to be socially beneficial, so that the exercise of political power does not become self-serving or an end in itself. Because of this approach to the exercise of political power, the talmudic rule clearly relates to a "war of free choice" or "voluntary war." It relates only to the initiation of hostilities where the element of choice is present. It is not intended to hamper the king in carrying out his primary responsibility of preserving the political society from external as well as internal enemies.

Attributing such an intent to the talmudic rule is largely contingent on the definition assigned to the term "voluntary war." In RASHI's view, "Every war is considered voluntary except for the wars of Joshua which were fought in order to conquer the Land of Israel."[12] It seems evident that, if this or a similarly broad definition is applied to the talmudic rule, the king would be unable to conduct even a defensive war against an aggressor state; that is, he could not take action without first receiving the assent of the Sanhedrin. This would place a clearly undesirable—if not dangerous and counterproductive—limitation on the king's freedom of action in responding to national security threats in an expeditious manner. An extreme position in this regard is apparently held by Jonathan of Lunel, who—in a fragmentary comment—reiterates RASHI's definition, with the following explanation: "That is to say, they would consult with fifty-five great sanhedrins as to whether or not they should go out to war."[13] This seems to imply that something on the order of a national referendum of tribunals—including the national, tribal, and major municipal courts—would be required to make the final determination to go to war.

Therefore, from a practical standpoint at the least, the latitude given to the king with regard to war-making powers must be somewhat expanded. Accordingly, in his restatement of the law, Maimonides provides that the king does have the authority to initiate a "mandatory war," which is defined to include "the defense of Israel against the oppressor that comes against them."[14] In all other cases, the king's authority to conscript an army is subject to the acquiescence of the Sanhedrin. Since the Talmud does not provide any rationale for the distinction between mandatory and voluntary wars—insofar as the authority of the court is concerned—we can assume that it considered the reasons to be self-evident.

However, Reuven Margaliot provides a rationale that reaches to the very core and essence of rabbinic political philosophy. He argues—in effect—that, since the fundamental purpose of the state is to preserve political society under conditions of order adequate to provide the tranquility necessary for man to occupy himself with his self-perfection, any arbitrary decision by the executive leadership of the state to jeopardize the lives of many of the members of society must first be weighed on the scales of justice.[15] Margaliot places the decision to go to a voluntary war in the same category as the capital trial of a large group of people. It becomes the responsibility of the court to determine whether the social good to be realized by the war balances the mortal dangers to be faced by the people who must do the fighting and dying. The people are not to become mere instruments of the state; this would subvert the very purpose of the state, which is to be the instrument of the people in securing a well-ordered society. The relegation of the responsibility for authorizing such a war to "a court of seventy-one"—the senate of the sages—serves as a counter to the otherwise unrestrained capability of the ruler to endanger the public for private purposes.

It is thus the judiciary that becomes the arbiter of the public interest, against the monarchy.[16] Furthermore, because of its special responsibility for and relationship to the people, the judiciary is recruited from the people—on the basis of merit, wisdom, and leadership ability as the primary requisites.

There can be little doubt that the heavy skewing of traditional rabbinic political theory in favor of the judicial system largely results from the corollary view that the rabbis are the heirs and bearers of the tradition of the sages—of the Sanhedrin. Sages and scholars are viewed as blessings to the community, whereas the king and high priest—and even the prophet—are considered necessary only in a rather negative sense. This perspective is perhaps nowhere expressed so poignantly as in the talmudic dictum that specifies the order to be followed in arranging for the ransom of persons taken captive by an enemy. "Our Rabbis taught: . . . A scholar takes precedence over a king of Israel, for if a scholar dies there is none to replace him, while if a king dies, all Israel are eligible for kingship. A king takes precedence over a High Priest. . . . A High Priest takes precedence over a prophet."[17]

While the emphasis on the judges and sages as the cornerstones of society may be at the expense of the other elements of political society, the traditional viewpoint on the matter should not be construed as mere parochialism. Throughout the literature, the rabbinic writers never lose sight of the ultimate purpose of the political society: that is, to secure justice and social peace. It is justice that remains the central concern, and it is in the dispensation of justice that man transcends the natural, and is seen as participating in the divine work. As the Talmud puts it, "every judge who renders proper verdicts for even a single hour, Scripture considers him to be at such a level as if he had become a partner with the Holy One in the act of creation."[18]

However—as has been shown—it is the Torah considered as the embodiment of the divine will that is the true centerpiece of rabbinic political theory. The desire to bring about the realization of a society built on the principles and precepts of the Torah motivates rabbinic thinking, and provides the unifying thread connecting its diverse skeins. This factor makes all rabbinic political theorists contemporaries—the time gap between them being rendered irrelevant by the continuum of tradition.

This brief study has attempted to shed some light on but a few of the many aspects of rabbinic political thought, which holds—as a fundamental tenet—the belief that "the moral laws of the Torah, the concepts of universal justice of the prophets, and the religious and spiritual philosophy of saints and sages throughout the ages can serve as the medium for the unification of knowledge and as a blueprint for an ideal society."[19]

NOTES

1. *Sanhedrin* 46a; *Yevamot* 90b. See also Maimonides, *Hilkhot Sanhedrin* 24:4; and Moses of Coucy, *Sefer Mitzvot Gadol*, "Lo Taaseh," # 208, p. 65a.

2. See Solomon ben Isaac, *Perush RASHI* [T], on *Sanhedrin* 46a; and Nissim Girondi, *Hiddushei haRAN aL Sanhedrin*, ad loc.

3. Chajes, *Torat Neviyyim*, p. 49.

4. Levi, *Yesodot haHalakhah*, p. 76.

5. Chajes, *Torat Neviyyim*, p. 31.

6. Malbim, *HaTorah vehaMitzvah* on Deut. 18:15.

7. Pinto, *Meor Einayim* on *Yevamot* 90b.

8. Chajes, *Torat Neviyyim*, p. 43.

9. Frankel, *Darkei haMishnah*, p. 9.

10. *Sanhedrin* 2a.

11. *Sanhedrin* 20b.

12. Solomon ben Isaac, *Perush RASHI* [T], on *Sanhedrin* 2a. See also Maimonides, *Perush HaMishnayot* on *Sanhedrin* 1:5; and Obadiah of Bertinoro, *Perush R. Obadiah miBertinoro* on *Sanhedrin* 1:5.

13. Jonathan of Lunel, *Perush Rabbenu Yehonatan haKohen miLunel al haMishnah vehaRIF leMassekhet Sanhedrin*, "Sanhedrin" 1:10, pp. 7–8.

14. Maimonides, *Hilkhot Melakhim* 5:1–2. See also Meiri, *Bet haBehirah al Massekhet Sanhedrin* on *Sanhedrin* 15b, p. 50.

15. Margaliot, *Margaliot haYam: Sanhedrin* I, # 29, p. 8.

16. See Levi, *Yesodot haHalakhah*, p. 104.
17. *Horayot* 13a.
18. *Shabbat* 10a.
19. Belkin, *Essays in Traditional Jewish Thought*, p. 14.

Bibliography

BIBLICAL TEXTS

Hamishah Humshei Torah. 2 vols. Edited by Solomon Z. Netter. Tel Aviv, 1958. This is a corrected edition of *Mikraot Gedolot* published in Vienna, 1859.
Humash Mikraot Gedolot. 5 vols. New York, n.d.
Mikraot Gedolot: Neviyyim uKetuvim. 10 vols. Reprint of Lublin edition. New York, n.d.
Soncino Books of the Bible. 14 vols. Edited by A. Cohen. Surrey and London, 1947–.
The Pentateuch and Haphtorahs. 2nd edition. Edited by Dr. J. H. Hertz. London, 1966.
The Twenty-Four Books of the Old Testament. 2 vols. Translated and revised by Alexander Harkavy. New York, 1916.

TALMUDIC TEXTS

The Babylonian Talmud. 18 vols. Edited by I. Epstein. London, 1978.
Sefer Ein Yaacov. 4 vols. New York, 1955.
Shishah Sidrei Mishnah. 3 vols. Eshkol edition. Jerusalem, 1955.
Talmud Bavli veYerushalmi. 20 vols. New York, 1959.
Talmud Yerushalmi. 3 vols. Zhitomir, 1866; facsimile edition: Jerusalem, 1968.
Tosefta. (Printed in *Talmud Bavli veYerushalmi.*)

MIDRASHIC TEXTS

Avot deRabbi Natan. (Printed in *Talmud Bavli veYerushalmi.*)
The Fathers According to Rabbi Nathan. Translated by Judah Goldin. New Haven, 1955.
Mekhilta. (Printed in Malbim, *HaTorah vehaMitzvah.*)
Mekilta de-Rabbi Ishmael. 3 vols. Edited and translated by J. Z. Lauterbach. Philadelphia, 1949.
Midrash Agadat Bereshit. Warsaw, 1876; facsimile edition: Jerusalem, 1962.

Midrash Rabbah. 2 vols. Jerusalem, 1969.
Midrash Tanhumah. 2 vols. Edited by Solomon Buber. Vilna, n.d.; facsimile edition: Jerusalem, 1964.
Midrash Tanhumah. 2 vols. Edited by Abraham M. Rosen. Warsaw, 1878; reprinted: New York, 1970.
Pesikta Rabbati deRav Kahana. Jerusalem, 1969.
Pirkei Rabbi Eliezer. Warsaw, 1852; facsimile edition: New York, 1946.
Sifra. (Printed in Malbim, *HaTorah vehaMitzvah.*)
Sifre al Bamidbar ve'al Devarim. (Printed in Malbim, *HaTorah vehaMitzvah.*)
Yalkut Shimeoni. 2 vols. New York, 1960.

MISCELLANEOUS RABBINIC AND OTHER WORKS

Aaron HaLevi of Barcelona (c. 1300). *Sefer haHinukh.* Edited by Charles B. Chavel. Jerusalem, 1966.
Abravanel, Isaac (1437–1508). *Nahlat Avot.* Jerusalem, 1970.
———. *Perush Abravanel.* (Printed in Maimonides, *Moreh Nevukhim.*)
———. *Perush al Neviyyim Aharonim.* Jerusalem, 1949.
———. *Perush al Neviyyim Rishonim.* Jerusalem, 1955.
———. *Perush al Neviyyim uKetuvim.* Tel Aviv, 1960.
———. *Perush haTorah.* Warsaw, 1862; facsimile edition: Jerusalem, n.d.
Albo, Joseph (c. 1420). *Sefer Ha'Ikkarim: Book of Principles.* 5 vols. Edited by Isaac Husik. Philadelphia, 1946.
Alfasi, Isaac ben Jacob [RIF] (1013–1103). *Hilkhot haRIF.* (Printed in *Talmud Bavli veYerushalmi.*)
Alsheikh, Moses ben Hayyim (c. 1507–c. 1600). *Torat Moshe.* 2 vols. Warsaw, 1865; facsimile edition: New York, 1966.
Almosnino, Moses (c. 1515–c. 1580). *Pirkei Moshe.* Jerusalem, 1970.
Altschuler, David (18th cent.). *Metzudat David.* (Printed in *Mikraot Gedolot.*)
Anatoli, Jacob (13th cent.). *Malmad haTalmidim.* Lyck, 1866; facsimile edition: Israel, 1968.
Arama, Isaac ben Moses (c. 1420–1494). *Akedat Yitzhak.* 6 vols. Tel Aviv, 1984.
Asher ben Jehiel [ROSH] (c. 1250–1327). *Perush Rabbenu Asher.* (Printed in *Talmud Bavli veYerushalmi.*)
———. *Tosafot haROSH al Sanhedrin.* Edited by Shraga Wilman. New York, 1969.
Azulai, Hayyim Joseph David [HIDA] (1724–1806). *Pnei David.* Jerusalem, 1959.
Babad, Joseph (1800–1874/75). *Minhat Hinukh.* 2 vols. New York, 1966.
Bahya ben Asher (d.:c. 1340). *Biur al haTorah.* 3 vols. Edited by Charles B. Chavel. Jerusalem, 1966–1968.
———. *Kitvei Rabbenu Bahya.* Edited by Charles B. Chavel. Jerusalem, 1970.
Belkin, Samuel (1911–1976). *Essays in Traditional Jewish Thought.* New York, 1956.
Ben-Amitai, Jacob. *Perakim beToldot haRaayon haMedini.* Ramat Gan, 1967.
Benamozegh, Elijah (1822–1900). *Yisrael vehaEnoshut.* Translated from the French by Simon Marcus. Jerusalem, 1967.
Berav, Jacob (c. 1474–1546). *Sefer Sheilot uTeshuvot.* Jerusalem, 1958.
Berlin, Naftali Zvi (1817–1893). *HaAmek Davar.* 5 vols. New York, 1972.
Botan, Abraham di (1545–1588). *Lehem Mishneh.* (Printed in Maimonides, *Mishneh Torah.*)

Chajes, Zvi Hirsch (1805–1855). *Torat Neviyyim* in *Kol Sifrei MAHARITZ Chajes*. 2 vols. Jerusalem, 1958.
Crescas, Hasdai (c. 1340–1410). *Or haShem*. Ferrara, 1555; facsimile edition: Jerusalem, 1970.
David ben Samuel HaLevi (1586–1667). *Divrei David*. Jerusalem, 1958.
———. *Turei Zahav*. (Printed in Karo, *Shulhan Arukh*.)
Diskin, Moses Joshua Judah Leib (1817–1898). *Hiddushei MAHARIL Diskin*. 3 vols. Jerusalem, 1971–1975.
Eidels, Samuel Eliezer [MAHARSHAH] (1555–1631). *Hiddushei Aggadot*. (Printed in *Talmud Bavli veYerushalmi*.)
———. *Hiddushei Halakhot* (Printed in *Talmud Bavli veYerushalmi*.)
———. *Sefer Hiddushei haMAHARSHAH al haTorah*. Edited by Zvi Hirsch Hacohen. Jerusalem, 1969.
Eldad, Israel. *Hegyonot Mikrah*. Jerusalem, 1958.
Eleazar ben Judah of Worms (c. 1165–c. 1230). *Perush haRokeah al haTorah*. 3 vols. Bnei Brak, 1981.
Eliezer of Beaugency (12th cent.). *Perush Yehezhel uTrei-Assar*. Warsaw, 1909; facsimile edition: Jerusalem, 1968.
Elijah ben Solomon of Vilna [HaGRA] (1720–1797). *Aderet Eliyahu*. Edited by Elijah Landau. Jerusalem, n.d.
Emden, Jacob (1697–1776). *Hiddushim veHagahot*. (Printed in *Talmud Bavli ve-Yerushalmi*.)
Ephraim Solomon of Luntshits (1550–1619). *Kli Yakkar*. (Printed in *Mikraot Gedolot*.)
Epstein, Barukh (1860–1942). *Barukh SheAmar: Pirkei Avot*. Tel Aviv, 1965.
———. *Torah Temimah*. 5 vols. New York, 1962.
———. *Tosefet Berakhah*. 5 vols. Tel Aviv, 1964.
Epstein, Isidore (1894–1962). *Judaism: A Historical Presentation*. London, 1959.
Epstein, Jehiel M. (1829–1908). *Arukh haShulhan heAtid: Sanhedrin*. Jerusalem, 1969.
Eybeschutz, Jonathan (1690/95–1764). *Tifferet Yehonatan*. Jerusalem, 1966.
Federbusch, Simon (1892–1969). *Mishpat haMelukhah beYisrael*. Jerusalem, 1973.
———, ed. *Torah uMelukhah*. Jerusalem, 1961.
Finkelstein, Louis (1895–). *The Pharisees: The Sociological Background of Their Faith*. Philadelphia, 1966.
Firer, Ben-Zion. *Hegyonah shel Torah*. 5 vols. Tel Aviv, 1967.
Frankel, Zacharias (1801–1875). *Darkei haMishnah*. Tel Aviv, 1959.
Gersonides, Levi [RALBAG] (1288–1344). *Milhamot haShem*. Facsimile of edition of 1560: n.p., n.d.
———. *Perush haRALBAG*. (Printed in *Mikraot Gedolot*.)
———. *Perush al haTorah al Derekh Biur*. 2 vols. Venice, 1547; facsimile edition: n.p., n.d.
Gipstein, Joshua (1883–1960). *Daat Torah: Biur al haTorah beDerekh haHigayon*. 2nd edition. Tel Aviv, n.d.
Gordin, Abba (1887–1964). *HaMAHARAL miPrague*. Ramat Gan, 1960.
Gordon, Samuel Leib (1865–1933). *Sefer Devarim*. Tel Aviv, 1972.
Gulak, Asher (1881–1940). *Yesodei haMishpat haIvri*. 2 vols. Tel Aviv, 1967.
HaLevi, Judah (c. 1075–1141). *Book of Kuzari*. Translated by H. Hirschfield. New York, 1946.

Hananel ben Hushiel (d. 1055/56). *Perush Rabbenu Hananel.* (Printed in *Talmud Bavli veYerushalmi.*)

———. *Perushei Rabbenu Hananel al haTorah.* Edited by Charles B. Chavel. Jerusalem, 1972.

Hanokh Zundel ben Joseph (d. 1867). *Anaf Yosef.* (Printed in *Sefer Ein Yaacov* and *Midrash Rabbah.*)

———. *Etz Yosef.* (Printed in *Sefer Ein Yaacov* and *Midrash Rabbah.*)

Hayyim ben Isaac "Or Zarua" (13th cent.). *Sefer Sheilot uTeshuvot.* Jerusalem, 1960.

Hen, Abraham (1878–1958). *BeMalkhut haYahadut.* 3 vols. Jerusalem, 1959–1970.

Heschel, Abraham J. (1907–1972). *The Prophets.* Philadelphia, 1962.

Hezekiah ben Manoah (13th cent.). *Hizkuni.* Edited by Charles B. Chavel. Jerusalem, 1982.

Hirsch, Samson Raphael (1808–1888). *Chapters of the Fathers.* Translated by G. Hirschler. New York, 1967.

———. *The Nineteen Letters of Ben Uziel.* Translated by B. Drachman. New York, 1942.

———. *The Pentateuch.* 5 vols. Translated by Isaac Levy. New York, 1971.

Hiyyun, Joseph (15th cent.). *Millei deAvot.* In *Perushei Rishonim leMassekhet Avot.* Jerusalem, 1973.

Hoffmann. David Zvi (1843–1921). *HaMishnah haRishonah.* Berlin, 1913; facsimile edition: Jerusalem, 1970.

———. *Sefer Devarim.* 2 vols. Tel Aviv, 1960.

Ibn Attar, Hayyim (1696–1743). *Or haHayyim.* (Printed in *Mikraot Gedolot.*)

Ibn Daud, Abraham (c. 1110–1180). *Sefer ha-Qabbalah: The Book of Tradition.* Edited by G. D. Cohen. Philadelphia, 1967.

Ibn Ezra, Abraham (1092–1167). *Perushei haTorah leR. Abraham ibn Ezra.* 3 vols. Edited by Asher Weiser. Jerusalem, 1976.

———. *Perush haKatzar leSefer Shemot.* (Printed in *Perushei haTorah leR. Abraham ibn Ezra.*)

———. *Perush Ibn Ezra.* (Printed in *Mikraot Gedolot.*)

Ibn Habib, Jacob (c. 1445–1515/16). *Hiddushei haKotev.* (Printed in *Sefer Ein Yaacov.*)

Ibn Kaspi, Joseph (c. 1280–c. 1340). *Matzref leKesef.* Vol. 2 of *Mishneh Kesef.* Cracow, 1906; facsimile edition: Jerusalem, 1970.

Ibn Nagdela, Samuel [Shemuel haNagid] (993–1056). *Ben Mishlei.* Edited by S. Abramson. Tel Aviv, 1948.

Ibn Shem Tov, Shem Tov (15th cent.). *Perush Shem Tov.* (Printed in Maimonides, *Moreh Nevukhim.*)

Ibn Zimra, David [RADBAZ] (1479–1573). *Perush haRADBAZ.* (Printed in Maimonides, *Mishneh Torah.*)

Isaac ben Sheshet Perfet [RIBASH] (1326–1408). *Sheilot uTeshuvot Bar Sheshet.* New York, 1954.

Jacob ben Asher (c. 1270–c. 1343). *Arbah Turim.* 7 vols. New York, 1959.

———. *Perush Baal haTurim al haTorah.* Edited by Jacob K. Reinitz. Bnai Brak, 1971.

———. *Perush haTur haArokh.* Jerusalem, 1969.

Jacobson, B. S. *Meditations on the Torah.* Translated by Z. V. Gotthold. Tel Aviv, 1956.

Jaffe, Mordecai (c. 1535–1612). *Levush haOra.* (Printed in *Otzar Perushim al haTorah.*)

Jastrow, Marcus. *A Dictionary of the Targumim, the Talmud Babli and Yerushalmi, and the Midrashic Literature.* 2 vols. New York, 1950.

Jonathan ben David of Lunel (1135–after 1210). *Perush Rabbenu Yehonatan haKohen*

miLunel al haMishnah vehaRIF leMassekhet Sanhedrin. Edited by Judah Kuperberg. In Vol. 2 of Sanhedrei Gedolah. Jerusalem, 1969.
Josephus Flavius [Joseph ben Mattathias] (c. 38–after 100). Complete Works of Josephus. Grand Rapids, 1977.
Judah ben Asher (1270–1349). Zikhron Yehudah. Berlin, 1846; facsimile edition: Jerusalem, 1968.
Judah Loew ben Bezalel [MAHARAL] (c. 1525—1609). Be'er haGolah. New York, 1953.
———. Derekh Hayyim. n.p., n.d.
———. Gur Aryeh. (Printed in Otzar Perushim al haTorah.)
———. Netivot Olam. 2 vols. Tel Aviv, 1956.
———. Tifferet Yisrael. Tel Aviv, n.d.
Kahana, Kalman (1910–). The Case for Jewish Civil Law in the Jewish State. London, 1960.
Kara, Joseph (b.:c. 1060–1070). Perush R. Yosef Kara. (Printed in Mikraot Gedolot: Neviyyim uKetuvim.)
Karo, Joseph (1488–1575). Bet Yosef. (Printed in Jacob ben Asher, Arbah Turim.)
———. Kesef Mishneh. (Printed in Maimonides, Mishneh Torah.)
———. Shulhan Arukh. 10 vols. New York, 1959.
Katz, Meshullam. Ikkar Tosafot Yom Tov. (Printed in Shishah Sidrei Mishnah.)
Katz, Reuven. Duda'ei Reuven. 2 vols. Jerusalem, 1976.
Katzenellenbogen, Samuel Judah [MAHARSHIK] (1521–1597). Shnaim Assar Derushim. Jerusalem, 1959. (Edition erroneously attributed to MAHARI Mintz.)
Kimhi, David [RADAK] (c. 1160–1235). Perush haRADAK. (Printed in Mikraot Gedolot.)
———. Perush RADAK al haTorah. Edited by Abraham Ginzberg. Pressburg, 1842; facsimile edition: Jerusalem, 1968.
———. Sefer haSharashim. Berlin, 1847; facsimile edition: New York, 1948.
Kluger, Solomon ben Judah Aaron (1785–1869). Imrei Shefer al haTorah. Lemberg, 1895; facsimile edition: Israel, 1971.
Kranz, Jacob (1741–1804). Mishlei Yaacov. Edited by M. Nussbaum. Israel, n.d.
Kuntzler, Saul. Toldot haMahshavah haMedinit. Vol. 1. Tel Aviv, 1962.
Leibowitz, Nehama. Studies in the Weekly Sidra: 5715 Annual. Jerusalem, 1958.
Lerner, Ralph. "Moses Maimonides." In History of Political Philosophy. Edited by Leo Strauss and Joseph Cropsey. Chicago, 1963.
Levi, Eliezer. Yesodot haHalakhah. Tel Aviv, 1967.
Lewittes, Mendell. The Nature and History of Jewish Law. New York, 1966.
Luzzatto, Moses Hayyim (1707–1746). Mesillat Yesharim: The Path of the Upright. Edited and translated by Mordecai M. Kaplan. Philadelphia, 1966.
Luzzatto, Samuel David [SHADAL] (1800–1865). Perush SHADAL al Hamishah Humshei Torah. Tel Aviv, 1965.
Maimon, Judah L. (1875–1962). Hiddush haSanhedrin beMedinatenu haMehudeshet. Jerusalem, 1967.
Maimonides, Moses [RAMBAM] (1135–1204). The Guide for the Perplexed. Translated by M. Friedlander. New York, 1946.
———. Mishneh Torah. 6 vols. New York, 1956. (Hilkhot citations in the Notes refer to this code.)
———. Moreh Nevukhim. Jerusalem, 1960.
———. Perush haMishnayot. (Printed in Talmud Bavli veYerushalmi.)

———. *Sefer haMitzvot*. New York, 1955.
———. *Treatise on Logic*. Edited and translated by Israel Efros. New York, 1938.
Malakhi ben Jacob haKohen (d.:c. 1785–1790). *Yad Malakhi*. Jerusalem, 1964.
Malbim, Meir Leibush (1809–1879). *HaTorah vehaMitzvah*. 2 vols. Jerusalem, 1956.
———. *Mikra'ei Kodesh*. 2 vols. Jerusalem, 1956.
Manasseh ben Israel (1604–1657). *The Conciliator*. New York, 1972.
Mantel, Hugo. *Mehkarim beToldot haSanhedrin*. Tel Aviv, 1969.
———. *Studies in the History of the Sanhedrin*. Cambridge, 1961.
Margaliot, Reuven (1889–1971). *Margaliot haYam: Sanhedrin*. 2 vols. Jerusalem, 1958.
Margoliot, Moses (d. 1781). *Mar'eh haPanim*. (Printed in *Talmud Yerushalmi*.)
———. *Pnei Moshe*. (Printed in *Talmud Yerushalmi*.)
Mecklenburg, Jacob Zvi (1785–1865). *HaKtav vehaKabbalah*. 2 vols. Jerusalem, 1969.
Meir Simhah haKohen (1853–1926). *Meshekh Hokhmah*. Jerusalem, 1926.
———. *Or Sameah*. (Printed in Maimonides, *Mishneh Torah*.)
Meiri, Menahem (c. 1249–c. 1310). *Bet haBehirah al Massekhet Sanhedrin*. 2nd edition. Jerusalem, 1965.
———. *Perush haMeiri al Sefer Mishlei*. Edited by M. M. Meshi Zahav. Jerusalem, 1969.
———. *Sefer Bet haBehirah: Perush Massekhet Avot*. New York, 1952.
———. *Teshuvot Rabbenu haMeiri*. Edited by S. A. Wertheimer and I. H. Daiches. Jerusalem, 1958.
Melamed, Ezra Zion. *Mavo leSifrut haTalmud*. Jerusalem, 1954.
Mendelssohn, Moses (1729–1786). *Biur Millot haHigayon*. Berlin, 1925.
Meshorer, Shabbetai (1641–1718). *Siftei Hakhamim*. (Printed in *Otzar Perushim al haTorah*.)
Meyuhas ben Elijah (c. 1150–c. 1200). *Perush al Sefer Devarim*. Edited by Michael Katz. Jerusalem, 1968.
Mindel, Nissan. *The Commandments*. 5th edition. New York, 1964.
Minkin, Jacob S. *The World of Maimonides*. New York, 1957.
Mizrahi, Elijah (d.:c. 1525). *Perush R. Eliyahu Mizrahi*. (Printed in *Otzar Perushim al haTorah*.)
Montefiore, C. G., and H. Loewe, eds. *A Rabbinic Anthology*. Philadelphia, 1960.
Moses of Coucy (13th cent.). *Sefer Mitzvot Gadol*. 2 vols. Venice, 1547; facsimile edition: Jerusalem, 1961.
Munk, Eli. *The Seven Days of the Beginning*. New York, 1974.
Nahmanides, Moses [RAMBAN] (1194–1270). *Hiddushei haRAMBAN leMassekhtot Makkot, Avodah Zarah, Sanhedrin*. Edited by M. Hirschler. Jerusalem, 1970.
———. *Perush RAMBAN*. (Printed in *Mikraot Gedolot*.)
———. *Perushei haRAMBAN al haTorah*. 2 vols. Edited by Charles B. Chavel. Jerusalem, 1969.
———. *Perushei haRAMBAN al Neviyyim uKetuvim*. Edited by Charles B. Chavel. Jerusalem, 1964.
Netanyahu, Ben-Zion. *Don Isaac Abravanel: Statesman and Philosopher*. Philadelphia, 1953.
Netter, Solomon A. (19th cent.). *Perush al Ibn Ezra*. (Printed in *Hamishah Humshei Torah*.)
———. *Perush al Targum Yonatan*. (Printed in *Hamishah Humshei Torah*.)
Nissim Girondi [RAN] (d.:c. 1380). *Hiddushei haRAN al Sanhedrin*. New York, n.d.
———. *Perush al haTorah*. Edited by Leon A. Feldman. Jerusalem, 1968.

———. *Perush haRAN al Nedarim.* (Printed in *Talmud Bavli ve Yeru-shalmi.*)
———. *Shnaim Assar Derushim.* Jerusalem, 1959.
Obadiah of Bertinoro (c. 1450–1510). *Perush R. Obadiah miBertinoro.* (Printed in *Shishah Sidrei Mishnah.*)
———. *Sefer Amar Neke.* Czernowitz, 1857; facsimile edition: New York, 1969.
Otzar Mamarim al haTorah. 2nd edition. Edited by E. L. Lavia. Jerusalem, 1962.
Otzar Perushim al haTorah. 2 vols. New York, 1965.
Pinto, Josiah (c. 1565–1648). *Meor Einayim.* (Printed in *Sefer Ein Yaacov.*)
Rabinowitz, Abraham H. *TARYAG.* Jerusalem, 1967.
Rackman, Emmanuel. *One Man's Judaism.* New York, 1970.
Rapa, Abraham of Porto (d. 1596). *Minhah Belulah.* Verona, n.d.; facsimile edition: Jerusalem, 1972.
Reider, Joseph, *Deuteronomy.* Philadelphia, 1948.
Rivlin, Eliezer (1889–1942). "Takkanot Tzibbur veSidrei Mishpat." In *HaMishpat haIvri.* Second series. Tel Aviv, 1927.
Rosenberg, Samuel. *Beer Shemuel al haTorah.* 2 vols. Jerusalem, 1973.
Saadia ben Joseph al-Fayyumi [Saadia Gaon] (882–942). *The Book of Beliefs and Opinions.* Translated by Samuel Rosenblatt. New Haven, 1951.
———. *Perushei Rabbenu Saadia Gaon al haTorah.* Edited by J. O. Kapah. Jerusalem, 1963.
Samuel ben Hofni Gaon (d. 1013/1014). *Perush haTorah leR. Shemuel ben Hofni Gaon.* Edited by Aaron Greenbaum. Jerusalem, 1979.
Samuel ben Meir [RASHBAM] (c. 1080–c. 1158). *Perush RASHBAM.* (Printed in *Mikraot Gedolot.*)
———. *Perush haRASHBAM haIkkari.* (Printed in *Talmud Bavli veYerushalmi.*)
———. *Perush haTorah asher Katav haRASHBAM.* Edited by David Rozin. Breslau, 1882; reprint: New York, 1949.
Schimmel, Harry C. *The Oral Law.* New York, 1973.
Sforno, Obadiah (1475–1550). *Biur al haTorah.* Edited by Zeev Gottlieb. Jerusalem, 1980.
———. *Perush R. Obadiah Sforno.* (Printed in *Mikraot Gedolot.*)
Shaare Teshubah: Responsa of the Geonim. Edited by W. Leiter. New York, 1946.
Shalom, Abraham (d. 1492). *Nevei Shalom.* 2 vols. Venice, 1575; facsimile edition: Jerusalem, 1967.
Sirkes, Joel (1561–1640). *Bayit Hadash.* (Printed in Jacob ben Asher, *Arbah Turim.*)
Sofer, Abraham (1815–1871). *Sefer Ktav Sofer al haTorah.* Tel Aviv, 1966.
Sofer, Moses (1762–1839). *Sefer Torat Moshe.* 2 vols. New York, 1960.
Solomon ben Isaac [RASHI] (1040–1105). *Perush RASHI.* (Distinguished in the Notes by [M]. Printed in *Mikraot Gedolot.*)
———. *Perush RASHI.* (Distinguished in the Notes by [T]. Printed in *Talmud Bavli veYerushalmi.*)
———. *Perushei RASHI al haTorah.* 2nd edition. Edited by Charles B. Chavel. Jerusalem, 1983.
———. *RASHI al haTorah.* 2nd edition. Edited by Abraham Berliner. Jerusalem, 1970.
Targum Onkelos. (Printed in *Mikraot Gedolot.*)
Targum Yonatan. (Printed in *Mikraot Gedolot.*)
Tosafot. (Printed in *Talmud Bavli veYerushalmi.*)
Tosafot Yeshanim. (Printed in *Talmud Bavli veYerushalmi.*)

Uzeda, Samuel di (c. 1540). *Midrash Shemuel*. Jerusalem, 1964.
Vidal Yom Tov of Tolosa (14th cent.). *Maggid Mishneh*. (Printed in Karo, *Shulhan Arukh*.)
Volozhiner, Isaac (d. 1849). *Milei deAvot*. Edited by Solomon Hillel. Vilna, 1888; facsimile: n.p., n.d.
Volozhiner, Joseph Duber (19th cent.). *Sefer Bet haLevi*. Warsaw, 1888; facsimile edition: n.p., n.d.
Werblowsky, R. J. Z., and Geoffrey Wigoder, eds. *The Encyclopedia of the Jewish Religion*. New York, 1966.
Yom Tov ben Abraham Ishbili [RITBA] (c. 1250–1330). *Sheilot uTeshuvot*. Edited by J. Kapah. Jerusalem, 1969.

Index

Aaron HaLevi of Barcelona, 49n, 84n, 94n, 121n
Abbahu, Rabbi, 14n
Abravanel, Isaac, 12, 50n, 58n, 69n, 70n, 71n, 82n, 83n, 89–93, 95n, 100, 103n, 104n, 105n, 118n, 126, 129n, 130n, 133, 135, 137–138, 139n, 140n, 142–143, 145
Aha, Rabbi, 2
Akavaiah ben Mahalalel, 29n
Akiva, Rabbi, 11, 13, 16n, 20, 27n, 40n
Albo, Joseph, 21–22, 32, 37n, 38n, 39n, 74, 82n, 89, 94n
Alfasi, Isaac, 120n
Alsheikh, Moses, 95n, 105n, 139n, 140n
Altschuler, David, 49n, 70n, 101–102, 104, 118n, 132
Anatoli, Jacob, 56, 94n
Asher ben Jehiel, 130n
Ashi, Rabbi, 2

Babad, Joseph, 85n
Bahya ben Asher, 70n, 72n, 118n, 119n, 120n, 121n, 139n
Belkin, Samuel, 28n, 150n
Benamozegh, Elijah, 61, 70n
Ben Zoma, 76, 83n, 133–134
Berav, Jacob, 2, 5n

Berlin, Naftali Zvi, 39n, 48n, 90, 130n
Buber, Solomon, 49n, 59n

Chajes, Zvi Hirsch, 38n, 71n, 82n, 85n, 110–11, 119n, 122n, 143–146
civil disobedience, 45–47, 79
Crescas, Hasdai, 12–13

Eidels, Samuel Eliezer (MAHARSHAH), 15n, 83n, 118n
Eleazar, Rabbi, 44, 59n, 100
Eleazar of Modi'in, Rabbi, 133
Eliezer, Rabbi, 39n, 101
Eliezer ben Jacob, Rabbi, 142
Emden, Jacob, 130n
ends and means, 20
Ephraim Solomon of Luntshits, 102, 104n, 133
Epstein, Barukh, 129n, 130n
Epstein, Isidore, 16n
Epstein, Jehiel M., 88, 140n
equality, 17–18, 36–37, 93
evil impulse, 9–10, 14
executive, 54, 62, 67, 79, 87–93, 141

Federbusch, Simon, 49n, 61
Firer, Ben-Zion, 122n

Frankel, Zacharias, 41n, 66–67, 71n, 146
free will, 10–13, 18

Gersonides, 12, 26, 49n, 55, 69n, 70n, 79, 83n, 84n, 93, 96n, 100, 108, 118n, 119n, 121n, 129n, 130n, 139n
Gordin, Abba, 27n

Hai Gaon, 46–47, 50n
HaLevi, Judah, 69n
Hanan, Rabbi, 44n
Hananel ben Hushiel, 49n
Hanina, Rabbi, 11, 15n
Hanokh Zundel ben Joseph, 85n
Hayyim ben Isaac "Or Zaruah," 40n
Hen, Abraham, 28n, 117n
Heschel, Abraham Joshua, 74, 81, 82n
Hillel, 18, 27n, 29n
Hirsch, Samson Raphael, 22, 27n, 29n, 30n, 34, 39n, 40n, 41n, 49n, 77, 114–115, 121n, 128, 139n
Hiyyun, Joseph, 71n
Hoffmann, David Zvi, 38n, 81n, 95, 127, 130n
Huna, Rabbi, 33

Ibn Attar, Hayyim, 56, 96n
Ibn Ezra, Abraham, 56, 70n, 91, 95n, 110, 121n, 133
Ibn Habib, Jacob, 85n
Ibn Nagdela, Samuel, 88
Ibn Shem Tov, Shem Tov, 84n
Ibn Zimra, David, 50n, 51n, 103n, 117n, 135
imitatio Dei, 9
Isaac, Rabbi, 115, 135–136

Jacob ben Asher, 58n, 59n, 139n
Jacobson, B. S., 4, 58n
Jastrow, Marcus, 59n
Jeremiah, Rabbi, 39n
Johanan, Rabbi, 2, 40n, 76, 83n, 136
Jonathan ben David of Lunel, 113, 121n, 147
Jose, Rabbi, 98–99, 103
Jose Taba, Rabbi, 134
Joseph, Rabbi, 112

Josephus Flavius (Joseph ben Mattathias), 53, 58n
Joshua, Rabbi, 39n, 132
Joshua ben Levi, Rabbi, 121n
Judah, Rabbi, 88, 93n, 94n, 98–100, 103n, 130n, 136
Judah Loew ben Bezalel (MAHARAL), 14n, 19, 27n, 28n, 59n, 71n
Judah the Prince, Rabbi, 29n
Judah b. Shalom, Rabbi, 36n
Judan, Rabbi, 68
judiciary, 54–57, 63–65, 81, 103, 107, 111–112, 116, 123–129, 142, 146, 148

Kahana, Kalman, 3
Karo, Joseph, 99, 120n
Katzenellenbogen, Samual Judah (MAHARSHIK), 14n
Kimhi, David (RADAK), 14n, 56, 70n, 91, 118n
Kranz, Jacob, 40n

Levi, Eliezer, 41n, 69n, 71n, 122n, 139n, 143, 150n
liberty, 18, 24
Luzzatto, Moses Hayyim, 28n
Luzzatto, Samuel David (SHADAL), 56, 59n

Maimon, Judah L., 3, 5n, 65, 85n
Maimonides, Moses (RAMBAM), 3, 4n, 12, 14n, 24, 26n, 37, 40n, 44–46, 48, 49n, 50n, 51n, 53, 55, 58n, 59n, 64, 69n, 70n, 76–77, 79, 82n, 83n, 84n, 88–89, 91, 96n, 98–99, 102, 103n, 112–113, 115, 117n, 120n, 122n, 130n, 133–137, 139n, 148, 149n, 150n
Malakhi ben Jacob haKohen, 103n
Malbim, Meir Leibush, 12, 16n, 19, 22, 25–26, 29n, 37, 38n, 47–48, 67, 70n, 71n, 72n, 84n, 89, 94n, 95n, 101, 104n, 105n, 116, 122n, 130n, 138n, 139n, 144–145
Manasseh ben Israel, 104n
Mantel, Hugo, 70n
Margaliot, Reuven, 98, 148

Margoliot, Moses, 37n, 39n, 119n, 120n, 121n
Mecklenburg, Jacob Zvi, 58n
Meir Simhah HaKohen, 14n, 117n
Meiri, Menahem, 24–25, 41, 46–47, 50n, 84n, 103n, 108, 122n, 133, 150n
Melamed, Ezra Zion, 71n
Mendelssohn, Moses, 58n
Meshorer, Shabbetai, 82n
Meyuhas ben Elijah, 55, 69n, 82n, 119n
Mizrahi, Elijah, 59n, 82n
monarchy, 88–91, 93, 96n, 97–103, 107, 116, 134, 141–142, 148
Moses of Coucy, 40n, 49n, 139n, 149n
Munk, Eli, 15n

Nahman, Rabbi, 132
Nahmanides, Moses (RAMBAN), 48n, 49n, 68n, 72n, 82n, 110, 118n, 119n, 125, 128, 139n
Nehorai, Rabbi, 88–89, 93n, 94n
Netanyahu, Ben-Zion, 95n
Nissim Girondi (RAN), 25, 51n, 63, 77, 83n, 94n, 108, 117n, 118n, 120n, 142–143, 145

Obadiah of Bertinoro, 58n, 149n
Oral Law, 32, 71n

Pinto, Josiah, 91, 101, 104n, 144
priesthood, 57, 61–68, 116, 134, 141
prophetic institution, 57, 73–81

Rabinowitz, Abraham H., 95n
Rackman, Emmanuel, 36
Rapa of Porto, Abraham, 55–56, 95n, 139n
RASHI. See Solomon ben Isaac

Rav, 85n
Rosenberg, Samuel, 121n

Saadia ben Joseph al-Fayyumi (Saadia Gaon), 14n, 29n, 73–74, 81n, 82n, 89
Samuel, 134–135
Samuel ben Hofni Gaon, 56
Samuel ben Meir (RASHBAM), 58n, 68n, 118n, 138n
Sanhedrin, Great, 2, 64, 66–67, 114, 120n, 125–128, 130n, 136–138, 143, 146–148
Schimmel, Harry C., 38n
semikhah, 2
Sforno, Obadiah, 37, 49n, 54, 57, 83n, 90, 129n, 130n
Shalom, Abraham, 30n, 94n
Simeon b. Gamaliel, Rabban, 129n
Simon, Rabbi, 15n
Slotki, Israel W., 59n, 130n
Slotki, Judah J., 121n
Solomon ben Isaac (RASHI), 49n, 50n, 58n, 59n, 68n, 70n, 82n, 103n, 109–110, 119n, 121n, 130n, 132–135, 138n, 142, 147–148

Tanhum ben Hanilai, Rabbi, 139n
Tarfon, Rabbi, 29n, 40n
theocracy, 53, 67–68
Tosafists, 79, 85n

Vidal Yom Tov of Tolosa, 39n

Yannai, Rabbi, 32
Yom Tov ben Abraham Ishbili (RITBA), 85n

About the Author

MARTIN SICKER earned his Ph.D. in political science from the Graduate Faculty of the New School for Social Research in New York. He has served as a senior executive in the United States Government, where he held a number of management and policy level positions, and has taught political science at The American University and George Washington University in Washington, D.C. He has written widely in the fields of political science and international affairs, and is the author of *The Making of a Pariah State: The Adventurist Politics of Muammar Qaddafi* and *The Strategy of Soviet Imperialism*. Dr. Sicker is now a private consultant and lecturer on international affairs, and resides in Silver Spring, Maryland.